THE FIGHTER PILOT—
one of "the happiest gang in the world"

JEAN OFFENBERG

JEAN OFFENBERG was the "best kind of warrior, a happy warrior", according to Group Captain Peter Townsend. He was a brilliant flier, the first Belgian to receive the DFC and the first despite his junior rank of flight lieutenant to lead a British squadron into action.

This book is his diary, sensitively recording the exploits of The Few with a fighter pilot's flair, compassion—and courage.

It tells of the men who faced death daily, alone in the sky, when a handful of Spitfires and Hurricanes defended Britain's cities against the hordes of Nazi bombers.

Lonely Warrior

The Journal of
Battle of Britain Fighter Pilot

Jean Offenberg, DFC

With a preface by
Group Captain Peter Townsend,
DSO, DFC and Bar

Edited by Victor Houart

Translated by Mervyn Savill

Mayflower

Granada Publishing Limited
Published in 1969 by Mayflower Books Ltd
Frogmore, St Albans, Herts AL2 2NF
Reprinted 1970, 1974

First English edition by Souvenir Press Ltd 1956
Copyright © Victor Houart 1956
Made and printed in Great Britain by
Hunt Barnard Printing Ltd
Aylesbury, Bucks
Set in Intertype Plantin

Contents

1	The Crossroads	11
2	First Victory	12
3	Retreat	16
4	Escape to War	19
5	"For the Duration"	37
6	"Bandits at One O'Clock"	42
7	Tangmere	57
8	Bader's Circus	96
9	Biggin Hill	117
10	Gravesend	144
11	Furious Autumn	173
12	Sometimes Unseen	198

PREFACE

by GROUP CAPTAIN PETER TOWNSEND,
DSO, DFC and Bar

THOUGH I NEVER HAD THE GOOD FORTUNE TO MEET
Jean Offenberg, I feel I know him well through the pages of
this book. I loved reading it. It moved me deeply, as much by
the gentle, gallant figure of its hero as by the simple buoyant
language in which his life as a fighter pilot unfolds.

The story of Offenberg rings so true that many memories of
those far-off days, now faded or forgotten, have been vividly
reawakened, not only in my mind but in my heart as well. I have
come across lots of old friends and found myself back in many
old haunts which I knew so well. Group Captain Woodhall was
once my station commander; Johnny Peel, Douglas Bader,
Michael Robinson were contemporaries; Léon de Soomer and
Jean de Selys were brother-officers in my unit, and since I have
come to Belgium, the names of Monsieur Gutt, Yvan du Monceau, Roy du Vivier, Mike Donnet and many others have added
to the number of friends I have found in this book.

When I read of the places that Offenberg knew, more memories begin to stir. It was at Tangmere, on the morning of that
fateful 3rd of September 1939, that I lay on the grass beside
my Hurricane, basking peacefully in the sun. As I lay there,
listening to the larks' song and watching the white clouds sailing
overhead, war was being declared. "The Ship" at Bosham,
Drem, Gravesend, Biggin Hill – these names, when I am reminded of them, take me back into another world, where I find
myself once more in that company of fighter boys, with Jean
Offenberg among them – the company to which he gives so
happy a description: "La plus joyeuse bande du monde."

As I read on, I soon formed a deep affection for Offenberg.
He was a typical fighter pilot, more serious than some, perhaps,
but delighting in the careless banter of his comrades and posses-
sing, himself, a turn of phrase and a wit with which he could
more than hold his own. I admired him for his sacrifice in leaving all behind him in his native land and making his way back to

the last remaining stronghold, England. It made me happy to think that there, among a people so different in many ways to his own, he came to feel at home and was welcomed with a warmth and kindness which, I like to feel, made up in some measure for what he missed in his own country.

Fighter pilots, as Offenberg rightly says, have so little in them of the military spirit. But he, for one, realised that he held in his hands, his own two hands, a weapon of terrible power. A single-seater fighter pilot is one with his machine. Flying to him is an unimaginable joy, but it carries with it the responsibility – and it is an awful one when you think of it – killing single-handed. He must decide for himself in the fleeting moments of aerial combat, when to kill, and whom to kill. It was not without question that Jean Offenberg's reason told him he had a right to kill. He believed, however, that it was his duty and he pursued it with all his might. But it is clear that his heart, close as it always was to God, told him that no such power was his alone. And so we find him, the redoubtable fighter pilot, coming humbly before his Creator, praying for his enemies and that he might be forgiven for all he did to them, yet trusting that what he did was right. I feel that Offenberg's humility and devoutness, which neither victory nor adversity could change, is the nicest thing about him. He knew the cure for pride, and for sorrow too.

Pyker, the true Bruxellois, often spoke of returning to his well-loved city. So close it seemed to him by air, yet, as he told himself, a whole world separated him from "là-bas," and there was a fatal irony in this thought. I feel sure that he saw through the tragedy of human conflict and suffering. He felt the loss of his friends deeply, but he showed no bitterness for his enemies. Death, the last enemy, could come through the bullets of his adversaries or through the dangers which are the very nature of an airman's calling. However it might come to him, he looked beyond it to a paradise where friend and foe alike could ultimately meet in "une heureuse éternité," and in this he surely understood much of the mystery and the meaning of Life.

Jean Offenberg was the best kind of warrior, a happy warrior. To him and his brave compatriots in whose country I have found such unfailing kindness, I pay a sincere and heartfelt tribute.

GROUP CAPTAIN PETER TOWNSEND.

PROLOGUE

JEAN OFFENBERG, WHOSE STORY THIS IS, IN THE course of his brilliant career fought with two squadrons of Fighter Command: No. 145 (Tangmere Station) and No. 609 (Biggin Hill Station), both in the zone of No. 2 Fighter Group.

This Group, in the van of aerial defence, protected the south-east of England and the London approaches. Offenberg, a lost child flung into this whirlpool, an impartial witness and willing actor in the tragedy, has left us a testament in the form of three old dog-eared notebooks which he often held in his hands, calloused by the controls of his Spitfire. They are cheap notebooks such as one buys in a general store in the suburbs of a great city. Day by day, in the simple graphic words of an airman, he told of his life as a fighter pilot.

A knight in exile, Offenberg found time between ops to record the names of his friends, the tale of his combats and patrols, the numbers of the aircraft he piloted and occasionally the exploits of some of his comrades.

I came across these notebooks, which had been mislaid for ten years, and read in them the account of his life during the two years he spent in England. It was as though with gentle fingers I had stirred a few warm ashes. . . . I suddenly felt that I loved him like a brother. I have written this modest book so that he shall not be forgotten by men, so that the years will not condemn him to oblivion, so that at the setting of the sun and at dawn those who watch and wait will remember him.

Jean Offenberg is dead, but dead pilots never grow old. He will always remain just as his friends knew and loved him, haunting the airfields and the runways in the shadow of fighter aircraft.

If there exists a paradise for dead pilots, Offenberg will be there beyond the blaze of stars, beneath a sky of peace where his enemy will never dive upon him out of the sun.

V. HOUART.

I
THE CROSSROADS

OFFENBERG'S STORY BEGINS ONE SPRING DAY IN 1940 on a small provincial airfield a few hundred yards from the old Belgian city of Nivelles. The runway, covered with coarse grass, with a deep and dangerous hollow to the south, had not the dimensions required of modern bases. And yet at that period it was a fighter base where the pilots lived contentedly in a comfortable mess not much larger than a pocket handkerchief and a block of huts where they had their quarters.... The aircraft were of the same standard as the airfield.... They were Fiat CR 42s, small Italian biplanes from which the pilot with his head outside the cockpit, fired his machine-gun through the propeller blades as in the good old days of the First World War. In the age of Messerschmitts and Spitfires, whose silhouettes were known only to leading specialist magazines, the Nivelles pilots of the famous Cocotte Squadron, a little late in technical progress, would have cut a splendid figure ten years earlier. Nevertheless flying these old Italian "crates" the day our story begins, the Nivelles pilots of No. 2 Group of the Deuxième Regiment d'Aéronautique did their duty as stout warriors. In a sky teeming with modern aircraft whose wings were adorned with sinister black crosses, they took off proudly and courageously, although they knew that the odds were against them, and without asking questions they were brought down....

And one morning the peace which had reigned so long in the air above Nivelles, the quiet garrison life swept by a great stir from the east. And Offenberg went to meet his fate. At twilight on the first evening of the war he wrote the first lines in his diary.

On the first page we find: "At the end of the war I wish these diaries and all my belongings to be sent to my parents.

On the 10th May 1940 their address was:

> 43, Square Riga,
> SCHAERBEECK (Brussels).

> Thank you, Jean.

Name: Offenberg.
Christian names: Jean, Henri, Marie.
Born: Laeken, 3rd July 1916.
Status: Bachelor.
Unit: No. 2 Group, 4th Squadron, 2nd Regiment d'Aéronautique."

2

FIRST VICTORY

10th May, 1940.

JOTTARD WOKE ME UP ABOUT ONE O'CLOCK IN
the morning by banging on the door like a maniac. Thinking
that one of the boys was larking about after a night out in town
I paid no attention. But when a solid fist shook the door I threw
off my blankets and called to this wretched fellow who was
waking everybody up: "What is it?"

"It's Alexis. Get up quickly. It's an alert."

"Go to Hell. If you can't find a better joke than that go back
to bed."

"No," insisted the voice, "it's not a joke, I assure you. Get up.
It's the real thing."

There was such a ring of truth in poor Alexis's voice that I
decided to get out of bed. I could hardly keep my eyes open and
the light hurt them. I put on a sweater and my flying suit and
went into the corridor where shadows were rushing about in the
ghastly light of the two ceiling lamps. Siraut, whom I met outside the block and who was officer of the watch, confirmed the
alert and went so far as to explain it by saying: "It's war." I was
a little abashed. Obviously like everyone else I knew that one day
or the other "they" would be coming. . . .

And then suddenly they came. Just like that . . . I thought of
our Fiats. What on earth could we do with those old death traps?
On my way to Squadron H.Q. I could not help thinking of my
family in Brussels. What would become of them? Bah! The
French would arrive and in the meantime we should halt the
Boches on the Albert Canal.

At headquarters we were told that we must be in readiness to take off at dawn and evacuate the airfield according to plan. It was too well known and would obviously be bombed at dawn. Our destination was the emergency airstrip of Brusthem near Saint-Trond.

I returned to my hut to collect my valuables and slipped them into a parachute pack. Should we ever return? No. I did not count upon it too much, and I felt a little sad as I cast a last glance at my room, the "bughole" as we called it, where I had lived so happily for the past few months.

About 04.30 hours, dawn broke in the east above the trees fringing the plain, and a few minutes later twenty-seven Fiats took off in groups of threes. One of the boys who remained behind waved wildly as I jolted off towards my take-off position. We flew over Wavre at 3,000 feet. Soon we saw Gossoncourt with its Fairey Foxes dispersed on the airfield ... and then Brusthem.

The props stopped one after the other. A strange mechanic came up looking rather distraught as I clambered out of my cockpit.

"They've just bombed Nivelles, Sir."

"But when? We've only just left there. It's not possible."

"It is, Sir. They telephoned through only a moment ago."

At that moment Jottard rushed over to me.

"Have you heard the news? They bombed Nivelles a matter of seconds after we took off. Stukas. They were Stukas."

Old Alexis was terribly excited. He was dolled up as though off to repair a breakdown and spanners of all sizes stuck out of the pockets of his flying suit. Jottard, the "gadget man" of the squadron, had no intention of abandoning his enormous private stock of tools.

"Don't worry," I said, taking off my helmet. "No need to worry. They're bound to bomb this, too. We've only got to wait like good children. I should like to go and have a good bash at those bastards!"

Although we watched the sky all day nothing appeared. It would have been a day like any other had we not been certain that the Boches would arrive at any minute. The only thing was not to be caught on the ground ... That would have been really stupid.

At my request, the Group Commander gave permission for me to take off with two wingers. I chose two sergeant pilots, Jottard and Maes.

We gained height by circling over Saint-Trond. The Fiats were slow on the climb ... I had plenty of time to admire the view below while keeping an eye on my altimeter. How should I react when the Germans came? It could not be long now. I suddenly felt chilly. Then a plane passed to port, a very elongated twin-engined aircraft with two tail units and black crosses surrounded by a thin white border—a Hun, my first Hun. My heart beat faster and I managed to wave to my two comrades. But they had seen him too and Maes, without waiting for orders, had broken away. I caught sight of his Fiat's belly against a cloudless sky the moment he dived on the Dornier 71. Why had he done it? Why hadn't he waited for my orders? For a thousandth part of a second I thought of our fighting instructions. I could not reflect for long, for Jottard pointed to a spot on the horizon and I suddenly saw a ragged formation of planes staged at various altitudes. Messerschmitts ... Instinctively I went into a spin, while two German fighters on my port beam broke formation. And then I cannot remember ... I do not recall diving between two Messerschmitts on a bomber whose rear gunner fired at me. I fired my first burst and then a second ... My starboard machine-gun jammed and I pulled out of the dive.

I found myself alone with no sign of friends or foes. It was as though a squall had passed, raising the dust and leaving behind it a few whorls and leaves torn from the trees. And now the sky was empty ... I was above the little town of Diest, the home of dark sweet beer which one drank in big pewter pots. I had lost nearly 5,000 feet without being aware of it. A glance at my watch showed that it was 06.45 hours. I was about to set a course for Saint-Trond when suddenly out of the blue a black "twin engine" passed below me. Remembering the lesson of my first combat I cast a hasty eye around me. Nothing to be seen ... He was alone and I began to chase him in a shallow dive. I do not know how long this lasted but I could not get enough speed and I was too far away to fire. On the Dornier's back I could see the gunner's turret moving occasionally sending me a ray of sunlight like the flash of a diamond. Above Maestricht I gave up the chase. Passing a finger across my lips I noticed a little dark patch on my glove. I had bitten my lower lip without knowing it.

A glance at Saint-Trond airfield, where everything seemed normal, and I flew on towards Brussels, following the main road, when another machine approached me slightly from the port side. It grew larger at every moment. It was a Dornier. A dive, followed by an Immelmann turn, and I was in a position above him. I had learned a great deal in the past few minutes. Unless I was well above him the speed of my Fiat would not allow me to close in on him without a dive. He passed on a level with me. His turret revolved. I waded in and opened fire just as tracers bore down on me from all sides like scarlet beads. The old Fiat vibrated and bucked from the recoil of the machine-gun. I did not know quite what to do so I went on firing. Spirals of black smoke began to pour from his port engine. He banked just as I pulled on the stick to avoid a red stream of tracers. Below me the Dornier was rapidly losing height. . . .

I landed at Brusthem at 07.45 hours after one hour and forty minutes of operational flying and a kill, happy to be still alive.

The airfield had not yet been spotted, probably because the Huns had not circled above it like vultures. I found a little peace again on the ground among the orchards whose fruit was not yet ripe . . . A peasant was busied at some obscure task in the backyard of his farm, whose walls must have been repainted for they were very white.

Our stocky Fiats lined up like strings of onions – not dispersed enough to my taste – had their wheels hidden in the tall grass. Both Jottard and Maes returned safe and sound. And then about 15.00 hours they arrived . . . Five Messerschmitts, flying at tree top level, flew in from the direction of the Liège road, making a deafening din and spitting all the fires of rage. I hardly had time to do a bellyflop . . . They had already passed over and my face was still buried in the grass. I was lying a few yards away from Alexis. I could see his questioning glance.

"Hmm," he said, "Those fellows haven't cleaned the pot yet."

"I still think it would be better to get out of here and to get all that junk airborne before they return," I said, pointing to our crates. "I . . ."

I did not have time to finish the sentence before we heard the whine of an engine coming from the south. Jottard and I exchanged glances and dived head first into the nearest ditch.

And the infernal merry-go-round began. Stukas dived on us, with their sirens wailing, hurting the eardrums as the bombs burst with a dull thud. I could hear crackling on the other side of the farm, which lay behind us. Perhaps it was the trees in the orchard. Jottard suddenly remembered the spanner which had slipped out of his boot as he sprinted towards the ditch. My heart seemed to have shrunk to the size of a cherry stone as I waited there powerless for the storm to abate. Then one by one the Stukas left for the east and a great calm descended upon the peaceful countryside. We scrambled out of our holes. No. 3 Squadron no longer had a single airworthy machine, and what yesterday had been their pride was now a huge pile of old iron, a junk shop of spare parts, a graveyard for aeroplanes. Ours were still intact, so only No. 4 Squadron could take off again.

In this scene of desolation some news arrived. Sergeant Pilot Roger Delannay, who left this morning as Goffin's "winger" on an interception patrol died in the ambulance on the way to hospital. Surprised by the Messerschmitts he was shot down with a bullet through his lung.

I felt like weeping. All our airfields have been bombed and shot up by machine-guns. Fort Eben-Emael has been put out of action by German parachutists. Night fell mercifully upon our grief . . .

3
RETREAT

11th May 1940

ESCAPING BY THE SKIN OF OUR TEETH FROM THE returning German bombers our last eight Fiats, all that remained of the Group, took off for Grimbergen, a small emergency airstrip near Brussels, where we touched down about 10.00 hours, not without having been subjected to the blind fire of the Belgian ack-ack north of Tirlemont.

Our orders were to intercept enemy aircraft above Brussels, my own city. I should have liked to pay a flying visit to my parents at Schaerbeeck, but it was hardly possible for there are very few fighters left capable of taking the air. With Jean de Gallatay, our Squadron Commander, and Goffin, Siraut, Jottard and the others I waited beneath the tired wings of the Fiat . . . waiting for what? . . . I don't know.

Everything seemed to have crumbled about my ears, as though I were in a huge house whose walls had just collapsed. And there I was sitting on the ruins, waiting for a voice, for a friendly hand, for some sign to give me a bearing.

16

At twilight we were ordered to leave for the west, away from the tragedy, in the direction of the sea. But why, since they would pursue us with their black crosses and their bombs?

Back there on the Albert Canal, Captain Glorie deliberately crashed his Battle on the Vroenhoven Bridge. And we, the last remaining fighters, had set our course for the setting sun.

Above Boom a "twin engine" passed to starboard, flying very low. I chased it for a few moments and easily caught up with it. It seemed stockier than the others and did not have that long pencil-like shape of a German bomber. At five hundred yards I was able to recognise the red, white and blue circles. The centre was red . . . it was a British Blenheim on the way home. A fighter arrived which I could not yet identify. It too seemed to be attracted by the bomber like an insect by the light. It was a French Curtiss which dipped its wings in greeting as soon as the pilot recognised our nationality. Hope returned. We are no longer alone in our distress and the presence of us three in this enemy-infested sky proves that the friendship of olden days has been renewed.

At Nieuwekerke, our new haven, we found three French Potez.

On the following day, Whit Monday, I did not take off. The Germans have forced the passage of the Albert Canal between Hasselt and Maestricht and parachutists have captured the Rotterdam airfield. Liège still holds out. Sitting with Jottard at the side of our Fiat, I am waiting for orders, which do not come. How peaceful everything is here and in this land of Flanders, where nothing speaks of war. Not an enemy formation has crossed our sky, and yet they are fighting to the east. . . .

My first mission was on the 13th. A patrol in the Tirlemont-Tessenderloo sector consisting of two flights of three aircraft.

On the Gossoncourt airfield, whose buildings seemed to have been lashed by a storm, a machine was still smoking as we flew over at 9,000 feet. The ack-ack defending Tirlemont went into action and shells burst all round us, a little too near for my liking. Fortunately their aim was bad and we got through. Hansel, my "winger," threw his arms up in despair. We made for home, avoiding flying over the big concentrations so as not to arouse the trigger-happy enthusiasm of the gunners below.

About 11.00 hours on the following day our six remaining Fiats, already slightly worn by three days of war, took off for Fleurus. They were to defend the station during the entrainment of French troops.

I waited for their return, curbing my impatience. And then we heard the sound of an engine ... Jottard was the first to spot them.

"They're Faireys," he cried.

"Faireys? There aren't any left, old man. I tell you those are Fiats."

"And I tell you they're Faireys."

In actual fact they were Fairey Fireflies, sent as reinforcements to our Group. They were all that the Air Staff could find to send us. After that there only remains the War Museum! The Fairey Firefly is a pre-1930 fighter biplane armed with two light-weight water-cooled machine-guns, with a cruising speed equivalent to about half that of the slowest German bomber. Perhaps the Germans would spare them. After all, one doesn't knock a poor child out of one's way.

When the Fiats returned there was one missing at roll call. The French adjutant has been brought down by the German fighters, and the victories of Jean de Gallatay and Michot do not make up for the loss of this brave fellow.

"How did it happen? Did you get to Fleurus? Where was he brought down?"

The five survivors seemed a little out of breath in the midst of the crowd which surrounded them and badgered them with questions.

"We got over Fleurus without any incidents. There de Moerloose left the formation to attack a Dornier which seemed to be there quite by chance."

"Did he get him at least?"

"Well, he thinks so. And we ought to believe him."

"And then?"

"And then we flew over Fleurus quite peacefully, wingtip to wingtip. I don't know how long it was but suddenly they were on us. Messerschmitts coming from all directions."

Oger had managed to take off his flying suit. Old Emile never gets excited easily and he gave us his version of the incident quite calmly.

"You see, from that moment I can't remember very much. It all went so quickly. A Messerschmitt was on my tail and I had only a split second to realise that I'd got to do something about it quick, and bloody quick at that. I banked, and saw at once that he could bank much tighter than my Fiat. We went on for a bit and I don't know how it happened but I suddenly found myself fifty yards behind him. But it may well have been another ..."

"And did you shoot him down?"

"When I thought that he must be annoyed at no longer being able to see me I gave him a little burst to let him know I was there on his tail. I must admit that after that I didn't see any more ..."

It's always the same story. As soon as there's a dog-fight one sees nothing more. It made me think of boxing matches I had at school with the boys. You did not see the fist until it arrived. The whole art is to see it coming, to forestall the attack by a fraction of a second and stop it with your glove. It must be the same thing here ... I must keep my eyes skinned. I must see. ...

The Group Commander decided late that afternoon to display the circles on the Fairey Fireflies out of bravado. But wasn't it a bit useless? Wasn't it slightly ridiculous to risk your life for mere showing off? What was the use? It would not settle anything and you would merely get shot down. Volunteers were called for. Everyone wanted to be in the party. Major Lemarche took Lieutenant Yves Dumonceau and Leroy du Vivier. The sky – fortunately – was free of the enemy. The Belgian gunners managed to bring down Leroy du Vivier near Keerbergen, north-west of Brussels. There, taking him for an enemy parachutist, the Belgian troops took him prisoner in spite of his Brussels accent and the boy returned by car this evening in a really foul temper.

A few minutes later the wireless announced that Holland has capitulated and that the Germans have crossed the Meuse in the region of Sedan, forcing the French fortifications.

Tomorrow we shall retire once more. Take-off is fixed for dawn, on a southerly course. ...

4

ESCAPE TO WAR

16th May 1940

I DID NOT SLEEP A WINK ALL NIGHT. WAITED once more on the tarmac with Jottard and Maes for the sun to rise. It was a very peaceful night disturbed only by the raucous drone of a far-off engine.

"The enemy is already at Wavre," said Alexis, standing up. "In a couple of days they'll be here and we shall be encircled, caught in a trap . . ."

"Nonsense, don't lose your nerve. As soon as we get a clear picture we'll fly to France. You'll see . . . And then it's premature to express an opinion while operations are still in progress."

I fell silent because I knew that I could not convince him and I knew . . . The Germans had overrun his village, Andenelle, back in the Meuse country, and it was better to leave him to his sorrow and his anger. At 03.50 hours I climbed into CR 23. I was dead tired and yet I had to take off in the half light where the sun had not yet dared to show its rays. Our six Fiats, the six last Belgian fighters – all that remained of the Group's effectives – were about to leave Belgium. I was the third to be airborne. Sleep vanished in the slipstream of the prop as soon as the wheels left the ground and I slipped into another world, beyond the darkness which closed behind me. I adjusted my helmet for the chinstrap was biting into my flesh . . . My eyes had already grown accustomed to the darkness and I could make out the wing struts vibrating . . . Beyond the windscreen nothing but the great invisible prop spinning in the void, snapping at the air . . .

For some strange reason my aircraft made me think of a man about to drown himself and who, already in the water, still clutches on to a few straws on the shore. Imperceptibly the light swung to this part of the world and the earth reappeared with its trees, roads, rivers and human beings. I found my bearings and glided gently down towards the airfield. Aelter. It was 04.50 hours by my watch. I did not take off again for France until the evening.

The first town I recognised was Armentières. Behind us, the known frontier and the familiar landscape disappeared in the dusk which glided across the fields, gradually blurring their traces here and there. In flights of three we flew over a formation of Fireflies, our Fireflies . . . Fighters giving cover to fighters. How absurd! When I looked down I saw them making heavy weather against the head wind. The leader of the second flight was Leroy du Vivier. I could imagine his frowning boxer's face looking for an opening, his solid shoulders and stocky body, glued to the seat of his Firefly. He must be livid at having to fly such an old tub.

And then Norrent-Fontes, our first halt in French territory. I was terribly stiff and exhausted after two sleepless nights. I was hungry and sleepy; I wanted to get my head down on a pillow and leave this world, sink into the abyss, die for an hour or two.

A voice whispered that we had won the Battle of the Meuse, that our fighters had beaten the enemy in the air. We were counter-attacking at Sedan ... So much the better. When I woke up I might perhaps be given a decent fighter. The French had some ... Yes, that was it ... A fighter ... A real fighter. To-morrow.

*   *   *

I woke up in a strange room with windows half open on to a place I had never seen before. Norrent-Fontes. I had never even heard the name on my school maps and yet there was an airfield a stone's throw from a village.

On the field I found Goffin gesticulating wildly ... The cause of this sudden exuberance was that another pilot had cast doubts on his yesterday's victory over a Messerschmitt 109. He had taken off with Moreau and Devalck from Nieuwekerke to escort a reconnaissance Fairey Fox and the Mes had as usual arrived like a whirlwind. Bah, it didn't matter a damn who had brought one down, he or one of his pals. The news I have just read in the French papers is not alarming. A phrase in the "Temps" however caught my eye: *"The battle as a whole presents itself as a vast mêlée. Long continuous fronts as we knew them in the last war do not exist ..."*

It is a vast mêlée which I don't understand. I only know one thing ... Brussels has fallen. The bastards are goose-stepping along the boulevards, perhaps in front of my house. Jottard cannot get rid of his rage and keeps swearing at the fate which has grounded us.

"When are we taking the air again?"

"Taking the air again. Out of the question, old chap," said Yves Dumonceau, who had been to hear the news. "We're leaving for the Fighter Training School at Montpellier. Tomorrow apparently ..."

Montpellier! But that's too far, we couldn't go any further because beyond that is the sea.

Charles Goffin protested angrily: "They're all crackers at H.Q. They've made a mistake. They must have put their maps upside down when they were playing their game of darts ...

21

Pij," he said, turning to me, "Pij, go and tell them where the north is . . . It's over there . . ."

His avenging arm pointed to a spot on the horizon which was hardly in the direction of the Pole star. "The sun hasn't forgotten to advance on the ecliptic as far as I know . . ."

"Over there, mon lieutenant," said Jottard, with a grin, "you'd fall into the drink."

There was a loud burst of laughter from the whole company, the laughter of a few Belgian pilots sitting in a circle on a strange airfield; the wind and the trees that limited our horizon must have learned that we were only boys of twenty.

18th May

Towards mid morning I was briefed by Major Lamarche to join the flight of six Fiats which were to report to Chartres, the great Armée de l'Air base. It is all very well racking my brains, trying to remmeber . . . Chartres only remains for me a cathedral in the centre of a town like any other. At 10.30 hours we took off and left the little Pas-de-Calais village behind us. I had difficulty in keeping my map balanced on my knees while looking for landmarks on each side. We passed the Abbeville-Amiens railway a little too far to starboard. Captain de Gallatay leading the first flight must have spotted this for he changed course. A few clouds made the sky less monotonous. Then the Seine appeared, describing an enormous bend which we flew over.

At the end of a gleaming stretch of water lay Paris, invisible that day . . . Dreux beyond a green patch of forest and then Chartres with the cathedral so familiar from my history book. We landed on the airfield which lies to the north of the town.

Unfortunately no one expected the Belgian Fiats. A French officer whose rank I never discovered explained to our Captain that the Belgian Armée de l'Air (sic) had to report to Tours. Good, on our way to Tours then . . .

"We'll get out of here quick," said our squadron leader. "As soon as we've filled up with juice we'll take off."

"What about our lunch, Sir," I asked, feeling a hollow sensation in my belly, "It's past midday. Couldn't we take off after a meal?"

He waved my suggestion aside.

"We'll eat at Tours. There are excellent restaurants on the banks of the Loire. Let's get going."

We took off as soon as we had filled up. The "Old Man" did not seem to fancy navigating that day for he simply turned westwards, found the railway line and kept it on our port side. Chateaudun ... And then it was all new to me for the map ended just south of that town. I knew that Tours lay somewhere on the Loire but I had not the least idea where. I stuck close to the others for I had no wish to get lost in this vast country which to me was a kind of fertile Sahara. A large town, a river, two railway lines ... We flew on until we came to a wide river running east-west ... That must be the Loire. The squadron leader signalled that we were going down. It was Tours.

Unfortunately they did not know what to do with us there. The French were not expecting us. ...

We ate in the mess before returning north once more for Chartres where they had now agreed to keep us.

Belgium is almost entirely occupied now and the German troops are smashing their way towards Abbeville.

****

Editor's Note.—At the request of the French Colonel Bladinier, the remains of his squadron shared with five Fiats the defence and protection of the base against a German threat which never matured. The Luftwaffe was in action much farther north, not far away, but giving air cover to the ground troops speeding towards the Channel ports. The Luftwaffe bombers ignored Chartres. On one occasion a reconnaissance patrol of three twin-engined Heinkel 111s found the airfield a tempting target and contemptuously dropped a few bombs before returning to their own lines. One of the fourteen bombs hit the airfield and made a large crater some yards from Fiat CR 26, tearing holes in the wings and buckling the undercarriage. At dusk on May 21st Offenberg and Sergeant Pilot Maes carried out a patrol at 15,000 feet in the hope of meeting an enemy who never came ... And yet ... less than an hour's flight away two armies were locked in a deadly struggle and men were killing each other to hold a strip of ground. Rushing headlong for Abbeville, the Germans reached Amiens and made the hoped-for break-through. The Belgian army, the British Expeditionary Force and the First French Army were cut off from the main body of the French forces.. ..

General Weygand became generalissimo of the Allied armies

in place of Gamelin. A last supreme effort to re-establish contact between the two armies of the Somme was defeated by the German panzers supported by Junkers 87 dive-bombers. The legend of the Stuka was born. . . .

From the Ardennes to the Channel the wreckage of allied aircraft strewn over the countryside testified to the tenacity of a handful of brave men who, in outdated machines, accepted battle, stuck on the tails of the powerful German formations and were brought down by the fighters. . . .

The R.A.F. retired across the Channel and operated sporadically from bases in South-East England.

The British land counter-offensive to break the encirclement having failed, the British troops fell back on Dunkirk.

The pincers closed tighter on the region where thousands of men were still fighting.

The fate of the Belgian army was sealed and all hope of saving it vanished. At the end of its organised resistance and pushed back to the sea, it fought with the British and French in a last stand of honour.

On the 28th May, King Leopold, before leaving his army, issued this last communique . . . *"We have been forced to capitulate. History will give the verdict that the Army did its duty. Our honour is unimpaired."*

On the mess radio Offenberg listened to the voice of the French premier accusing King Leopold of felony and high treason. Around him reigned an atmosphere of uncertainty and dismay, heavy with apprehension. Offenberg began to doubt.

The battle of France was about to begin . . . The Belgian army would reform – in France apparently – since the Belgian Government at Limoges had decreed it. Despite all these ordeals the morale of the pilots was high. They were convinced that the Seine was impassable and that even if Paris fell the allies would win a decisive battle on the Loire. Had not Joffre planned to lure the Germans to the centre of France so as to crush them to the last man?

But Paris was not defended and Le Havre fell.

On the 11th June our fighters received orders to leave the zone of battle which was hourly drawing nearer. So, while somewhere fighting was going on in the French sky, while the Luftwaffe mercilessly pounded all military and other objectives situated between the sea and the Swiss frontier, Offenberg and his com-

24

rades were ordered to report to the airfield of Mérignac near Bordeaux.

Who gave the order? Offenberg does not mention any details in his diaries. In the mist that clung to the edge of the airfield he took off once more for the south, leading four Fiats piloted by the youngest members of the squadron: Aubert, Deiperdange, Gheyssens and Bobby Bladt.

The 17th June at 13.00 hours, Marshal Petain made his speech to the French nation: *"People of France, it is with grief in my heart that I have to tell you to stop fighting. . ."* He announced his intention of suing for an "armistice between soldiers." He spoke of an honourable peace and of lies which had done us so much harm. His voice trembled and seemed very remote. . . .

Offenberg and his fellow-pilots, gathered round a small wireless set forgotten by the owners in the villa where they were quartered, were dismayed.

The voice of the Marshal died away.

A tragic silence. Then the incredible, the heartrending, the fantastic happened: the Marseillaise was played: *"Le jour de gloire est arrivé . . ."* Everyone felt like weeping.

But there remained a last bastion, the fortress and hope of Europe. A great voice was raised: "The battle which General Weygand has called the Battle of France is over. I think that the Battle of Britain has begun . . ."

In the darkness of their room Jottard and Offenberg exchanged glances and understood each other.

****

19th June

It is all over now. The Germans will come southwards invading the immense strip of territory along the Atlantic coast. A clause of the armistice which is to be signed stipulates that the French authorities will not let their former allies capable of bearing arms leave French territory. There remains but one thing to do, to reach North Africa where the French forces will continue the struggle. I caught hold of Jottard just as he was getting ready to leave for Mérignac and decided to find out if I should be alone in my attempt to escape.

"Alexis, I'd like a word with you," I said.

"I know exactly what you're going to say," he replied. "I, too, have no intention of remaining here and waiting for them. We can't let ourselves be disarmed like that and return to Belgium. What are we going to say to them back there when they question us? We've got to get out of here as quickly as we can."

"What do you intend to do?"

"I don't know yet. What about you?"

A thought suddenly crossed my mind. I was forgetting that we had the means of leaving. It was so simple that I hadn't even thought of it.

"Alexis, what about the Fiats?"

Jottard smiled and slapped his thighs.

"Of course, that's obvious. The Fiats. What an idiot I was not to have thought of it. There are still five and that's more than we need. Come on . . ."

Jottard never wastes much time once he has decided upon something but on this occasion I found him a bit too premature. After all, I was an officer and my superiors were still there. I managed to persuade him to follow my suggestion and to go and get the blessing of our leaders. All we received was a douche of cold water.

"But you're mad, Offenberg. If you leave without orders you will be posted as a deserter. Don't make your case any worse by pinching a Fiat into the bargain. I forbid you to leave, do you hear? I forbid you to move from here. We are leaving Mérignac for Montpellier this afternoon – right, that's all . . .'

On the station the pilots, idle and bewildered, consoled each other by getting their miseries off their chests. The most fantastic rumours were flying around. The seeds had already been sown. A few of the boys were being harangued by one of our lieutentants who sat gesticulating on an old jerrycan.

"You haven't the right. The king has surrendered and the army has to follow his example. If you leave, you'll be deserters . . . Your duty . . ." and so on and so on.

Jottard, without wishing to let himself be convinced, accused me of having been too honest by asking permission.

"The Fiats were there," he grumbled, "we'd only got to get into the cockpit, swing the prop and buzz off. Now everything's in the air . . .' Then, pointing to the officer who was speaking, he added: "And that cretin won't lift a finger."

We had to find some way. But what? I racked my brains but I could think of nothing until I was told that if I liked I could fly to the next base in a Simoun. We were going to help evacuate the French aircraft still on the Mérignac airfield. What aircraft?

Block 151s or Simouns? I took the chance of getting to know these two types and Jottard, who never said a word, did three circuits on a Caudron Simoun and two on a Bloch 151. He whistled as he rejoined me.

"Well, is it okay?" I asked.

"It certainly is, old man. Much better than I'd hoped." And he went off with a broad smile on his face.

After a quick bite we loaded our gear in the Simoun and reached Montpellier two and a half hours later.

There, too, the atmosphere among the Belgians tended towards defeatism. All documents had been burnt and the soldiers had been disarmed. They even went so far as to tear up all the parachutes.

The few wretched Belgian aircraft which had arrived here, God knows how, were dismantled.

"We must manage to get the Simouns filled up," I said to Jottard, who suddenly appeared.

"I've already done it," he replied. "We've got enough juice to reach Corsica."

"Have you got any maps?"

"Not a chance. I've made a rough drawing on a slip of paper. Here, look. I've marked Corsica."

He handed me a strip of rather crumpled paper with a few black pencil markings.

****

Editor's Note.—On the following day, 20th June 1940, about 16 hours, two small single-engined aircraft with French markings took off one after the other from the airfield of Montpellier; course due south and a slight cross wind. They were airborne, seemed for a moment to be checking their course, then headed for the sea. Offenberg and Jottard had made their choice. . . .

Three hours later the two machines reached Cap Corse. They followed the high frowning mountains for some minutes along the sea shore before finding the entrance to the bay of Ajaccio. Since they had no idea where the airfield was, they flew along the shore of the bay and over the town, until suddenly it appeared to their tired eyes.

No one was particularly surprised to see them arrive. A French naval officer took them aboard his corvette, which was anchored in the roadstead. They strolled for a while round the basins where the fishermen had spread their nets, before returning on foot to the airfield. They were given quarters in the guardroom. At dawn, after filling up with petrol, Offenberg and Jottard set out on the next stage which should bring them to Phillipeville in Algeria. Their goal was a small town on the Moroccan frontier to which the Belgian Training School had retired with its officers, instructors, pupils and a part of its material.

Sétif, Maison Blanche and then Algiers ... Relisane on the Oran road where they were given a warm welcome by some French officers.

(In his diary Offenberg quotes the names of Captain Mages and Adjutant Ducas.)

At Relisane, Jottard, taking off in a strong wind, pushed his stick a little too far forward as he was taxi-ing; the propeller hit the ground and broke in pieces. Using his brakes, he managed to avoid turning turtle. . . .

Offenberg taxied over to him.

"Shove your things in my Simoun. We'll go on in one 'crate'."

"No – I refuse," replied Jottard. "To have such a lovely machine and then to leave it. No, no and no. There must be some Simoun props somewhere in the neighbourhood."

"With your messing about, we're going to lose a lot of valuable time. There's plenty of room for two in a Simoun. Don't be such an obstinate mule."

But Jottard refused. He wanted a prop, and an adjustable one at that, for the blades were shorter.

At Oran they did not find the requisite part. Nor at Algiers. No propeller, no propeller ... The Armée de l'Air had apparently forgotten to stock up its North African depots with the necessary parts for Caudron Simouns.

A French officer suddenly grew suspicious of these two pilots in slate-grey uniform who were flying about Algeria, said very little and behaved as though they belonged to a private air force of their own where no orders were given, but discussions took place between a second lieutenant and a sergeant who seemed to be as thick as thieves. They were forbidden to fly.

After a rather difficult interview during which they insisted that they had received orders to join the Belgian contingent at Oujda, they obtained permission to fly there – but by the shortest and most direct route. Jottard bowed to the inevitable and gave up all hope of finding a spare prop. South of Oujda town was the Angades airfield, still under construction but now abandoned to the evacuated Belgians.

It formed part of the *bled*, the parched desert where no trace of vegetation relieved the drab landscape. Trainees, specialists and non-commissioned officers were quartered there in great discomfort. There was an epidemic of dysentery and those who did not catch the disease sold articles of equipment to the Arabs which could be found on the following day in the native bazaar in the town.

Offenberg and Jottard arrived as heroes in this winderness.

Familiar faces and well-known voices. . . . They were back in their tribe. That evening they were already disillusioned for there was nothing to show that the people there had made up their minds to continue a war which most of them considered to be irrevocably lost.

Demoralised and no longer knowing what to do, Offenberg and Jottard had a final council of war eating *babas au rhum* in Simone Segui's pastry shop among a number of trainee pilots who seemed to be living in this establishment. There was one answer – the Simoun, destination Gibraltar. The trainees would leave for Casablanca and try to find a ship. On the following day when Jottard went over to the little aircraft parked between two hangars at the edge of the field he found that the magnetos had been removed. He beckoned to Jean.

"Pij. The swine have taken out our magnetos. We can't take off. I wonder who pulled that dirty trick." Offenberg thought it must be the French.

Jottard disagreed and thought it must be the work of a compatriot who was jealous of their initiative. Taking a pair of pliers from his pocket – he always carried his tool kit with him – Jottard completed the sabotage by systematically cutting all the cables within reach.

"If we can't take off with the Simoun," said the good Alexis, "no other blighter will."

In his rage he cut the cables, ripped out the plugs and flattened them with a hammer.

No one ever took off in the little Simoun No. 360, which was abandoned on the hard soil of Angades airfield in Morocco.

The two unlucky comrades took the afternoon bus. It was a blue bus belonging to a Courtrai company which the Wevelghem Flying School had requisitioned on the 10th May. Since then it had followed the school, had found a berth on the cargo vessel which carried the Belgian war material from Marseilles to Oran and at the moment served the Belgian officers between Angades and the Hotel Simon at Oujda where they were quartered.

In the town the atmosphere was one of departure and desertion. Small groups of Belgians seated on the café terraces sipping their *menthes à l'eau*, discussed matters in the hot sirocco which blew from the desert.

Offenberg suddenly had a brainwave. One of his uncles lived in Buenos Aires. Perhaps he could get the necessary papers to leave for the Argentine if he went to their consul in Casablanca.

A phone call. Nothing doing, the consul was very nice but unhelpful. In the narrow streets of the Oujda suqs they met three bored trainees who, having been left to their own devices for some time, were wandering about the town in search of problematical distraction.

"What the hell are you doing here?" said Offenberg going up to them.

The pupils who had broken camp were not scared by this resolute and sympathetic-looking lieutenant. Was he not the hero of the day, the man who had stolen the Simoun, the only one who did not fear to speak openly to his superiors of the choice he had made. They could say anything to him.

"Yesterday evening, sir, Lallemand, Ortmans, Limet and a few others from the 82nd left without leave for Casa – in a train full of Polish Pilots . . ."

"How many were they?" asked Offenberg, suddenly interested in the news. "Don't tell me that the pupils thought that out on their own. Weren't there any officers with them?"

"Yes – I recognised Captain de Hemptinne at the first aid post on the station platform. And Lieutenant Picard, and I think there were a few others, but, you know, in the excitement of leaving we may have missed one or two. . . ."

So they left without telling anyone. After all, the decision had been made. Had they themselves not decided to fly to Gibraltar in the Simoun.

"What time's the next train for Casa?" asked Jottard.

The pupils who had been wandering about the town seemed to know everything that was going on in Oujda.

"At 10.10. The train from Algiers for Casa stops here."

"Good. Thanks. Are you coming, Alexis?" said Offenberg, suddenly in a hurry. "We've just got time to pick up our gear. No good wasting time here."

The following day, July 1st, Jean Offenberg and his inseparable Alexis Jottard reached Casablanca. They had not gone 500 yards from the station when they caught sight of a group of trainees on the opposite pavement.

Alexis gave a shout which made half the passers-by turn round. Their comrades saw them and rushed through the traffic at the risk of their necks.

"Well, what have you found out?" asked Offenberg.

"Nothing, sir. It's extremely difficult to get a ship for Gib as we haven't got the necessary papers. Apparently the Belgian consul can't give us certificates of nationality or permission to leave. He has promised to do his best for us."

"What about the British? Is there a British consul in Casa? Have you seen him?"

"No, but Captain Cajot has."

"Is he here?"

"Yes. We met him yesterday quite by chance. We went in a body to the Consulate and Henri Limet went on twenty yards ahead. We followed him, slipped into the gardens and then Henri gave us the sign to make ourselves scarce. We hid among the trees in the shrubbery. Two seconds later Limet reappeared on the step, put his two fingers in his mouth and gave a magnificent catcall. He had simply noticed Cajot at the Consulate entrance and thought that he was merely in Casa for the purpose of taking us back to Oujda. On the contrary, he was trying to arrange matters for everyone. He, too, has made up his mind to leave."

Offenberg, as the senior officer present, took control of things, meeting Baudouin de Hemptinne and his group.

After some hours spent in finding ways and means of leaving, the Belgians suddenly discovered a method which, although perhaps not a certainty, was worth trying.

The Poles were authorised by the police to sail in a cargo boat leaving that evening and their leader agreed to smuggle the Belgians aboard. They were given metal badges with the white eagle of Poland and these were soon to be seen on caps and uniforms in place of the Belgian lion.

The *Djebel Druse*, a cargo ship, was tied up at the quayside. At the gangway a few members of the police were checking up, calling out in Polish to the embarking soldiers. They ignored the silent Belgians. The Poles talked at the tops of their voices, arguing the toss with the police.

At 21.00 hours, a couple of ruffianly looking sailors pulled up the gangway. The ship's engines began to throb and the ship left the quay. On deck, fourteen Belgian airmen suddenly smelled the fresh wind coming from the Atlantic, a scent of adventure and liberty. A few French airmen had also managed to slip through with the Poles and on board there was even a Spahi officer in a magnificent scarlet burnous with an arrogant monocle stuck in his left eye.

The following afternoon, the cargo vessel anchored in Gibraltar roadstead beneath the protection of the legendary rock, and half the Polish group received orders to leave the ship.

A British homeward-bound cruiser would take them to England in two days. Order countermanded.

The cruiser had a full complement and could not take this additional group, which returned to the *Djebel Druse*, led by the French Spahi. Not until two days later was the entire group transferred to a British cargo vessel, the *Har Sion*.

For two days they had warmed themselves in the Gibraltar sun on the upper deck of the *Djebel Druse*. Their sole distraction had been the beehive activity of the port, the take-off of British aircraft from the airfield at the foot of the rock and the infernal din from the naval ack-ack which on two occasions, beneath their eyes, shot an Italian Savoia into the greyish water of the bay.

And then, one by one, the ships left port and made for the high seas in convoy formation under the protection of two destroyers, real watchdogs, circling round their merchant charges.

On board the *Har Sion* which cruised between five and six knots, life settled down, enlivened by Jottard's sense of humour; his iron morale was a blessing for his comrades. It was wonderful weather and most of their days were spent on deck. Alexis, feeling that he was a navigator, checked the daily course. Every three hours he verified the speed of the ship and sent one of the trainees on to the captain's sacrosanct bridge to get the course from the enormous compass. As soon as he had the necessary information, the pupil returned and gave him the course.

"We're sailing 345° West, Captain," he said with a salute.

"Good," replied Alexis, "pass me the map."

From God knows where, he had found a marine chart. Making a swift mental calculation, measuring the distances on his thumb, and having plotted his position he proudly announced to the awed company: "We're here!"

His finger indicated a spot in the middle of the map where there was absolutely nothing marked except the depths in fathoms.

The food on board was disgusting and moreover rations were short. They were constantly hungry.

Sometimes a lucky fellow found some potatoes, which were immediately steamed, cut into thin slices and shared.

On the 15th July, Offenberg, leaning against the rail in the bows, suddenly spotted land. England. . . .

"Alexis," he cried, "land ahead!"

Alexis, who continued his role of navigator until the bitter end, checked the time and wrote it down in Offenberg's diary. It was 16 hrs. 14′ 40″. The following evening, after a long wait off-shore, probably while the roadstead was being cleared of mines, the *Har Sion* and her cargo of deserters drew alongside the appointed quay in the port of Liverpool. A few moments later, fourteen Belgian airmen stepped ashore in England, the last bastion of Europe's fortress. Fourteen aviators who had come to take part in the greatest epic of modern times, the majority of whom would never see the towns and villages of their native Belgium again. They had burnt their boats. They were alone in the centre of the citadel in an alien world. They were like sailors lost in an immense ocean, peering in the darkness for the golden gleam of a lighthouse.

A friendly hand led them to a naval rest-house in the port quarter. They ate and went to bed—real beds with sheets, mattresses and springs. It was the first time for a fortnight, writes Offenberg. Sleep, that transitory death, accorded them the blessing of oblivion.

Editor's Note—

THE LUFTWAFFE, WHICH HAD JUST WON A CRUSHING victory in Western Europe, allowing a few weeks' respite to the tired pilots of the R.A.F., took advantage of the time to carry out a redistribution of its units on the newly conquered airfields.

Looked upon as a kind of miracle, the evacuation of the British Expeditionary Force from Dunkirk – resulting in the return to England of 350,000 men – was a defeat which was equivalent to a victory. "Operation Sealion," whose objective was the invasion of the British Isles, was being prepared at the German General Staffs. Boats and barges cruised on the calm waters of the canals in the direction of the Channel ports, while the invincible Luftwaffe received orders to achieve the mastery of the sky.

Three Luftflotten were to take part in the operation. Luftflotte No. 2 was to operate from bases in Holland, Belgium and north-eastern France under the orders of Kesselring. Luftflotte No. 3 was in the north-west of France and No. 5, of lesser importance, occupied the Danish and Norwegian airfields. In this way more than 3,500 enemy aircraft were assembled, only waiting for the order to take off and launch an assault upon the English sky, to destroy the airfields, radar stations and factories and to sweep the remaining fighters out of the air. The *Adler Angriff* would start at any moment. While waiting for the final assault, the Luftwaffe tested the adversary's defences, mostly under cover of darkness. They were light, unimportant missions destined to harry the civilian population, to determine the position of airfields and other objectives and to train the German crews. Numerous Allied ships still used the Channel under the protection of a few vague fighter patrols and, what was more effective, by a few balloons on steel cables, flown from the decks of the ships. These ships became the daily target for the Luftwaffe.

The R.A.F., which had lost a quarter of its pilots, reorganised itself as best as it could while volunteers from all parts arrived in the British ports.

For the average Englishman, the man in the street, the great battles of Norway, Belgium and France had been far-off conflicts in other countries, fought under other skies. The Expeditionary Force in France was the only one which had a slight bond with all these events. Genuinely astonished by the lightning German victories, the English were convinced that, in one way or another, they would muddle through as they had always done.

But one fine June day, a terrible awakening was in store for them. After the evacuation of Dunkirk, Great Britain realised that she was alone, terribly alone, in the great struggle, and that only twenty miles of water separated her from the panzer divisions of the Third Reich. The whole world was expecting the end of an empire which was now on its knees. The following dawn, from all points of Europe, the Luftwaffe planes took off in an attempt to annihilate the grandeur of Britain. But the world had not taken into account the tenacity of the British people, who staggered to their feet and dug in their heels. The great voice of Churchill boomed out above the grief, doubt and bloodshed. "We shall fight on the beaches, we shall fight in the streets, and we shall fight in the hills, we shall never surrender." And the volunteers assembled and formed themselves into groups. The ack-ack gunners, the balloon barrage crews, the soldiers on the beaches, took up their action stations. In the rear, women took the places of the fighting men. It was not an army about to fight, it was a whole race which had risen against the immensity of the oncoming tide.

The squadrons of Fighter Command, reinforced and re-grouped under the command of Air Marshal Sir Hugh Dowding, waited for the battle to begin. The fighter pilots stood by their aircraft ready to "scramble." And they were no longer alone, for liberty is a great word for which men are always prepared to be killed, and its appeal has never been uttered in vain.

Already young people from the overrun European countries had assembled. Pilots who, without being summoned, came of their own accord to ask for a place in Fighter Command. They were promised nothing since they asked for nothing. Clothed in Air Force blue uniforms, they proudly bore on their shoulders the names of the countries whom they had come to represent – France, Belgium, Poland, Czecho-Slovakia, Norway. The Poles had come a long way. After fighting desperately in 1939 in old fighters which were as outdated as those of the Belgians, they had reached Roumania. There, internment and escape, to France. In company with exiled Czechs, they volunteered for the Armée de l'Air and, flying Moranes, took their revenge for the ruins of Warsaw. After the French debâcle they made their way by devious routes to England.

A few adventurous Americans had also come to offer their services to the R.A.F., bringing with them all the nonchalance of their generous hearts. Belgians, too. . . .

The first Belgian fighter pilot to reach British territory was a tall, thin youth with childish features, Roger de Cannart d'Hamale, a sergeant pilot of 19, who arrived on the 20th June 1940. Three days later a small group, consisting of Lieutenant Jacques Phillipart, Instructor Pilots Maurice Buchin, Giovanni Dieu and Gonney, known to his friends as "Mosquito," landed at Plymouth. Having made France during the retreat, they were employed in ferrying French machines between Tours and Mont-pellier and between Istres and Mérignac, where they were the day Offenberg took off with his Simoun. From Mérignac they flew to Bayonne and found a berth in a Dutch cargo vessel. The most important group arrived from Montpellier where, after witnessing the most demoralising scenes, six pilots deserted by borrowing a staff car and driving to Port Vendres. They embarked on the S.S. *Apapa* on the 23rd June. These were Van den Hove d'Ertsenryck, Seghers, Leroy du Vivier, Rodolphe de Hemricourt de Grunne, Georges Doutrepont and Vicky Ortmans. At Gibraltar the group was increased by two more fighter pilots, Roger Malengrau and François de Spirlet. Together they disembarked at Liverpool on the 7th July. In "Pijker" Offenberg's group there were only two commissioned officers apart from himself: Alexis Jottard and Baudouin de Hemptinne. All the others were trainee pilots.

Nevertheless, other groups were on the way and a large contingent of officers, instructors and pupils left Oujda-la-Sordide and sailed across the Atlantic. A few others slipped on board the last ships to set sail from the French ports. The battle of Great Britain was about to begin and Belgium would be represented, thanks to a handful of deserters. The list was not very long:

With Fighter Command:
 Pilot Officer M. Buchin
 Pilot Officer J. Phillipart
 Pilot Officer G. Doutrepont
 Pilot Officer Van den Hove d'Ertsenryck
 Pilot Officer A. Jottard
 Sergeant Pilot R. de Cannart d'Hamale
 Pilot Officer R. de Hemricourt de Grunne
 Pilot Officer J. Offenberg
 Pilot Officer B. de Hemptinne
 Pilot Officer F. de Spirlet
 Pilot Officer E. Seghers
 *Pilot Officer D. Leroy du Vivier
 *Pilot Officer R. Malengrau
 *Pilot Officer V. Ortmans
 *Pilot Officer W. Van Lierde

With Coastal Command:
 Pilot Officer J. Kirkpatrick
 Pilot Officer A. Van Wayenberghe
 Pilot Officer L. Dejace

Pilot Officer L. Javaux, observer
Pilot Officer R. Demoulin
Pilot Officer F. Venesoen, gunner
Pilot Officer H. Gonnay
Pilot Officer A. Michiels, observer
*Pilot Officer G. Dieu
*Pilot Officer H. Lascot
*Sergeant Pilot L. Heimes, gunner
*Pilot Officer O. Lejeune
*Pilot Officer L. Prevot
*Pilot Officer Ch. Roman

The names marked with an asterisk are of the survivors who returned to Belgium after the war.

5

"FOR THE DURATION"

Liverpool.

WE GOT UP VERY LATE AND BREAKFASTED QUICKLY before changing our remaining Belgian and French money. (I ought to say my remaining money for Alexis, who is not particularly economical, did not have a penny in his pocket.) Our trainees were not very rich either and we shared our funds as pals by turning out our wallets.

A British Army officer, who must have been on duty in the port of Liverpool, told us in the late afternoon that we were to report to Tenby, a camp where the Belgian personnel were being collected. We asked for details as best as we could and, after checking the order, found that we had to take the last train for Cardiff and the Welsh mountains. We could not find the location of this town with the strange name on a map of England. Tenby.

"It must be near London," insisted Jottard, who had not the slightest idea of the geography of England.

"Perhaps it's on the south coast."

"I should prefer Cornwall," said someone else, "with its rocky coast, creeks with warm sand and . . ."

"As regards sea bathing I have a feeling that you'll soon be taking it in the Channel," said Alexis, "there's a war on."

The British officer returned and handed us our papers and railway tickets.

"Ask him where Tenby is," said Jottard, who did not understand a word of English, giving me a dig in the ribs. "He must know where it is."

So we learned at last that Tenby was a seaside resort in Pembrokeshire, in Wales.

As soon as we arrived on the Welsh border, the names of the villages we passed through, with their strange and improbably Celtic syllables which none of us Belgians could pronounce, formed a good subject of conversation in our two compartments.

"What about that one?"

"Wait, I'll spell it out to you. Take it down. S-k-y-d-i-r F-a-w-r. Are you certain we're still in England?"

"And that one?"

"Llanishen. There's no question about it. It's a beautiful language."

Thus, at the top of our form, we reached Tenby camp after a night spent in Cardiff.

At the camp we found about fifty Belgian army officers from a great variety of regiments. Lancers, Chasseurs, infantrymen and others, most of whom had got away from Dunkirk.

The airmen were not represented in this medley. In fact, that afternoon, our group was told that a mistake had been made – a little mistake which could be put right immediately. This was a centre reserved exclusively for the army. We were rounded up, given new tickets and itineraries, and at 19.00 hours we left for the Royal Air Force camp at Gloucester.

I do not know whether the saying is true that travel broadens the mind, but there are moments when it is grossly exaggerated. Cursing our misfortune, we reached the military base at Innsworth in the middle of the night, after crossing Gloucester in a most uncomfortable truck. We were standing and banged our heads against the metal bars of the roof each time the wheels went over a bump in the road. We arrived at last at an R.A.F. station where we began to feel a little at home.

We passed the guardroom whose windows were blacked out. A thin streak of yellow light came through the door. We could make out the sentry.

"It's an R.A.F. man," said a voice. "He's wearing a blue uniform."

One of the trainees – Limet, I think – tried to lift the flap to see better.

"It's not an airfield," he said. "There are no crates, only huts."

"That's okay. We don't want an aircraft. We want a bed and something to eat."

Despite the lateness of the hour we were given some sandwiches and hot cocoa. And then a bed. . . .

When you are hungry and doubled up with weariness, it is surprising how little it needs to make fourteen men happy. Before falling asleep I hear a voice say that some Belgians and Poles arrived at the camp two days ago.

* * *

On the 13th July, Baudouin de Hemptinne, Alexis Jottard and myself left Innsworth camp, for after passing our medicals in London, we had all three been accepted as fighter pilots. Baudouin and I are to be commissioned as pilot officers, which corresponds to second lieutenant at home. Only Alexis has not definitely been given a rank for he is a sergeant in Belgium and Captain de Soomer, who remained in London as assistant to our Air Attaché at the Embassy, has promised to do his best to arrange matters. If he can't manage it, I should prefer to remain a sergeant so as to be with Jottard, for we are very good pals.

"Don't worry about him, Offenberg," said de Soomer as we left. "We'll fix it up. You can leave for No. 6 O.T.U. with your mind at rest. The Air Ministry will send you your papers in a few days. Good luck!"

"But sir, – we haven't any decent uniforms. Look!"

He had to admit that we were not a pretty sight. The journey had put paid to my only uniform. There was an enormous stain of oil on the left breast pocket and the seams had gone in places.

"As soon as you've finished your retraining at Sutton Bridge, come and see me and we'll find you some really smart uniforms."

"But that will be a long time. They might keep us there for months."

"Months," he laughed. "Weeks, days. A few miserable days and you'll be joining an operational squadron with Fighter Command."

"Hurricane or Spitfire?"

"The Air Ministry will decide that."

So now I am a pilot in the R.A.F. and I have never in my life flown an English machine. It won't be long now.

In fact it was not long at all. On the following day, after spending a far from restful night in a King's Cross hotel – I was woken twice by the earsplitting wail of sirens – I took the train for Sutton Bridge.

I arrived at this airfield feeling a complete rookie, shy as hell, wondering how we were going to be treated by the British airmen.

The entrance barrier to the camp was lifted to let a military truck through just as we arrived. Two Hurricanes flew low above the buildings, chasing each other.

"Real aircraft," said Jottard, his eyes lighting up. "Look Jean, real fighters – what do you know?"

"The sort of fighters we ought to have had at the start."

"The Schaffen boys had them," replied Jottard.

"But how many."

"A dozen."

"We didn't need a dozen. We needed dozens and hundreds with eight machine guns like those. I guarantee if we'd had them you wouldn't be here now. Give the gentleman his marching orders."

The "gentleman" was the corporal of the guard who gave us a suspicious glance. He probably distrusted these three fellows chattering in an impossible language, clothed in uniforms he had never seen. (I am wearing an Alpine beret instead of a cap.)

"Belgians?" he asked.

"Oui – I mean yes."

He checked our papers while Jottard tried to spot the aircraft in the sky. Vapour trails at a great height were making magnificent white arabesques. Baudouin, calm and phlegmatic, smoked a cigarette until the Corporal had finished his conversation on the telephone.

At last we were allowed to enter the camp, escorted by a Redcap.

"This way, sir."

Baudouin threw away his cigarette and picked up his suitcase. Jottard ceased looking at the sky and followed us.

The real war is about to start for us.

*   *   *

This morning the postman brought me a letter. On the envelope stood "On His Majesty's Service." It was a letter from the Air Ministry addressed to Pilot Officer Offenberg, J.H.M., from a certain Charles Evans who signed himself as my obedient servant.

Here is the letter in its original text:

Sir,

I am commanded by the Air Council to inform you that they have approved your appointment to a commission in the General Duties branch of the Royal Air Force Volunteer Reserve and you will be appointed in the rank of Pilot Officer on probation with effect from 30/7/40, the date on which you reported for duty at No. 6 O.T.U. Sutton Bridge.

The appointment will be for the duration of hostilities.

I am, Sir,

Your obedient servant,

I am officially a British officer. Jottard arrived like a whirlwind.

"Pij!" he shouted. "Pij – I'm an officer!"

He began to dance a jig round me, waving a piece of white paper just like mine. Jottard is indestructible and incorrigible.

"Wait a minute," I said. "Anyone would think you'd won the big lottery. What does your paper say?"

"I think it says I'm appointed pilot officer for the duration of hostilities."

For the first time he realised the situation ... the duration of hostilities.

"But then I'll be a Sergeant again when it's over," he said.

"Of course you won't. They won't take your rank away from you, you'll see."

"Well, when we return to Belgium what shall I be? An officer or a sergeant?"

"My dear Alexis, I couldn't care less. I don't know how it will turn out. It's better not to think of it."

Alexis is not very happy about his future, either now or at a later date. After the war he wants to marry his fiancée Lulu for whom he bought a ring in Sétif during our stay there.

"You see it would be much easier to get married as an officer than as a Sergeant. And, besides, it would look more serious at

Andenelle with all the people there who know me. Ah, if only Lulu could know . . ."

Alexis is an optimist with an unshakeable faith in our future.

"How many flying hours have you got on Hurricanes?"

"Not enough. What about you?"

My face fell.

"Very few, I was sent solo on a Hurricane the day after I arrived and I've now got about 18 hours flying time. In any case, that's quite enough. She's a piece of cake. You ought to have been there yesterday afternoon. I was in a flight with Dawbarn and Solomon when we attacked three Blenheims flying near by. What a chase! We banked between the sheds and over the chimney pots of the mess. It was terrific."

"What about your English?" said Jottard.

"My English? Oh, I get by. What about yours?"

"Usually I don't understand a bloody word they say on the radio, but it'll come. I've finished my firing, formation and navigation tests. I was nearly frozen to death on my altitude test. For a moment at 25,000 feet I thought I'd been changed into a block of ice.

"As far as I can see we're pretty well okay. All set to go. What about Baudouin?"

"He's the same as us."

Alexis made a gesture which left no doubt as to the state of preparation of our friend Baudouin.

A week later, after a trip to London to buy uniforms and a few indispensable personal articles, we received orders to report to No. 145 Squadron at Drem in Scotland.

6

"BANDITS AT ONE O'CLOCK"

Editor's Note.—Drem. A Scottish village with little white-washed peasant houses in the foothills on the south shore of the Firth of Forth estuary. In the distance the slopes are covered with heather which turns the landscape a velvety purple beneath the sunny August sky. In England the battle for the mastery of the sky, the crucial battle upon which the fate of Europe depended, was in full swing. The newspapers and the B.B.C. communiques reported the brilliant actions of the R.A.F. fighters which were holding their own with the Luftwaffe all along the south coast. Hundreds of German aircraft, escorted by Messerschmitts, bombed the airfields and the ports while Spitfires and Hurricanes, guided by radar, intercepted, broke up the enemy formations, making them pay dearly for every bomb they dropped on Britsh soil. At Drem, apart from the newspapers and the radio, it was like being at a peacetime airfield on a fine summer's day.

Offenberg, de Hemptinne and Alexis Jottard, all three in impeccable uniforms of the best cut, arrived on the 17th August 1940, at the little station of Drem. A car was waiting to take them to the airfield where the grass still glistened in the early morning dew.

The station adjutant was delighted to see them for they were the first Belgians to be stationed there.

"Oh, I know the Belgians," he said, as he wrote down the routine details in the arrival book. "I was a pilot in the '14-18 war and I spent several days' leave in Brussels after the Armistice. It's a lovely city. There you are," he said, closing the big black book. "You are now attached to the station at Drem, No. 145 Squadron B Flight."

"Who's in command of 145?" asked Offenberg.

"Robert Boyd – unfortunately you won't be meeting your mates yet. They're all on leave. As you probably know they arrived two days ago. They're having a rest now and I can tell you it's a well earned one. Your huts are ready for you. Settle in at your leisure and we'll all meet for lunch in the mess."

Offenberg, who of course had never seen an R.A.F. Operational Squadron, wanted to know what the 145 was like. Was it an old unit or had it just been formed?

What were the pilots doing at the moment?

The elderly officer told them that 145 Squadron was an old one which had been disbanded between the two wars and reformed at Croydon at the end of 1939 with Blenheims. When the R.A.F. sent half squadrons to France, B Flight went across the water. Then, after leaving Croydon the twin-engined Blenheims were exchanged for Hurricanes, the squadron operated from Tangmere, an airfield on the south coast, and covered the evacuation from Dunkirk. It had been on convoy duty in the Channel for several weeks. On the 11th August it took part in

43

the furious air battle over Portland and on the 15th left Tangmere for Drem.

"Many victories?"

"A host of victories. I don't know all the pilots for I only
caught a glimpse of them the day they arrived. But I know that
Boyd has already shot down twelve Jerries and that Peel must
have five or six to his credit. The squadron as a whole has a
scoreboard with forty Swastikas. They're terrific fellows, the
boys of the 145. A bit rough," said the Adjutant with a smile,
"But you'll soon find that they're a fine bunch."

"Who's in command of our Flight?"

"B Flight. Wait a minute. (The Adjutant rummaged in one
of his drawers and brought a bundle of papers. He pulled out
a sheet on which was typed a list of names.) B Flight – let's see.
Oh yes. Boyd. No, I'm wrong. Boyd's in command of the Squadron now since he replaced Johnny Peel who was wounded and
brought down on the 8th. I don't think there's a flight commander yet for B Flight. But never mind," he said philosophic-
ally, "they'll choose the best fellow they've got."

Baudouin de Hemptinne, accustomed to the rigid regulations
of the Belgian Air Force, protested: "They've only got to ap-
point the senior in rank."

"You're wrong there," said the Englishman. "It's war-time
and a man's rank has nothing to do with it, unless he happens to
be the best. You'll see, it will be the best pilot who will be given
B Flight."

The three Belgian pilots settled in during the next few days,
paying several visits to the neighbouring town of Edinburgh.
Jottard even went for an afternoon's fishing in a mountain burn
and brought back some trout.

On the 21st August the whole squadron was present in the
mess when the three Belgians came in to lunch. They were exactly as Offenberg had imagined them – young, noisy and gay.
They wore their tunics over pullovers without collar or tie and
flying boots. The introductions were quickly made. Jean could
not catch all the strange sounding names as he shook hands:
Storrar, Dunning-White, Sykes, Honor, Weir, Newling, Faure.

A young fair-haired rather short youth came up to Offenberg,
put out his hand and said: "I'm Franck Weber," and added in
rather halting French "Welcome to 145. I am Czech and I served
in France."

The Squadron foregathered round Squadron Leader Adrian

Boyd, D.F.C. and bar, who, two days later, to keep his hand in, shot down a Heinkel III which was marauding over the Firth about ten miles from Edinburgh.

The three Belgians took part in the alerts like the others and flew on reconnaissance patrol over the Scottish coast.

On the morning of the 30th Boyd was called to the telephone. He came into the crew room.

"Gentlemen, we're off tomorrow morning. Here is the briefing for the three flights."

"Where are we off to?" asked Mike Newling.

"Dyce," said Boyd with a good Scottish. R, "near Aber..r.. deen."

"Hell, we shall freeze to death there. And we shall never see a blasted German crate."

"Oh yes we shall," said Boyd. "No. 5 Luftwaffe is sending a lot of recce Heinkels along the east coast. I bet we'll get one before the week's out."

The following day Boyd's Red Section (in which Offenberg was No. 3) took off for the north-east. The four Hurricanes set their courses above the Firth of Forth. They skimmed over the water for about ten minutes before climbing. With a map on his right knee, Offenberg followed the new itinerary over coastal towns and fishing villages ... St. Andrews. ...

"The best golf course in the world," said Sykes as they crossed the bay.

Carnoustie, Arbroath and Montrose, a French sounding name, Aberdeen and Dyce. Forty-five minutes' flight over the most marvellous landscape in the world, skirting the Scottish mountains.

****

8th September

Control reported an unidentified aircraft twenty miles out to sea, north-east of Aberdeen, flying in a southerly direction, estimated altitude 15,000 feet. By now I am quite used to the English method of registering height in feet. Sometimes it amuses me to divide the number of feet by three to find the metres. 15,000 feet of course automatically becomes 5,000 metres.

"Come on Pyker," called Sykes, rushing towards one of the three Hurricanes, whose engines had been started up by the mechanics.

A moment's hesitation and I ran towards one of the machines. Cockpit closed, temperature in order. . . . To starboard Sykes had ordered chocks away and had begun to taxi. The three of us, with Storrar as the third, sped across the airfield at full gas not quite into the wind. What did that matter? We had to make it snappy if we wanted to intercept the Jerry.

Sykes called up Control.

"Blue Section airborne."

"Blue Section set your course 090, angels one five."

Angels of course in crew jargon means something quite different from heavenly beings.

Angels one means a thousand feet. Angels one five meant 15,000. We climbed to 17,000. After a few minutes Control gave us a new course – 110°. I glanced at my instrument panel. We were told to circle, for the "bandit" was somewhere near our position. According to my watch we'd been flying for thirty-two minutes when suddenly, two miles ahead, slightly below us, I caught sight of a twin-engined aircraft flying in a south-easterly direction above the clouds.

I pressed the button of the intercom., and announced:

"Blue One to Blue Two – bandit at 1 o'clock below us."

"I can see him," replied Sykes.

The clockwork deference which the British Aviators have adopted to denote the positions of other aircraft is an excellent invention. It is based on the axis of the machine, twelve o'clock being ahead and six o'clock to stern. An aircraft at three o'clock therefore is exactly on the starboard beam.

Sykes, who has been in many types, ordered us "Line abreast." We turned a little to starboard, diving towards the bomber whose double tail unit I could now distinguish. It was a Dornier 215. One had to be careful of these solitary marauders which are generally very heavily armed. We closed in on him fast.

"Section attack."

We were still a mile away from the German bomber. Sykes dived while I banked slightly to starboard and Storrar followed suit to port. Our section fanned out above the bank of cloud through which we would catch an occasional glimpse of the sea. As on a practice flight, Sykes, who had arrived at the right distance, coldly announced:

"Opening fire."

A fraction of a second later the bomber replied.

Sykes gave a burst or two and then broke away. Three-quarters to stern I went into the attack when the German, trying to escape, banked violently to the left and flew into Storrar's field of fire. I do not think he saw our number three who sprayed him with his tracers. The Dornier pilot gave up the struggle and disappeared into the cloud.

Having lost sight of him, we got into formation, keeping a weather eye open. Sykes reported to Control. We found our quarry again after two minutes. He came out of a cloud to port.

"Blue Section echelon to starboard."

Storrar slipped beneath my Hurricane and took up his place on my right about a hundred yards to stern.

The hunt was on and my two partners exchanged comments over the intercom. in short curt phrases.

"Hurry up before he disappears again."

"Okay, I'm going in."

And Sykes waded in. He began to fire at 400 yards from the Dornier. The bomber did not reply.

I fired as soon as Sykes broke off and left me a clear field. I got the Dornier's tail in my sight and did not press the tit until I was forty yards from his double unit.

Storrar arrived too late. The German in a slight dive took refuge in the protecting cotton wool of another cloud.

We looked for him for another ten minutes but without result.

Tired of the engagement we returned to Dyce in close formation without knowing whether the bomber was shot down or whether he managed to crawl back to base.

18th September

I have just returned from patrol and am still in my gear as though I had returned from the moon, a Mae West slung round my neck. I noticed Nigel Weir and Sykes discussing with the mechanics on the tarmac.

We had flown over the sea in vain for more than an hour and I had finally decided to return to Dyce for my engine temperature had risen to 105°.

We all went into the briefing office.

"Well," said Squadron Leader Boyd, standing up, "you were unlucky again, eh?"

"Yes," I replied, "we went as far as the mouth of the Moray Firth without seeing a thing apart from a few trawlers."

The telephone rang. Boyd took off the receiver.

"Hullo. Squadron Leader Boyd here."

There was a silence.

"It's for you, Pyker," he said, handing me the 'phone.

It was Baudouin de Hemptinne on the other end of the line telling me that he was in the mess and had just received a letter from de Soomer in London. He had a lot of news.

"Important?"

"Yes. Buchin has been shot down. Come and join me and I'll give you the details."

"I won't be long. I'll slip out of my things and be with you in ten minutes."

Boyd gave me permission to leave. He asked me why I was so excited.

"It's Baudouin, sir. He's received news from my Belgian comrades who are in No. 2 Group."

"Have you many pals there?"

"No, not many, but most of them are personal friends and I like to know what happens to them."

"Good," said Boyd, picking up his cap. "You're taking off with a formation at 16.00 hours. Until then, do what you like. Be seeing you."

In the mess I found Baudouin still reading his letter.

I sat down in a comfortable airchair and sighed.

"Tell me the news."

Baudouin handed me the letter and, after a few seconds' hesitation, said in a slightly gloomy voice :"Philippart and Doutrepont have also been shot down. But, here, read for yourself. Where's Alexis?"

"He's flying."

"Well, he'll hear on his return. In any case, there's no particular hurry."

I took the letter and learned, sentence by sentence, the news of all these fellows who had joined the Free Forces almost at the same time as ourselves. Poor Maurice Buchin was the first casualty among the Belgian aviators with the R.A.F.

Posted to No. 213 Squadron at Exeter on the 25th July, with Lt. Philippart, they were sent to patrol over Portland on the 11th August. With another squadron they intercepted a formation of 150 German aircraft composed of Junkers 88's and Heinkel 111's escorted by Messerschmitts. Buchin flew as No. 2 in Philippart's section and they both obtained a confirmed victory.

Two Junkers 88 were shot into the sea.

Three days later, the 15th August, the South Coast radar station announced seven enemy formations (some two to three hundred aircraft) approaching the Hampshire and Dorset coast. Eight squadrons, among them No. 213, were in the air, consisting of 150 Spitfires and Hurricanes. An air battle developed near Portsmouth and Portland. It was a savage dog fight. Sixteen Messerschmitt 110 and four Stuka Junkers 87 were shot down. Buchin was reported missing. He was the first Belgian aviator to be brought down over England. Philippart, as though to avenge the death of his comrade, had three victories confirmed, bringing down three Me 110s and damaging a fourth in the course of the battle.

On the 22nd August, Philippart at the head of the Yellow Section of No. 213 Squadron intercepted a German formation above Exmouth at 20,000 feet and managed to bring down another Junkers 88. On the 25th his aircraft was hit and he baled out over the Channel. Not until the dawn of the 28th was his body washed up on a South Coast beach.

Baudouin, who had stood up, went over to the big window which looked on to the gardens and stared at the Scottish mountains outlined against the sky. We were alone in this impersonal room which was like every other R.A.F. mess.

"Baudouin," I asked, "was Philippart married?"

"Yes. His wife is Irish. They have a child."

"Hmm."

The letter also said that Rodolphe de Hemricourt de Grunne, who was with Eugene Sèghers in No. 32 Squadron, has three Germans to his credit. On 16th August he shot down a Me 109 and the following day, when a German formation attacked the Biggin Hill H.Q,. Nos. 32 and 610 Squadrons intercepted it, Rodolphe brought down his second Me 109. On the 18th August he achieved his third success with a Do 17 but paid dearly for it this time. He was brought down by the fighters, baled out and was badly burned. Sèghers was shot down into the sea on the 24th August. He got away with an enforced bath, went up the next day and had his first success three days later.

Captain Vandenhove d'Ertsenryck and "Boy" Leroy du Vivier of No. 43 Squadron each shot down a Stuka in cloudy weather. Vandenhove then proceeded to damage a Me 109 which he chased over the Thames Estuary. On Monday, 2nd September, Roy was put out of action; he was shot down and wounded in the leg.

Vandenhove, the only Belgian representative now of No. 43 Squadron, distinguished himself on 4th September by shooting down two Me 110s in quick succession – one confirmed, one probable. But a third Jerry hit his fuselage with a shell and four machine-gun bullets. Vandenhove was covered with glycol; the black smoke prevented his seeing but he managed to make a forced landing on a South Coast airfield. He was shot down for the second time on the 8th and once more managed to land in a field near Ashford, his plane riddled with bullets. Six days later he was posted to No. 501 Squadron at Kenley and the following day his new Squadron commander took him up as his No. 2, Red Section. They waded into a score of Do 17s above Ashford and Vandenhove received a burst which destroyed his cooling system.. The engine temperature rose. . . . He tried to land his Hurricane but at 200 feet his aircraft blew up and crashed into the River Stour. It was 12.45. . . . Vandenhove was killed.

Baudouin de Hemptinne did not stir and was still staring at the flowers in the garden. He stood there, his hands in his pockets, waiting for me to speak.

"Where was Vandenhove on the 10th May?" I asked.

"At Schaffen, I think. No. 2 Squadron of No. 1 Group. Have you read the passage about Georges Doutrepont?"

"I'm coming to it."

Doutrepont joined No. 229 Squadron at Wittering on the 4th August after ten days retraining at the No. 7 Fighter School (O.T.U.) at Hawarden, near Chester. The squadron was commanded by an Englishman, Banham. On the 9th September it was moved to Northolt, west of London. Two days later the formation took the air to intercept a formidable armada composed of thirty Heinkel 111s and twenty-five Me 110s, protected by fifty Me 109s. Doutrepont brought down two bombers in the ensuing fracas and with a couple of pilots of Blue Section, in which he flew No. 2, shot down a He 111. The German aircraft landed in a field.

On the 15th Semptember, Doutrepont took part in his second important engagement. At 20,000 feet over Maidstone No. 229 Squadron established contact with twenty-five Me 109s. Blue Section – Doutrepont was still flying No. 2 – attacked a group of German fighters flying above the others in order to prevent them diving on the rest of the squadron. In the course of the fight No. 1 of his section baled out. Eye-witnesses who with typical English phlegm were watching the battle from the ground, saw a Hurricane dive and crash onto the station buildings of Staplehurst in Kent. Its pilot, the Belgian airman Georges Doutrepont, was killed in combat. . . .

"What do you think of it?" asked Baudouin, turning towards me. Of all the squadrons of Fighter Command we had to be posted to one stationed in the quietest sector of the British Isles while our pals get themselves killed in the South.

I, too, thought of all these chaps who were fighting so bravely in this battle where no quarter was given, in a perilous sky where no day passed without some adventure.

I nodded.

"Baudouin, we can't stay here. We must go and ask to be transferred to No. 2 Group. Let's go and see Boyd and explain things to him. I'm sure he'll understand."

We returned to the squadron. The Commander was in one of the sheds discussing with the chief mechanic, who saluted and left as soon as we arrived. Boyd was wearing his flying boots and "Mae West," that rubber belt so typical of the American actress's charms.

"Anything wrong?" asked Boyd, who saw at once that we had something important to ask him. Since my English was better than Baudouin's, I acted as spokesman.

"Yes sir, we've just received news of our friends down south. We should like to get transferred to some unit in No. 2 Group. Can you help us?"

"Ah, so that's it," said Boyd with a smile. "Fellows out for blood in my squadron, eh? Tough guys . . . who like a scrap. So much the better, that's an additional reason for keeping you both in my squadron."

"But sir . . ."

"Don't you worry, Pyker," he said, giving me a friendly tap on the shoulder. "A transfer isn't necessary. In a fortnight we're going back to the old fighter territory."

"We're leaving for the south?"

"Yes, to Group 2. Does that satisfy you?"

"Yes sir."

"Well, in the meantime, I've been bequeathed a new commander for B Flight . . . An Australian named Bungey . . . In a day or two you'll fly a Hurricane to Drem . . . That one," he said, pointing to one of the machines. "No. 2683. You'll leave it there and I'll send a Fairey Battle to pick you up. On the way back you'll stop at Montrose, meet Bungey and bring him back here. O.K.?"

He did not wait to hear my reply, but went on:

"Go and get ready. In two minutes we're taking a trip along the coast. The three of us . . ."

We were already some way off when Boyd called me back, shouting at the top of his voice to drown the noise of the engine which had just been started up.

"Pyker, you remember that Heinkel 111 a fortnight ago? Storrar and Sykes both insist that you hit him. You can count it as 'damaged.' And now make it snappy!"

24th September

I have been waiting almost two days for the Fairey Battle which Boyd was to send here to Drem to pick me up and take me back to Dyce. I know hardly anyone on this airfield and the two days have been very dreary and monotonous. I have just learned to my delight that Pilot Officer Rawbone of my squadron has just taken off from Dyce. Sitting on the edge of the runway facing the Control tower I keep scanning the sky in the direction of the Firth of Forth. The wind has a salty tang which it has probably absorbed from the grey waters of the North Sea. Some stray gulls are flying majestically over the airfield. . . .

After about half an hour's wait the Battle appeared like a Jack in the box over the water, skimmed the shed at about fifty feet before zooming and getting into a position to land. Rawbone, to my amusement, succeeded in pulling off the finest "pancake" of his career, letting the Battle sink like a stone from at least ten feet. Luckily the "crate" was solid and the undercarriage stood up to the shock, otherwise I should have been there for another couple of days.

Rawbone, who parked his machine facing the tower, was carefully inspecting his wheels and shock absorbers as I came up.

"Hullo, Rawbone, what was eating you? Not a very Gosport landing I feel."

Rawbone, a tall youth of twenty with a cheerful face marred by a small scar at the corner of his mouth, looked up over the wheel.

"You're right. This tub's a bit different from the Hurricane. Just as I pulled the stick to flatten out I realised that I was to high."

"Why didn't you give her a burst of gas ... You could have put her down further on ..." I slipped under the wing to take a look at the shock absorbers.

"I thought of it," said Rawbone, "but then I said Hell, pulled the stick full back into my belly and shut my eyes. There was a big bump and Bob's your uncle. I was down."

Seeing that things were not as bad as he had anticipated and not bothering his head unduly about such trifles, Rawbone flung his helmet in the cockpit and putting on a rather rakish cap calmly announced with a smile on his lips: "Let's go and grab a cuppa."

"You're crackers," I said, annoyed by this proposal. "I've been sitting here on my pack for two hours and now you want to drink a cup of tea."

"But it's only ten o'clock and we've the whole day before us. What can we do once we get back to Dyce? Come on ... it'll do you good."

It is pointless to argue with an Englishman when he feels that it's teatime. If there were ten Stukas bombing the field or Jerries landing a couple of miles away he would still be capable of going for his cup of tea. So without any more argument I took the placid Rawbone off to the canteen. Only after inflicting upon his stomach two cups of the tasteless brew and eating four biscuits did he decide to take off for Montrose flying the school-boy route. As soon as we landed he insisted that he knew of a nice small restaurant, the George Hotel. . . .

However, an officer in a leather jacket came up, dumped his pack and introduced himself.

"I'm Flight Lieutenant Robert Bungey and you've probably come from Dyce to fetch me. Well I'm all set."

Rawbone looked at me and I felt that he was going to say that he wasn't by any means ready. But he changed his mind.

"All right. Let's get going then."

As we walked towards the Control tower Bungey, who was walking next to me, said in his odd drawling Australian accent:

"Are you from 145 Squadron?"

"Yes, sir, B Flight, yours."

"By your accent I can tell you're not English," he said, shifting his valise to his other hand.

"No, I'm Belgian. There are three Belgians in B Flight."

"Have you been in action yet?"

"Yes, I have one German confirmed and a second damaged."

Wishing to change the subject, I added "There are also a Czech and an Anglo-Argentine in B Flight . . ."

"Well that's fine. I'm a Digger. We shall be a fine bloody Russian salad and there won't be any chance of getting bored. You can call me Robert or Bob if you like. What's your name? I thought I heard Offenberg just now."

"Yes, but everyone here calls me Pyker."

"That's an odd name. What does it mean?"

How difficult it would be to make him understand all the nuances of the Brussels street kids' jargon.

"Oh, I've never really found out," I replied. "It's a name they sometimes give in Brussels to boys who are born there. It's unimportant."

Rawbone flew us to Dyce for lunch despite his desire to visit the George Hotel in Montrose. He even managed to put the Battle down as lightly as a feather. A perfect three-point landing.

2nd October

I was in the mess with Dunning-White and Bungey. Leaning against the bar we listened to the wireless blaring out an old dance hit. Dunning-White knew it and hummed the words:

> *My honey and me*
> *And baby makes three,*
> *We're happy in my blue heaven . . .*

"Good dance tune, eh, Pyker?" said Bungey, doing a few steps. "Why don't you go dancing tonight at the Caledonian?"

"We can't buzz off to Aberdeen at 9 in the evening," I grumbled. "Anyhow, I'm ops at 6 tomorrow and I want to be fresh and fit."

"Don't be such a mutt, Pyker," advised Bungey. "You don't go out and you take things too seriously. You never drink much either. . . ."

"And when he does he always takes a big dose of Eno's afterwards," interpolated Dunning-White. "It may be wonderful for the health but I'd rather die a slow death."

At that moment I saw Jottard's bright face in the doorway.

"Hi, Alexis, come and have one," I cried.

Jottard, who had been looking for me for about ten minutes

announced that de Hemptinne had shot down a Heinkel 111 over a convoy.

"When?"

"Half an hour ago. I was at the squadron when he came back from a protective patrol over a naval convoy. Lucky devil, old Baudouin!"

I was thrilled. I went on asking Alexis questions although he was a trifle breathless from running to tell me the news.

"Did he get him single-handed?"

"Naturally. He was alone. It was dusk when he took off. Boyd sent him up at about 19.45 hours and he picked up the convoy 20 miles north-east of Aberdeen at 15,000 feet. It was half light. He saw a twin-engined bomber within range. Apparently the moment he announced it to Control you could have heard a coin drop in the Ops room . . . they were waiting religiously for the result of the combat.

"After making the first attack he passed within 50 yards of the machine. Baudouin had just time to make out the shape . . . it was a Blenheim. The Group Captain was just telephoning to ask who had sent Blenheims over the convoy without notifying him. Apparently he could be heard giving them a rocket 200 yards away . . ."

"And did Baudouin bring down the Blenheim?"

"Apparently not . . . He missed it."

I was furious. This habit of sending Hurricanes up in the half light – a machine that was designed to fight by day – seems to me a monstrous and dangerous waste of time. Night fighters are the Achilles' heel of the R.A.F. defence. Although the Spits and Hurricanes can hold their own with the enemy during the day, as soon as night falls all that remains are the searchlights and the ack-ack guns.

Only eight so-called night fighter squadrons. Two equipped with Defiants and six others with Blenheims exist at the moment. These squadrons started their career as day fighters and went on until the authorities realised that in this role they only succeeded in being decimated.

Then they were transferred to night fighting.

The Beaufighters are only coming into operation very slowly and are not available yet in sufficient numbers to have much operational significance.

In view of the restricted numbers of specialized night fighters, the Hurricane and Spitfire pilots fly operational at night.

55

Extremely regrettable accidents have already been reported from all the fighter groups and Baudouin de Hemptinne's adventure is only a minor incident in the annals of night fighting.

Baudouin, whom I found in his hut, told me exactly what happened.

"I was over the convoy, which I could see quite clearly in the moonlight. Then I saw the exhaust flames of a twin-engined aircraft. I attacked and realised too late that it was a Blenheim." Baudouin straightened his tie at a small mirror on his night table. He was forced to bend down to see what he was doing. "It was too late. I had already fired two bursts . . ."

"A ridiculous business," I said sympathetically.

"Absolutely ridiculous," replied Baudouin, getting into his tunic. "Control didn't even know that the Blenheims were in the neighbourhood. Luckily it's damned difficult to aim at night. I missed them . . . It's the first time that such a thing has pleased me." He took my arm. "Are you coming? I haven't eaten yet as I've been too upset."

"But Alexis told me that you'd shot down a Heinkel."

"Well, I think I did. But if you hear that I've succeeded in shooting down a Blenheim I shan't be surprised."

In the corridor leading to the mess horseshoe staircase we met Dunning-White.

"Good show, Belgy. They've found your Heinkel. It fell on the beach a few miles south of Aberdeen. But you're a lousy shot. You didn't manage to kill a single Jerry and they've all been taken prisoner."

At the bar Baudouin paid for the first round and Boyd for the second. Had not the squadron commander betted that we should shoot down a Jerry before we had been a week at Dyce? In actual fact it had been a month . . .

Boyd called for silence and hitched himself on to the bar.

"Gentlemen," he announced, "I've lost my bet and I'm a good gambler. I'll wager another bet this evening. Before ten days are out I bet we have another kill. Any takers?"

Everyone was ready to take him on. Before the bets were made, Group Captain Finlay Crear, commanding Dyce, made himself heard above the turmoil.

"Mind your eye, boys, don't bet with Boyd. The 145 Squadron is leaving here. You're off to Tangmere in a few days time."

"Did you say Tangmere?" asked Dudley Honor. "Tangmere near a certain Chichester, down south?"

"That's precisely what I said."

"And did Boyd know?"

"I think so."

The whole mess was flabbergasted. The cunning of their squadron leader left them speechless.

"The dirty dog. To think I've bet that rogue half a pint," roared Dunning-White, who would probably have stood a round of ten without a bet.

"Let's debag him."

"Come on then."

Boyd was too quick for them. Jumping down from the bar, he made for the door, fled along the corridors, being chased to the accompaniment of loud laughter by the others.

I could not help thinking of a lot of college boys having a grand lark.

7
TANGMERE

10th October

AT 12.40 HOURS SQUADRON-LEADER BOYD, LEADING No. 145, touched down on one of the Tangmere runways, followed by his flock. We landed after covering the stretch Dyce-Tangmere in three hours and five minutes flying time, including a stop at Church Fenton. The squadron has been given its old quarters and now has a place worthy of it in No. 2 Fighter Group. Most of the pilots who have been with the squadron for some months feel quite at home on this airfield, from which they operated until the 15th August, but for the others the change is a radical one. In Scotland it was an extremely calm sector and suddenly without transition we have been plunged into the greatest aerial affray of all time. . . .

Dunning-White came into the dispersal hut at the extreme north end of the field, rubbing his hands.

"Finished with messing about, my young friends. This afternoon the war begins. It won't be long . . . You'll only have to wait an hour or two to wish you'd never come here."

Personally I wanted nothing better than to see the Luftwaffe bombers appear. But in the meantime I thought it best to get comfortably settled in and take a look round our new home. Everyone had landed safely. Bungey had already chosen an armchair and installed himself in a corner of the hut as though he had never been anywhere else. He admired the rustic scene which was to be our view from now onwards, a huge field stretching as far as the eyes could see, with cows grazing. In the distance we could make out some farmhouse roofs behind a screen of trees.

To the south I knew that there was a beach and beyond the sea the enemy coast ... The grey waters of the Channel, that large stretch of sea separating two worlds will in future be the arena where we shall settle accounts.

"Do you know this part of the world, Bungey?"

"Me? I've never been here before."

"And yet you settle down like a lord in your armchair and look completely at home. Aren't you going to take a look round the joint? At least come to the mess and bring your precious goods and chattels."

Bungey grumbled. He is fair-haired and has the face of an obstinate woodcutter.

"Not worth while," he said. "There'll be a 'scramble' as soon as we're filled up. Take a pew," he said, pointing to an armchair. "We can settle down this evening."

He was perfectly right, for within an hour Control gave the order: "Scramble!" Jottard appeared with half his gear and leaped into his plane. I wondered where he had come from.

My mechanic strapped me in. With an automatic gesture I checked the controls and tried the cockpit roof to see that it was functioning properly ... On my right a trail of grey smoke was coming from Boyd's machine. His prop glistened in the sunlight. One by one the pilots started their engines, raising a huge cloud of dust. I pressed on the self-starter, the prop turned jerkily and then suddenly began to whirr. Twelve aircraft were soon lined wing to wing on the extreme north of the main runway.

Boyd pushed his throttle full home and was off, followed by his two wingers. Then came the second section and the third. They had not yet reached the middle of the runway before I released my brakes and gave the engine full gas.

As soon as his four sections were airborne Boyd rallied them and gave orders for them to take up Formation A of our Tactical Manual.

Our twelve aircraft followed the coast eastwards as far as Beachy Head, then turned back south on orders from Control.

I was what the Luftwaffe pilots call the *kugelfanger*, known irreverently in the R.A.F. as Tail-end-Charlie, while the two wingers of my section were the weavers who roamed up and down the flanks protecting the lords who flew in the centre of the formation.

Boyd grew irritated when the Control Officer at Tangmere with his B.B.C. announcer's voice calmly told us we could return home. It was probably a false alarm, he added.

This did not prevent the loudspeakers in the ops room from emitting a torrent of abuse for anyone who happened to be there to hear. Most of the pilots were very disappointed on their return to the dispersal, where Bungey at last took up his valise to find a place in the mess.

Tangmere was an air base in peace time, and enjoyed a comfort which was not to be found on all the R.A.F. airfields. The officers have individual rooms in a hut situated about a hundred yards from the mess where we are to take our meals.

It did not take me long to find out the distractions available at Tangmere when one was not flying.,. "But between ourselves," said Mike Newling, who gave me the tips, "those moments are extremely rare."

"A few miles away," he said in a bored voice, "there's a little town with a main street and a cathedral. There are a few pubs but they're not very interesting. The cinemas aren't bad, that's all."

"How do you mean that's all?" I asked. "Isn't there anything else?"

"You can go and bathe at Bognor or visit Brighton, if you like, where there's a good music hall called the Hippodrome. And then there's always the 'Old Ship'."

I wondered what sort of a ship it was, but Mike explained. It was really the name of an old inn at Bosham, a nearby village.

Boyd, who had just come into my room, flung himself on my bed and interrupted Newling to describe the place for me.

"The old ship is a pub. A splendid pub kept by an even more splendid woman. Nancy is a great character."

"It's completely out of this world. In a village where the clocks stopped when Admiral Drake beat the Armada. We'll take you along there one of these evenings."

"What is there to do there apart from drinking beer?"

"It's difficult to explain. You see, Pyker, it's a club for fighter pilots, the company is pleasant and they make you welcome. We spend very restful evenings there. There's nothing better for the nerves, as you'll find out yourself."

"And where is this dream spot?"

"A few miles from here – beyond Chichester," said Newling as he left the room. "It's a kind of pirate's den. Cheerio, Pyker, see you tomorrow."

"Cheerio," I replied as he shut the door without banging it, which was rather unusual for him.

Boyd got up from the bed where he was sitting.

"I'm going to get a good night's rest. We shall need it. The war begins again tomorrow. Cheerio, Pyker. Have a good sleep ... and don't forget tomorrow we shall be hunting big game."

11th October

After the first dawn patrol over the Isle of Wight – I was in Blue Section with Baudouin and Bungey, but we did not make contact with the enemy – we returned to Tangmere for breakfast. It was not yet nine o'clock when Boyd took us up again to 30,000 feet. As there was no heating in the Hurricane I almost froze to my seat and found difficulty in using the controls. Ice soon formed on the windscreen and we were obliged to come down a bit. Far away to the west we could see long vapour trails, but despite Boyd's requests, Control forbade us to go and take a closer look because it was not in our sector.

We took off four more times and each time I was "Tail-end-Charlie."

12th October

At 30,000 feet I flew behind the others. They were staged ahead of me in a sky where not the smallest cloud broke the blue monotony which hurt the eyes. Boyd, leading the group, gave the orders over the intercom and kept in touch with Control, which reported bandits at twenty miles from our actual position. Bungey, my flight commander, who was weaving on our starboard flank, kept up an uninterrupted commentary, telling us his impressions.

Banking eastwards into the sun I thought for a brief second that I had caught sight of some aircraft. Should I inform the squadron commander? And supposing I was wrong? I pressed the intercom button all the same.

"Red 1, I think I can see aircraft in the sun."

Before I had even finished my message the Hurricanes ahead of me scattered in all directions. As I let go the transmitting button I heard a medley of cries.

"Break away, break away . . ."

"I'm behind you. Carry on."

A glance in my mirror. A Messerschmitt. I pulled the Hurricane over to the left and dived. The Me had missed me but I had disengaged only just in time. Another fraction of a second and he would have brought me down. The sky was suddenly like a hornet's nest. I do not know how long the battle lasted – ten or fifteen minutes maybe – but to me it seemed an eternity. My ears hurt, my head was buzzing and the sweat made my clothes stick to my body despite the icy temperature at that altitude. Twice I got in a quick burst of about two seconds. The Jerries broke off now and below me, far below, I could see the white blossom of an open parachute descending. Calm returned on the short waves. The reassuring voice of Boyd rallied his sections and gave them a rendezvous over Selsey Bill.

Then I heard: "Red 1 from Yellow 1. My No. 2 has gone down in a spin. I didn't see anyone firing at him."

"Probably passed out."

"Red 1 from Blue 3. Blue 2's been shot down and baled out."

"That's Thorpe."

"He'll be okay."

Thorp was fished out of the drink, but Sergeant Pilot Wadham had not fainted. His body was recovered in the wreck of his Hurricane with a machine-gun bullet in his head.

That afternoon on our second patrol Boyd and Dudley Honor separated from the squadron just as the Messerschmitts dived on us; they went down to 15,000 feet, intercepted an Arado 196 and despatched it into the sea.

Upstairs where I had remained a gigantic ballet developed, in the course of which I could not get into a favourable firing position, for these Messerschmitts are so much faster and more manoeuvrable than our aircraft at these high altitudes.

Pilot Officer Rawbone brought down an Me 109 and went up in my esteem, for I was still irritated with him after the Drem affair. Mike Newling hit a second but did not dare to follow when the German dived, leaving a trail of smoke.

During the past two days I have been in three different fights without any certain results, despite a few bursts at close quarters into the swastikas. I hoped to be luckier this morning. We had been flying in zig-zags over the sea south of the Isle of Wight for half an hour, when the Controller of the Tangmere sector notified Boyd that there were bandits for him. In action the squadron commander is normally the only one to use the radio and speak to Sector Control. It is useless for the others to transmit while chasing the enemy. By merely listening I learned how many of the enemy there were in the neighbourhood, their altitude and the direction of approach. Boyd replied curtly: "Red Leader okay" to each message from Control. When the interception took place it became worse than Radio Luxembourg, and if someone transmitted for four or five seconds with nothing particularly interesting to say while the tracers were flying all round him, nobody could interrupt him before he had finished his message. By that time it was more than probably that the warning would not interest him in the least, for it was surprising the number of bullets one can pump into the fuselage of an aircraft in four or five seconds.

Thus we all kept radio silence and let Boyd speak and act for us. We only had to follow him and keep our eyes skinned.

The Messerschmitts dived on us before we were aware of their presence from out of the sun, where no one had spotted them. It may have lasted a couple of seconds. A few yellow noses, some black crosses, and here and there in the sky the white silk of a parachute. They swept past like meteors, preceded by a jet of tracer bullets. I followed their dive without being able to catch them up. Only Boyd had time to get on the tail of one of them and to rip open its belly, from which a long red flame poured.

Control had nothing further for us and we returned to Tangmere.

At the dispersal everyone discussed the fight like spectators coming from a football match in the dressing rooms of the Union Saint-Gilloise or the Racing Club.

Boyd was furious because he maintained that no one had followed him down.

"You're wrong," said Dunning-White, who looked more and more like a corsair (the butt of a Colt stuck out of his boot at knee level). "I dived on the first crate I saw and sprayed him from at least 200 yards."

Mike Newling corroborated this.

"We've only one missing, and that's Macazec, the Czech. He was brought down flying Tail-end-Charlie. In any case no one saw it happen."

The telephone orderly came over to Boyd, whispered something in his ear while the squadron leader wiped his neck with a handkerchief.

He told us with a smile that our Czech comrade, who had been brought down unnoticed by us, had baled out and was almost safe and sound: he had a few splinters in his legs but would be all right after a few weeks in hospital.

In the truck which took us back to the mess, Nigel Weir, a great clown on occasions, made us a little speech in an Oxford accent on the chase in general and aircraft in particular.

"The task of the warrior has always been the same," he began. "It is the systematic extermination of the infidel. Today new methods and effective weapons have been put at the disposal of the enthusiasts of this interesting little sport. Among these I must mention that the fighter plane is unrivalled. However . . ."

A violent jolt, which made all of us hit the ceiling, interrupted his speech. Then, quite imperturbably, he continued:

"However, as I was saying, this instrument is not perfect, and there are certain things which it refuses to do, namely (a) to look behind so that it is not shot down stupidly, (b) to place itself at a point exactly 200 yards from the nearest Nazi airman, (c) to make the necessary firing corrections, and (d) to fire the machine-gun.

"On account of these grave imperfections, for which I blame the scientists, His Majesty's Government has seen fit to engage the services of a certain number of gentlemen like you and I to carry out missions in order to rectify the four points I have just quoted. . . ."

The arrival of the truck at the mess door put an end to this lesson by Professor Nigel Weir, professional fighter pilot.

19th October

My flight commander, Bob Bungey, having suggested that a couple of days' rest would not come amiss, we went to see Boyd to get his blessing.

"Where do you think of going?"

"To the Old Ship at Bosham to sleep for forty-eight hours."

"And you won't stir from there?"

"No, but in the event of Mr. Churchill needing Offenberg or myself," said Bungey, already looking very holiday-like in his sun glasses, "don't hesitate to give us a ring."

And so we spent two marvellous days in that old inn which the years seem to have forgotten at the edge of a creek, into which the waters of the Atlantic do not dare to thrust their waves. In front of the inn there was a porch and a small garden with a crazy pavement path and a few dying asters.

It is very "Olde English" with its oak beams, blackened walls and a few lanterns from caravels which have been cast upon its beaches.

In the old days the sailors came to quench their thirst here after their privateering – pirates or corsairs with faces bronzed by the sea wind. Today the inn is the rendezvous of the Tangmere fighter pilots, who come to drink a pint or two when dusk falls on their airfield. The old walls then hear stories which must thrill their 300-year-old plaster to the marrow and remind them of the good old days of piracy.

I spent two days of complete rest putting my ideas in order. Bungey spoke of his native land, Australia, to which he wishes to return one day "unless one of those bloody Huns pumps an explosive bullet into my guts."

His advice is very precious, for he has many combats to his credit, and last night, leaning on the bar where the beautiful Nancy presides, we discussed fighter tactics and the respective performances of Hurricanes and Messerschmitts.

"What we ought to avoid," said Bungey, his face cupped in his hands and his elbows on the counter, looking at Nancy, who seemed to smile at him, "is flying in sections of three. We ought to fly in pairs like the Germans do. The leader can then fire, knowing that his rear is protected."

"We must try and convince Boyd, that's all," I replied.

"Yes, that's all. But . . . there you are." He changed the subject and said to the barmaid: "Same again, Nancy, please."

25th October

For several days I have been training with Dunning-White, since we have been given permission to fly in pairs. Several times Tangmere Control reported unidentified aircraft over the Isle of

Wight, but we never managed to make contact with them, for each time we reached the spot the Germans had disappeared. Every day, however, we could see vapour trails to the south, probably over Brittany.

This morning we took off as a squadron under the command of Boyd. Apparently he will soon be leaving us to become Chief Instructor of a fighter school. Pity, for I get on very well with him.

After twenty minutes' flight Dunning-White, who flies as Blue 2, announced black specks on the horizon, coming in from the south. We were at 30,000 feet, well above the muck.

Boyd reported bandits to Tangmere Control, but once more for some obscure reason they refused permission to intercept them and called another squadron in the sector to go and attack the Huns.

It was ridiculous, for we could have cut them off had we turned eastwards.

In the earphones we could hear far-off voices calling, giving orders, commenting on the situation.

The other squadron lost sight of them. Bad luck!

In the afternoon we took off again. An enemy formation had been reported very high, at 30,000 feet, forty miles south of the coast. We climbed like madmen to 29,000 feet, in the hope of being above them at the moment of interception.

Unfortunately, when we spotted them they were still above us. I counted fifteen Me 109s at about 32,000 feet.

"Red 1," Boyd called to Control. "We're too low and too late. We shall engage at a great disadvantage. Blue 1," he added, "watch the sun. That's where they'll come from."

"Blue 1," okay."

The German aircraft, in open formation, slowly circled above, pretending not to have seen us. What was going on? They could not have failed to spot us. This was something quite new.

We went on climbing towards them.

Suddenly a voice cried: "Red 1 from Yellow 3, I've got three on my tail."

"It's Yale. Where the hell is he? Red Section follow me."

The three leading aircraft half rolled and there was a few seconds' pause. Yale called again: "They've got me. I'm baling out. Cheerio."

Little Yale was the rear man, and without doubt he could not keep up with us. No one would have noticed the incident except the German squadron, which remained aloft, refusing to attack us, while three of them fell upon Yale.

On the way home, as we were flying over Selsey Bill, Baudouin de Hemptinne reported engine trouble, but thanks to his skill as a pilot he managed to put his Hurricane down in a field. He jumped out of the cockpit and ran off. Two minutes later it burst into flames.

27th October

Without having time to attend Mass, as I do each Sunday, I took off with the whole squadron in Blue Section led by Bob Bungey, with Alexis Jottard as our No. 3.

At 15,000 feet someone announced a formation much higher to starboard, but Tangmere Control reassured us by saying it was a squadron of Spitfires also on patrol.

At 32,500 feet I was literally frozen and my numbed hands could hardly feel the controls. Over Halton, Boyd, whose eyesight is phenomenal, reported a dozen Messerschmitts a few thousand feet below.

I tried to remain calm but my heart pounded furiously. In spite of my oxygen mask I breathed stertorously as though the air were suddenly lacking in my lungs.

Boyd dived with his section and a split second later Bungey followed. I did not follow suit, in order to remain with my leader. Ahead of me Boyd's No. 2, my Czech pal Franck Weber, was firing into the tail of a Messerschmitt; it did a violent half roll and spun earthwards.

At the moment I arrived, the Mes, which had dispersed, put on full gas in a rapid climb, knowing that we could not keep up with them at high altitude.

Bungey continued to follow them, although he kept losing distance. From about 600 yards, hoping for a lucky shot, I fired a burst, without success.

We climbed back to 30,000 feet and Alexis told me in highly unofficial language what he thought of our bloody Hurricanes.

It is really not very amusing to fight at these heights in Hurricanes. It is freezing in the cockpit. The Spitfires managed to establish contact and the combat went on some way off while our almost exhausted fuel reserves forced us to set course for home.

Dudley Honor and Sergeant Sykes were obliged to land in

open country, having used up their reserve tanks. They both got away with it.

About 17.00 hours, in the same section, I climbed once more to 25,000 feet. We had not been up five minutes before a formation of Mes dived on us out of the blue without Control having signalled their presence in the neighbourhood. We were over the south coast of the Isle of Wight. At the instant I half rolled to the left, I saw a Spitfire in a vertical dive with a long trail of smoke pouring from his tail. Poor fellow!

Three Mes, who had missed us, now shot over our heads, trying to split us up by putting on full gas. Bungey immediately went in pursuit. I dived steeply and got one of the Germans on my zoom.

My throttle was full open. The radio made a terrible din.

"Your bird, Pyker. To port."

"The bastard."

"Where are you, Red 3?"

"Cheers, you've got him."

I did not listen any more. I heard nothing. I had the Jerry for a moment in the luminous dial of my gonio. I was 300 yards away and allowed for a slight deflection. 200 yards . . . I pressed the tit and the tracers spat. The Me, probably hit in one of its tanks, exploded and pieces of the body flew into the air. Black smoke was coming from his right wing. I blacked out . . . My helmet pressed on my skull until I thought it would explode and my ears were terribly painful. And then there was nothing but the empty sky and a few calls on the radio. I had been flying for an hour. I had better return home without bothering about the others . . .

At Tangmere three pilots were missing at roll call and Alexis Jottard was among them. At 19.00 hours No. 2 Group notified us that the two sergeant pilots of No. 145 had landed in the fields, but there was no news of Jottard. His name was taken off the board.

We realised that not a single pilot had spotted the Me 109s which had attacked us out of the sun.

****

Editor's Note.—Deeply upset by the death of his best friend, Offenberg paid a visit on the following day to Father Greenstock, the Catholic Chaplain at Tangmere, and asked him to say a mass for the repose of Alexis's soul. Realising the depth of Offenberg's grief, the chaplain consoled him as best as he could but his words were not enough to make up for the loss of a real friend.

"You were very attached to Jottard?" asked the priest, placing a hand on his shoulder.

"Yes," said Offenberg. "He was my best friend. He had so much confidence in me that in the old days we even renewed the gesture of William Tell. He let me fire my revolver at an apple on his head. And then we've been like brothers over here. We are so alone here in England."

The chaplain, who could do no more for him, took him to Chichester, the little town about five miles from the airfield, and introduced him to a family he knew, in the hope of cheering the airman up.

The mother was a Belgian, and in her native tongue she managed to find some words to solace his grief. At dusk he returned on foot to the airfield.

As he walked alone through the English countryside, beneath the foreign sky which he defended every day, he realized in his heart of hearts that perhaps he too would never return to Brussels. This was the first time that the idea of death had entered his head. The first time. . . .

At the end of a deserted avenue a thin strip of light betrayed the guard room.

"Good evening, sir," said a corporal, saluting him.

"Good evening. Anything new?"

"No, sir. Oh, yes . . . A type from 145 Squadron shot down a Jerry this afternoon."

"Do you know the name of the pilot?"

"Dunning-White, sir."

"Good show."

He could not get to sleep.

About two o'clock in the morning he got up and sat at the rickety table on which he had placed a few objects he had saved from the wreck and wrote to Alexis's parents.

This letter, which we reproduce, is a poingnat document, a humble but admirable page in the story of the small Belgian Air Force.

The letter was addressed to the next of kin of Alexis Jottard and to his fiancée, Lulu Sacré.

17, rue Pré-des-Dames,
Andenelles, Andenne (Belgium).

The authorities will no doubt have informed you before this letter reaches you of the sad news that our dear Alexis is missing.

I wanted to write you these few lines, that you might know the events in which he has been mixed up during the last six months of his life.

Before the war I was in the same squadron as he at Nivelles, the 40/II/2, and I have known him since 1938. The German advance forced us ... (Offenberg here recapitulates everything that had happened since 10th May, 1940.) On the 10th October the squadron was sent south to Tangmere, Sussex. It was the worst sector of all. We made several sorties without ever meeting the enemy. However, on Sunday, 27th October, 1940, at 17.15 hours, we saw several German fighters well above our heads. Alexis was in the same section as myself. After the operation we found that Alexis was missing at roll call. I believe he was brought down by the Me 109 which I shot down in the course of the engagement. It happened five miles south-east of the Isle of Wight.

Since then I have heard no news of him. It was one of the saddest moments of my life. We were very close and we were like brothers for we knew few people in this country, where the people incidentally are very kind and life is very comfortable.

I have had a mass said for the repose of Alexis's soul, and I shall have several more said.

He always behaved like "a stout heart." If he left France to come and fight in England it was in the hope of contributing to the liberation of his country, his family and his fiancée.

Try to console yourselves with the thought that life is only a passage here below and that we shall meet our dear ones once more in Paradise.

I too was in this country urged by the same desire. I say "was," for one day when you receive this letter I too may be on the list of missing or disappeared.

You may have heard Alexis speak of me. My name is Jean Offenberg and my parents live at 43 square François-Riga, Brussels.

I say adieu, begging you to say masses and prayer for Alexis and myself.

P.S. Your son's luggage will be entrusted to the Belgian Embassy, 103 Eaton Square, London, as soon as it is found because it went astray on the journey from Aberdeen to Tangmere. Alexis had £30 deposited in Lloyds Bank Ltd., Cox & King's Branch, 6 Pall Mall, London, S.W.1. I think that this money, too, will be handed to the Belgian Embassy.

****

1st November

Ops this morning without success. Boyd had engine trouble at 10,000 feet while we were climbing above the coast east of Portsmouth. He came down in a slow glide and the formation broke up and landed. Boyd put his Hurricane down in a field. Immediately after he landed – we had not even got back to the crew room – white vapour trails could be seen in the sky over the Channel. They were at least 30,000 feet.

Nothing doing for us.

Another sortie this afternoon with B Flight detached from the rest of the Squadron.

We climbed into the sun above a layer of scattered clouds. I read 20,000 feet on my altimeter when Nigel Weir called: Red 1, Bandits overhead at 2 o'clock.

"O.K. I've seen them."

What a wonderful sight, it was better than Hollywood.

A veritable swarm of aircraft was flying to the west of the formation and far too high above it.

We banked to draw closer to them when from out of the blue a Me attacked us from the rear. I saw him too late in my mirror.

He broke away underneath our formation and I dived immediately to find myself 400 yards behind him, almost on his tail.

I fired a burst which must have hit for he turned away seawards streaming glycol.

A bit of the pilot's cockpit broke away and he dived.

I followed him and gave him three more bursts which finished him. In spite of my orders I followed him down but lost him in the clouds over Selsey Bill; he was flying westwards in the direction of his airfield.

At 17.00 hours I took off on my third patrol. Enemy formations had been reported south of Brighton but we saw nothing. It must have been a false alarm.

This evening in the mess I learned that the Me 109 I attacked this afternoon crashed near Selsey Bill. The pilot had not received a scratch. I prefer it like that. I shall go and have a look at it tomorrow.

2nd November

As I thought, it was my Messerschmitt which landed in the open country near Selsey Bill.

I went to see it this morning. Dudley Honor, the Anglo-Argentinian who speaks better Spanish than English, drove me in his ancient Austin. I can never understand why he keeps that old bus in repair. At home it would long since have found its way to the scrap heap. On his way he told me that he had brought his camera because he wanted to take the star photo of the year: the victor and the vanquished.

Finally, after asking the way at least a score of times, we discovered the field in question.

The Messerschmitt was there.

It seemed quite undamaged. The engine had been hit . . . probably by my first burst. The village policeman came up and when Honor told him that I was the man who had shot it down, he said that he had all the German's effects safely under lock and key. He rode off on his bicycle and returned a little later with the pilot's parachute, helmet and Mae West. He handed me all these objects as a war souvenir. I could not refuse and I confess I am pleased to have these relics.

Honor took the historic photo and we returned to Tangmere. The pilot was apparently a "Herr Major" for whom the war was now over, incidentally quite a "big wig." As usual, we had hardly returned than we took off on an interception patrol with Sykes. It's about time that the British realise that a formation of two is more than essential. In threes one of them always gets shot down.

Tangmere, 5th November

I have been on numerous patrols during the past few days with de Hemptinne. On several occasions we spotted formations of Mes but they were always far too high.

They never attacked us. What is the matter with them? I am quite at a loss to understand.

6th November

Dawn patrol. I was Tail-end-Charlie and we cruised at 16,000 feet over Plymouth. A few strato-cumulus below us did not entirely obscure the view and I could distinctly see a few ships in the port. I could smell Germans in the offing. There were a host of vapour trails above the Channel. All the Führer's fighters must have been in the neighbourhood.

I tightened my helmet and removed the safety catch from my guns. O.K. Everything in order.

Suddenly I saw three Mes ahead flying almost at the same altitude as myself. They attacked us. They had some guts ... Three against twelve. The others could not be far away. A glance in my mirror. Nothing behind. The whole squadron dived.

I remained aloft with another Hurricane (I think it was Boyd's). We must not get excited. The two of us ought to get one.

Suddenly two Mes streaked below us making for the west.

"Pyker take the starboard one. Wade in."

"Tally ho!"

I dived on my opponent. He spun down towards the sea. I caught him before he managed to take cover in the clouds and gave him a burst of 150 bullets from 200 yards. To my dismay I saw some tracers coming from three-quarters astern. Another Hurricane was chasing the same Messerschmitt. So as not to collide with him I stopped firing and pulled hard on my stick. Then I tried to get on the Jerry's tail again. Black smoke was already pouring from him and he dived seawards where he exploded in a magnificent fountain of spray half a mile off Shoreham.

I saw a red patch in the water and a poor devil swimming. I notified the Ops room so that they could send the Air Sea Rescue to fish him out of the drink.

After forty minutes flying I landed at Tangmere. Boyd, who was flying the other Hurricane, maintained that he did not fire a single burst.

Thursday, 7th November

I am off this afternoon and I am going to the pictures with Baudouin de Hemptinne in Chichester. It is a small provincial town where nothing ever seems to happen.

On our return I learned that 145 Squadron almost in full strength had been attacked by fifty Mes west of Plymouth. A spectacular dog fight ensued in which five pilots of B Flight were shot down: Nigel Weir, MacConnell, Ashton and Bungey the Australians are unhurt for they managed to bale out in time; Captain Sykes crash-landed and is only slightly wounded.

The results are not particularly good for such a show since the only Jerry shot down was a Junker 87, easily accounted for by Pilot Officer Riley of A Flight.

De Hemptinne and I have once more missed a pretty party. And all for a trip to the pictures!

Friday, 8th November

This morning we received orders to intercept a lone German flying twelve miles from the south coast. Three of us took off: Dudley Honor, de Hemptinne and myself. After forty minutes spent in patrolling the shore in line abreast without seeing anything suspicious, I decided to change formation.

"Blue Leader here. Disperse. Free for all. Good luck."

"O.K. Message received."

I had been on my own for some time when I saw an Me not far away dodging in and out of the clouds apparently enjoying this game of hide and seek. A funny place to play all the same.

I gave my Hurricane the works. He must have been two miles away when he changed course due south. Nothing doing. He was too far away and my fuel was running low. I made for home and wrote "nothing to report" in my flight log book.

This evening there was a big dance in the mess. Since the Australian Bungey, Baudouin and I knew no one we went to the pictures in Chichester.

9th November

Patrol with Bungey. He's a grand chap. I should like to fly as a pair with him for good. Perhaps he has inherited it from his Australian ancestors, but I can feel that he likes killing; this is not the case with the other members of the Squadron. I think he loves a scrap and to spray the enemy planes with his tracers. I should like to bet that he laughs himself sick when a Jerry aircraft is blown to smithereens in front of his eyes.

But he is a marvellous shot and after all . . . we're at war.

There were clouds from 1,000 to 22,000 feet. It was lunacy to try and intercept anything in such conditions. As we came down we suddenly saw a Ju 88 two hundred yards ahead. We were at 13,000 feet. The Junkers was flying due south while we were on course 190°. A whole formation might never have seen him in these accursed clouds.

"Bungey, Tally ho, get cracking."

"Wade in."

I dived on to the bomber and gave him a burst from port and from a little below. He dived. I followed him and found myself on his tail. The German put on speed. I had to give him a second burst while doing a roll. I missed him and he disappeared into the clouds where it was pointless pursuing him. Moreover I had lost Bungey and I returned alone to base. I found him there on my arrival.

It was pure chance meeting a bomber at that particular spot where the clouds were a trifle less dense. I fired 1,200 cartridges. I was allowed a "probable," for Bungey insisted that flames were pouring from the right side of his fuselage.

Sunday, 10th November

I attended Mass at the camp. At 10.15 we took off for Portland Bill and on reaching 25,000 feet I saw thirty Mes about 7,000 feet and above us to starboard.

They adopted their strange new policy of neutrality. There were thirty of them in full daylight above us and they didn't even attack us! It's obvious that the good old days are over. Two months ago they would have dived on us without a moment's hesitation. Now they fly very high in close formation as though on exercise.

It was useless trying to reach them. At that height we should not be on equal terms with the Mes. When shall we be given Spitfires?

Nevertheless they must realise that their peak is passed. Too bad for them!

****

Editor's Note.—The Battle of Britain, that epic which aroused the admiration of the whole world, was drawing to a close.

Since October the Luftwaffe had reserved its bombers for

night attacks and the daylight offensive was now entrusted to the fighters and fighter bombers, usually operating in dull weather. These tactics posed new problems for Fighter Command and for the fighter pilots entailed many fruitless patrols at high altitude. Towards the end of the month, the Luftwaffe was forced to realise that the British Fighter Arm was very far from having been eliminated and that their ultimate defeat was by no means a certainty.

Göring's airmen called it a day and only ventured over England under cover of darkness. Offenberg had fought well and had long since been accepted by the whole of No. 145 Squadron.

He had been given his nickname: Pyker. In Belgium when he had flown the diminutive Fiat CR 42s at Nivelles his pals had called him "Pij," a typically Brussels expression. In that city ... "Pij" is almost a compliment. The British, hearing de Hemptinne and Jottard constantly called him this, anglicised the word and in future he was invariably to be known as "that old Pyker."

Some people even forgot his real name. He was known by this nickname which a mechanic had painted on the orange Mae West he had worn for days and nights on end when he was in readiness waiting for the order to "scramble."

Pyker this exile this sympathetic deserter who was such a decent fellow, was popular at Tangmere. He became anglicised like his name, drank tea and adopted English customs. He had many friends and began to feel less lonely. He had thought only once of death, on the night Jottard was killed. Now it was all over. Life, he wrote, was a short passage here below and since death would take him when his time came he was ready. He was at peace with his God, in whom he believed devoutly, and at peace with his own conscience which did not reproach him. Death held no terrors for him.

From 10th November onwards he only made a few notes each day in his diary. Missions, patrols with his heterogeneous squadron, composed of some British, three Poles, a Czech, two Belgians, an Irishman, a Scot and a Rhodesian. He met Messerschmitts but they refused to fight and when he arrived too late for a big scrap he was genuinely disappointed.

Towards the end of November, for the first time since the start of the Battle of Britain, he flew as far as the coast of Brittany with Dudley Honor and Peacock, a new pilot.

"*I have seen the coast of France,*" he wrote. It was not without emotion that a few miles away he saw the friendly coast of

75

Brittany. For him France was almost home. He spent two days of his leave in London, the 19th and 20th November, but bored with the capital he returned to Tangmere. This airfield near the seashore was to a certain extent his home since he had no family in England. His family was now the squadron. His brothers were the pilots. On quiet evenings he walked to Chichester and called on Father Greenstock, the Catholic padre in whom he had found a friend. The priest often took him to visit the Lydon family at 32 Melbourne Road. They lived in a typical British suburb where the little houses were all identical and all have their small gardens.

It was good to sit in front of the log fire. Jean rediscovered an atmosphere that he had long lacked and almost forgotten. Mrs. Lydon reminded him of his mother and pretty young Sheila was almost a sister for him.

Nothing in him at those moments betrayed the cool-headed killer he could be when flying his Hurricane in combat. He no longer looked at his hands, which were roughened by the cold of great heights, by tugging at the controls of his fighter. He did not look at his hands as he stretched them out to the warm fire because they reminded him of the button of his machine gun – the little button which released a hail of death.

At the Lydon's he wanted to forget. During those brief moments he wanted merely to be the tall twenty-two-year-old he really was.

But the war pursued its course, less exciting now perhaps. In the air above the Channel, with Dunning-White, Bungey and the others – those whom the English began to call "the few" because they were so very few – he sought the reluctant foe who appeared but seldom and then always hidden in the cloud and refused to fight.

December arrived. London had often been bombed by night. but London was a long way from Sussex.

On 11th December, however, he took off with Bungey as his mate. Control soon reported a non-identified aircraft south of their position and ordered them to go after it.

They spotted vapour trails in the dusk and saw a Heinkel 111 at 20,000 feet. Offenberg reported the fact to Control.

"Bandit in sight. Am going in to attack." And to his winger Bungey:

"Come on, Bob, cover me."

"O.K., Pyker. Wilco."

Offenberg was the first to fire. Glyco immediately streamed from the German's port engine and the gunner, probably wounded, stopped firing. The Heinkel veered off to the south, rapidly losing height. Pyker fired his remaining ammunition for he was afraid of losing the Hun in the semi-darkness, then handed over to Bungey who made two close attacks.

The left wing of the Heinkel caught fire but the flames were soon extinguished. The bomber had slowed down its pace and was still losing height. Neither Offenberg nor Bungey had a round of ammunition left. They could not despatch the enemy bomber, but it seemed to have had its coup de grâce. They followed it down to 2,000 feet where they lost sight of it in the darkness and the clouds. The British Control at the moment reported that it had disappeared out of their screens.

They were twenty miles from the French coast. The Heinkel would never get back to its base.

On his return to Tangmere Offenberg, who had been invited to dine in London that evening, gave up his place to Baudouin de Hemptinne.

"I think I did right," he wrote. "I shouldn't have enjoyed myself after what happened today."

Christmas Eve arrived. The sector was very quiet. Not a Jerry had been seen for a week. This was a very long time for Pyker. This was the first Christmas he would be spending away from his family. He wandered about the deserted mess at Tangmere, not knowing what to do with himself. Nearly all his pals had gone off on leave. He had nowhere to go and he felt terribly lonely.

He was idly turning over the pages of a magazine when Eric Faure, one of the pilots just off on leave, saw him in his corner.

"Well, Pyker, aren't you going anywhere for Christmas?"

"No, I'm staying here. Where do you expect me to go?"

"Why don't you come with me to Dunmow in Essex. Come on. You'll be very welcome down there."

He did not spend Christmas alone after all. Eric Faure took him to Dunmow and Pyker was received with open arms by Mrs. Gibbons and her two daughters, Bridget and Judy, in their small cottage.

He spent a wonderful Christmas Eve among people who had been strangers yesterday but who treated him as a friend of long standing.

"Once when he happened to say 'But I'm a foreigner' Bridget, the elder of the girls, replied: "You mustn't say that. You're not a foreigner, you're one of the boys."

Offenberg returned to Tangmere. The two days he had spent at Dunmow seemed all too short but he was glad to be back in the officers' mess with his old friends, the pilots of 145 Squadron, that band of gay companions who had so little of the military spirit about them. Their hair was far too long, they wore bright silk scarves, and the eldest of them was twenty-five. They did not ask for a long and properous existence. As long as it was exciting, that was all that mattered.

They knew how to drink hard and if death were to efface the gay smile on their lips they had the consolation of knowing that their end would be a speedy one.

They were the gayest bunch in the world. Always ready for a skylark on any pretext, ready to go to parties, to any party to which they were invited. There only needed one to be organised ... But as soon as the alert sounded on the tannoys they were ready in a second to rush to their Hurricanes, to start their props, climb into the dangerous sky and fight at odds of one against five. If one were shot down, he baled out, returned to base and was airborne again in a couple of hours at the latest, in another Hurricane formation defending that strip of England which he had been called upon to defend.

Pyker loved and admired all these men with whom he lived at such close quarters.

Each time he left the station, even for few hours, something seemed to be missing. Then he was happy to find Dunning-White again in flying boots, sitting on the steps of the hut which served as the squadron office. He was delighted to find that Bungey had not been shot down despite the mistakes he was bound to have made on his last mission. Sitting on the Squadron commander's desk Dudley Honor, in far from regulation kit, was singing an Argentine air. He stopped when Pyker came in.

"Hullo, Pyker. Back at last, eh? Go hide your head. We've been in a murky scrap with fifty Jerries over Plymouth and you weren't in the party."

"You had a scrap?"

"Sure. A pretty scrap, and I nearly got shot out of the sky. I'm sorry you weren't with us."

"So am I, Dudley. You can be quite sure of that."

Offenberg spoke fluent English by this time. He had no need

of books or special courses. His highly orthodox English, full of slang expressions, would have made an Oxford don shudder. He had learned it in 145 Squadron, sitting in old weather-beaten armchairs, by the Hurricanes when his section was in readiness for a "scramble."

He learned it in the air when he flew in close formation with his peers, the fighter pilots. Between two sorties, on the 5th January, they heard that their old faithful Hurricanes were to be replaced by Spitfires.

He suddenly realised that Spitfires were not so vital now that the Luftwaffe pilots rarely came over the South Downs, his fighter section. Squadron Leader Boyd had handed over No. 145 to Johnny Peel.

The buzz ran round the Squadron that the fighters were soon going to pass over to the offensive. Sweeps were to be organised over the Continent, perhaps even over Belgium. Yes, the Spits were very welcome. The war was a long way from being over and there would still be some good fighting.

Three days after these rumours, the 9th January 1941, to be accurate, No. 145 Squadron (at 10.40 hours precisely) received orders to take off for one of the first attacks on the Continent.

Offenberg rushed to the cupboard to get his helmet. Bungey stopped him.

"Sorry, Pyker, it's not for you."

"Why?"

"Continentals are not allowed to take part in missions of this type. Air Ministry orders. It's too dangerous for you should you happen to be shot down. Sorry, Pyker, old man."

With death in his heart, Offenberg watched his pals get into their Hurricans for the last time. The Spitfires were arriving on the following day.

In pairs, the fighters took off. They flew for a while and then climbed to get into formation. Then they disappeared in a southerly direction out to sea.

Pyker, alone on the rain-soaked tarmac, waited a long time for them to return, his eyes on the clouds into which they had vanished.

He was still there when they returned.

"Well, Pyker, old man. It's a piece of cake. We didn't see a thing the whole trip. We met nothing."

"Nothing at all?"

"No. Not even ack ack . . . all over Brittany. An absolute picnic, I tell you."

****

Tangmere, 10th January

The first Spitfires have arrived, ferried by fellows attached to the factories, I think. We have five and I have just tried one. It's a fabulous "crate" and very easy to fly, particularly for aerobatics. Johnny Peel was livid because I did an Immelman thirty feet above ground over his flight. What a type! This evening the Nazis bombed Portsmouth. The fighters of 145 were sent up at once but Control kept me grounded for some reason. On their return, Dunning-White told us that he had a crack at a Heinkel 111. Only a flight lieutenant of No. 65 Squadron managed to shoot one down. A bad show.

16th January

Lunch was barely over when a two-section patrol was ordered off the Isle of Wight to protect a convoy of warships. I was on it. The truck took us over to dispersal.

Six Spitfires took off. Joe Backman led the formation while I was Blue Section leader. We flew very low over Bognor. The weather got steadily worse and the visibility at ground level was 500 yards. To cap everything, radio reception was bad. In fact, as I had expected, we did not find the convoy, which was not at the spot indicated.

We circled for some minutes, but in vain. We could see nothing and the weather was deteriorating rapidly, particularly towards the south. We returned to base after an hour and a half's fruitless flight. The snow began to fall gently.

In the mess the most marvellous letter in the world was waiting for me. Not even a letter, a simple card with a Red Cross heading telling me that my parents are in excellent health. I replied to them at once through the same channel.

****

Editor's Note.—The whole of January passed uneventfully. Between two spells of bad weather, Pyker flew on patrol over the South Coast or trained with Bungey and Sergeant Gardiner – a newcomer whom Pyker calls a martyr.

Squadron Leader Johnny Peel left after a short period of command and was replaced by Leather.

Mike Newling, one of the veterans of the Squadron, got his D.F.C.

Nearly every evening Offenberg went to Chichester or to Brighton to the theatre or the pictures. He was bored to death.

His close pal Franck Weber, the Czech from Prague, was given a Czech squadron and left Tangmere on the 26th January. New pilots arrived and Pyker was more bored than ever.

While No. 145 Squadron was being re-equipped, clouds darkened the South Downs; every day the depressions arrived from the Atlantic bringing a grey gloomy sky with showers of rain and snow.

The bad weather of that January reduced the activity of the R.A.F. to almost nil.

The R.A.F. had won the first round and was licking its wounds. The air supremacy won during the tough fights in the Battle of Britain was an accomplished fact. The British people could breathe again and take a brief rest. . . . Operation Sea Lion, the invasion of Britain, had been called off indefinitely by the Führer and his advisers.

Each time the sky cleared and flying was possible the Spitfires were ferried to Tangmere and delivered to 145 Squadron.

Offenberg familiarised himself with his new combat plane, the fabulous immortal Spitfire whose thoroughbred outlines he had so often admired.

This unwelcome respite was forced upon him. He was obliged to get used to his new machine which he considered he already knew. He stormed and cursed, felt useless and was unhappy.

New young pilots from the training establishments had come to fill the gaps in the squadron or to replace the veterans who were sent for a long rest.

Offenberg remained at Tangmere. Not for a moment did he think of leaving the Squadron. Does a workman leave the factory where he works every day?

To court death every day and to laugh at it is the profession of an airman. For Offenberg it was more; it was a sacred duty.

He remained at Tangmere and flew with the youngsters, taught them the art of aerial combat, gave them the benefit of experience which he had learned the hard way.

"Take your bearings from the sun before take off so that if

your compass is shot out of action over the sea you won't have to row too long in your rubber dinghy. Don't climb with the sun behind you because you'll only do it once. When you're chasing a few isolated Mes, beware. The Jerries don't usually put all their eggs in one basket and you can think yourself lucky if half the Luftwaffe isn't watching you."

Sitting in dispersal the greenhorns listed to the veteran pontificating.

"Remember, my lads, when you're attacking a formation. If possible leave a couple of crates above you to serve as cover and keep your eye on the sun ... there's probably a Jerry up there."

He knew the tactics of the Mes by heart.

"The Jerries will roar over the Squadron without the least intention of diving on you. Don't think for a minute that it's because they're scared. It's simply because they adore types which do what you are doing at the moment, lagging behind the formation.

"Then you'll see a couple of them dive at 45° in front of you but out of range of your machine guns. Don't fall into the trap. *Never*, I say *never*, follow an enemy fighter on his own ground and if you hear machine-gunning break and break fast. Break, do you understand? You will never hear that sound except when someone's firing on your tail and unpleasantly close at that. ..."

The newcomers learned fast from their contact with Offenberg, Dunning-White and the other old hands. The whole Squadron now had Spitfires. Even the "rookies" did well on them.

But there were still things for them to learn, things that are not to be found in the training manuals or at Flying School, things which are told among pilots on fighter airfields and which the wind carries away ... Signs in the air that the enemy is near ... The art of keeping a cool head in the flurry of a dogfight. When to use the radio and when to keep silent ... "If you see an enemy diving on your pal and you want to lose him as a friend you have only to give a panic call on the radio: '*Look out there's a Messerschmitt on your tail.*' If you say that you can be quite sure that all the Spits within fifty miles of your position will embark upon the craziest aerobatics. For God's sake be specific. Say rather: '*109s attacking Red Section*' or '*Look out Red 1 or Red 4.*'

"If you can't say it calmly it's better to say nothing at all and to let your pal get out of it as best he can.

"A panic message is the greatest crime a fighter pilot can commit for he risks breaking up a host of formations.

"Remember it is better to attack a lone Me from 95° starboard and not directly from astern. You can be almost sure that the fellow is looking to port for it is more natural to turn the body and the aircraft to the left. Remember that enemy planes never fly alone. They fly in pairs or in fours. If you can see only one take a good look round to spot his winger ... and LOOK BEHIND YOU."

Offenberg took the young ones with him every day in formation over the Sussex coast — the coast he now knew so well and which he had seen from so many unorthodox angles between two bursts of tracers.

By their daily contact with the veterans the tenderfoot pilots Clarke, Grundy, and Turner learned the tricks of the trade, of that dangerous game which is played in a circus under the biggest "top" in the world. Sometimes in order to instil the fighting spirit in them the flight commanders — Britishers — took them on an operational trip over the French coast.

They returned from these sweeps with broad smiles like kids who have been given a bright toy to play with for an hour.

Pyker listened to them and envied them. He was not allowed to go on these sweeps and it grieved him.

He knew that the interception patrols would never be the same again. The streams of bombers would never return to his sector as in the good old days of the Battle of Britain which he already called "the last war." He grew used to the Spit but missed his old friend the Hurricane which was superior in a dogfight because it could break faster.

During this month of enforced inactivity he grew even more English. With the new squadron commander, Squadron Leader Leather, and Eric Faure he went once a week to Goodwood to become initiated in the Royal and Ancient game of golf. He spent his evenings with the Lydons in Chichester.

****

17th February

Six Spitfires took off at dawn and I was the leader of Green Section. Control led us to 15,000 feet above the clouds and calmly told us that an enemy formation was there ... probably below us. The only trouble with Control was that below us there was nothing but cloud. The Huns may have been in them but we couldn't see a thing.

The leader decided to go down and return to base. As was to be expected, I lost my two wingers in the clouds. A dangerous game!

When I saw the earth once more I was at 12,000 feet, and decided to glide down to the coast. Over Beachy Head I found one of my wingers and we made our way together back to Tangmere, hedgehopping and following the shore.

****

Editor's Note.—That same evening, Offenberg put on his best suit and had his buttons polished by old Jack, his orderly.

He flung his greasy oil-stained flying suit over the single chair that graced his hut.

The officers of the squadron were all invited by Squadron Leader Leather, the new C.O., to Midhurst. In all the cars available this bunch of pirates burst into the old "Spread Eagle."

Noisy, happy and excitable despite their smart uniforms, they sat down at the tables. They flirted with the barmaid as she served them with their beer.

Jean and Bungey played darts with the locals; the only men there were those who were too old to fight.

And the old walls heard all the old yarns of Messerschmitts, tracers, smoke trails in the distance, weavers and stories which only pilots could believe.

Very late that night the gang returned home singing in their ancient rattling crocks.

*   *   *

At dawn six Spitfires of 145 Squadron were patrolling at 25,000 feet over Sussex as though nothing had happened.

A great surprise on the 21st February ... The Group Captain in command of Tangmere Base announced that in future foreigners were allowed to participate in offensive sweeps over the Continent. The war ... a new war ... was about to begin. Life was good. The grey English sky with all its clouds and cloying mists had cleared for him.

And in actual fact the weather gradually improved. The

Squadron, in great form, was ready to resume the battle. Offenberg patrolled the coast two or three times a day but never met the enemy.

With Bungey he played at war in mock air battles, "chasing each other," as he writes, "round big clumps of cumulus." He kept up on his diary. About this time he wrote: "British public opinion is becoming more and more favourable to King Leopold III. There is considerable evidence that the accusations made against him were a tissue of lies.

"I was wrong to doubt the integrity of our King when he capitulated on the 28th May 1940." (*In the diary.*) He summed up his activities and found that he had taken part in 112 sorties and patrols since he had arrived in England.

****

Monday, 10th March 1941

A patrol has been ordered by Group Operations to protect a convoy of coasters off the south coast.

When Leather approached the blackboard in the crew room to chalk up the names of those who would form the section everyone fell silent. It was a long time since we had been on ops.

I felt that every pilot would like to be one of them. Who would he choose?

In capital letters the Squadron Commander wrote:

> No. 1 PYKER
> No. 2 MACCONNELL
> No. 3 SYLVESTER

Two veterans and a newcomer.

We picked up the convoy south of the Isle of Wight. There must have been about twenty-five ships down there below. I could not understand the sense of their formation but it must have been some method of mutual protection. I thought of Lallemand's letter which I received a few days ago, telling me that the *Har Sion*, the ship which brought us to London, has been sunk in the Atlantic. I felt very sorry.

Sylvester stuck close to me for a change. But why will they persist in making us fly in threes? I should have felt more comfortable alone with that old fox MacConnell to protect my tail. All that Sylvester risked was to get shot down by the first Me that attacked us.

Leather ought to change this type of formation. The Mes understood long ago that the basic formation was the pair. Those fellows never fly in threes. After an hour's circling above the convoy, I led my section back to Tangmere.

I had hardly left the runway when I noticed out of the corner of my eye another section of Spits taking off. They were probably going to replace us over the convoy.

Jack, one of the mechanics confirmed this. Bungey and de Hemptinne were in the section. When they returned an hour later Bungey came into the crew room terribly excited.

"We got one of the bastards – and Gundry's made his first kill. It was money for jam."

"What about Baudouin?"

"Baudouin and I kept the enemy off."

This is how it happened.

Hardly had they arrived over the convoy than fairly dense clouds began to form. To the south the sky was completely overcast. They were at 15,000 feet when the sector announced an enemy aircraft flying at 10,000 feet along the South Coast about twenty-five miles out to sea. They were given a vector. Bungey and his wingers looked carefully but could see nothing. Then suddenly at two o'clock a Junkers 88 came out of the clouds at about 12,000 feet. The section took up its action position and No. 3, Gundry, was to receive his baptism of fire.

"Green leader, tally-ho!"

The hunt was on. But the Ju 88 had caught sight of the three Spitfires and immediately turned south in a slight dive. Green 1 attacked the bomber at the moment it turned, firing a three to four-second burst and breaking away at 100 yards. Green 2 – Bungey – followed suit, and during this attack from three quarters astern the rear gunner of the bomber ceased firing. The Ju continued its course southwards and finally straightened out of its dive at 1,500 feet.

Bungey must have killed the gunner. The bomber could not return his fire and was defenceless. The crew in the bomber must have been sweating with the terror of men who feel that death is at hand. There would be a few red gleaming tracers, a vast explosion and it would be the end.

The two first Spitfires re-formed on the bomber's tail, slightly above it.

De Hemptinne called young Gundry on the intercom.

"Green 3, wade in. Push your attack home and fire when

86

you're certain of hitting him. Don't be scared: he can't fire."

The novice dipped his wings and came down in a magnificent sweep, finishing on the tail of the Ju 88. He fired a long burst – far too long – making his break so near the enemy's tail unit that he nearly ran into it. When he pulled out he was only 50 feet above the water.

At this moment, in a fight which had only lasted a few seconds, the Junkers flew into the clouds near the coast, to re-appear a little lower down, and crashed into the sea.

Green Section re-formed and returned for home a few feet above the waves.

15.00 hours. The whole squadron took off on an offensive patrol between Boulougne and Cap Gris-Nez. This is the first time I have operated with a wing of four squadrons. No. 145 was top cover at 30,000 feet. One almost dies of cold at that height. We saw nothing, not even the coast, but it was a pleasant day all the same.

13th March

The sky does not look like clearing up. Yesterday morning, to kill time and to give myself some illusion of flying, I spent a couple of hours on the Link Trainer. It works very well by instrument but if they think that I have time to look at my instrument panel when I have Me 109s on my tail they make a great mistake. I'm bored.

This afternoon about 15.00 hours we took off on a mission over France in wing formation. We were protecting Stirlings, which were bombing the station or the factories of Lille, I don't know which.

We crossed the French coast at Hardelot at 30,000 feet, for once more No. 145 was top cover. Near Arras I saw about twenty Mes flying much lower, at 20,000 feet perhaps, across another Spitfire formation. The wing leader spotted them and gave the order to No. 145 to go down and attack them. Although we dived at once we could not engage them in a combat, for as soon as they saw us one half began to flee in a climb to the south-west while the other carried out a masterly half roll and went down in a vertical dive. We re-formed and flew off peacefully in the direction of Lille. We were not far from the Belgian frontier, and, if I am spared, I thought, I should one day see my home-land again.

Above the target, which was visible below, I could see three Stirlings flying in from the north-west on a south-easterly course. They would pass over Lille.

I should not like to be in those fellows' shoes. Me 109s cavorted at all heights round us in small formations. As soon as a Spitfire section looked like attacking them they made off. They had no intention of getting involved in a dog fight. What a yellow-livered bunch.

In any case they must have been given orders to bring down laggards, for they circled round our formations like mosquitoes with black crosses painted on their backs.

No. 610 Squadron, also stationed at Tangmere, operating at a height of 20,000 feet, lost patience and when a pair of Mes flew below them at right angles a section broke away and dived in pursuit. The two Jerries crashed somewhere near Bethune. We lost one Spitfire.

****

Editor's Note.—The Luftwaffe resumed a tentative offensive against the South Coast airfields. Ju 88s and Heinkel 111s slipped across the English coast under cover of darkness. Tangmere was attacked several times. At dawn on the 16th March, when Pyker arrived at dispersal he was shown his plane riddled with shell splinters and out of action.

The squadron had not yet rediscovered the rhythm of the last months of 1940, for transfers were still in progress. The great figures of the squadron disappeared one by one. The old corsair, Peter Dunning-White, was appointed Flight Commander to No. 615 Squadron; Johnny Ashton, D.F.C., from Newcastle, joined No. 64. All these war-scarred pilots – the best of them since they were still alive – were sent to stiffen new squadrons or to reinforce others. The expansion of Fighter Command was an urgent necessity and there was a need of experienced pilots to lead the new generation.

19th March

At about 10 o'clock in the morning Jean Offenberg was sitting at No. 145 dispersal discussing flying techniques with Nobby Clarke. Winter seemed to be on the way out and it looked like being a fine day with a mild sun shining through the windows, bringing a little light into the untidy room.

An A.C. put some coal in the stove in the centre of the room, looking at the pin-ups on the walls with a glint in his eye. Above all these capacious bosoms someone had had the bright idea of sticking a poster showing a Dornier 17 being attacked by a Spitfire against a sky-blue background.

In any case this warlike picture had little success with the newcomers and if from time to time eyes wandered to the Dornier's double tail unit with the black crosses they never remained there for more than a second.

Eyes were lowered, opened wide, a hand would push back a cap, letting a keen face suddenly be seen.

Camplin and Sylvester were playing darts despite roars of protest from Nobby Clarke, who, in the doorway, was in a bad position should one of the darts go astray.

"For God's sake stop that silly game!"

"Why should we stop? It's fun."

"If one of you aims a bit this way, I shall get one in the eye."

"Don't worry. We know how to throw. Besides we aim off a little towards the door because of the draught."

"In God's name, that's just what I'm afraid of. With players like you I'll have my chips."

Clarke was quite serious. This man who, when Control gave the order to scramble, would rush to his Spitfire and hurl himself in the toughest dog-fight where he risked being shot down by cannon fire a score of times, was terrified of these six-inch darts which the sergeant threw at the red and black circles of the dart board.

"Give them a break, Clarke. Let them get on with their game."

"You won't go and explain to the quack if these morons blind me, Pyker."

The door suddenly opened, letting in a draught of fresh air, and the jovial face of "Chiefy" appeared. The chief mechanic was Flight Sergeant Barrister, a rather untidy figure in a tunic too large for him and very baggy trousers.

"Hi, Chiefy, what's the gen?"

"Not an airworthy machine?"

"Have you lost a spanner? I haven't been in your bloody shed."

"No, gentlemen, it's not that. It's better or maybe worse. It all depends on you. I've just come back from the sergeants' mess and do you know what I've heard?"

"You know damn well we don't. Come on, give."

"Well, a new Wing-Co has just arrived, walking very slowly."

"Perhaps he isn't in any hurry."

"No, this one has no legs."

A legless wing commander? A pilot with no legs? There was only one of them in the R.A.F. – Bader, Douglas Bader.

Bader at Tangmere! The type who always took with him a host of fighters when he went on ops.

Offenberg, like everyone else, knew the fantastic story of this fellow who, had he wished, could have sat in a comfortable chair for the rest of the war, but who preferred the most dangerous profession in the world and continued to be a fighter pilot. And what a pilot! He must have at least fifteen Jerries to his credit.

Bader at Tangmere. That probably meant a lot of changes.

Yes, a lot of changes. That afternoon, after a few minutes flight before lunch in a Spitfire, Bader gave orders for Nos. 610 and 145 to take off.

He led the formation along the coast as far as Dungeness. No. 610 flew at 25,000 feet and the twelve Spitfires of No. 145 were a little higher and to stern with their backs to the sun, here Bader told them to remain. Offenberg flew in a pair with Leather, the squadron commander. Bader, who was lower down with Ken Holden and his boys, called on the radio and ordered No. 145 to stay put until he called on them.

"Let the Huns attack first. Let them attack 610. Don't dive until I tell you. Silence now."

Below, when he dipped his right wing, Pyker could see Bader's Spitfires over the coast of France near Boulogne.

Once more no enemy appeared.

It was infuriating to be in such a good formation, so well placed to make a whirlwind descent on an enemy who had not spotted you. If only the Saint-Omar fighters would put in an appearance.

Ops at Tangmere called Bader.

"Dogsbody. Nothing in the sector. Return to base."

"Okay, Beetles. Just one more minute. You never know."

Up there a dozen pairs of eyes from No. 145 scanned the strip of French coast which stretched as far as they could see. But they could see nothing from the shore to the horizon, not a machine. No luck. They must go home.

Offenberg slept badly. After a few drinks in the officers' mess, chiefly from curiosity to catch a glimpse of the new wing commander, Jean retired to bed, for he was on ops at five next morning. And even if there was nothing on the screen Control usually sent a patrol for a spin along the coast. Offenberg had slept badly because the Luftwaffe has been very active. At 23.00 hours a few bombs fell on the airfield and the Beaufighters had kept up a hellish shindy all night, taking off and landing, particularly as those fellows only worked individually. If only they had taken off in a squadron and made a fine din before disappearing into the night, one could then have got a little sleep. But instead of that they kept on taking off throughout the night. As soon as one had gone and you had dozed off another one came in to land.

"You'd think that Pike does it on purpose," said Sergeant Camplin in the truck which took them to dispersal at the other end of the field.

Pike was in command of the Beaufighter squadron, the night fighters who shared the field with three squadrons of day fighters.

"You know," said Sykes. "For all the damage they do we might just as well let them bomb at their leisure. It would make one hell of a row once and for all and then I should manage to get some sleep when they left."

Half an hour later Offenberg and his two wingers were airborne. Dawn was breaking. They flew wingtip to wingtip seawards, passed over Littlehampton and began to climb on a southerly course. Here and there they could see a few white horses in the Channel below.

Tangmere Control called. Offenberg had difficulty in understanding, for there was much disturbance.

"Hullo, Pyker. Non-identified aircraft at 15,000 feet. Ten miles south-east of your present position. Vector 140°."

The three Spitfires turned.

An unidentified plane over the Channel at this hour? It must be a German. Good!

Since Offenberg had no confidence in the altitudes given by Control and preferred to get between the enemy and the rising sun, he veered off to port on course 130°, climbing as fast as he could to reach 20,000 feet. The three Spitfires almost hung on their props.

At 20,000, Pyker flattened out and reduced his engine, which had begun to overheat. He could see nothing except the vast expanse of sea, changing colour now in the intensified light.

Suddenly Sykes called him.

"Pyker. Two o'clock below. A bandit."

Offenberg looked and began to laugh. An enormous warm-hearted laugh. For the last ten minutes he had had one idea in mind, a single thought: to find the enemy, to find the enemy ... No, it was too much.

The enemy, that lone marauder coming from the rising sun in the bright halo of an early morning sky, was a Beaufighter. One of Tom Pike's accursed Beaufighters returning home. One of those lousy night fighters which had disturbed everyone else's rest.

It was too much! On the intercom Sykes called down all the wrath of heaven on this son of a bitch who had played such a trick on them.

Camplin went further and asked Pyker to attack him all the same. But Pyker laughed up there in the sky. He automatically plugged in his radio and in the ops room at Tangmere the girls who pushed the round discs representing aircraft on the huge controller's table suddenly heard an enormous burst of laughter interrupted by obscenities from Camplin and Sykes.

The little WAAFs tried not to laugh for the controller in his glass cockpit turned a baleful eye on them.

"Hullo Pyker. Beetles here. Are you getting on with the war or are you coming home?"

"Okay, Beetles. Coming home. There's nothing about."

* * *

That afternoon Pyker was warming himself in the sun with his feet on the portable wireless. The set had been there from time immemorial and no one remembered the name of its owner. Everything had happened to it since it was there and Barrister, the chief mechanic, whom the pilots ordered to change the batteries when necessary, maintained quite seriously that the only use to which it had never been put was to serve as a football. And that was only because it hurt the feet. Offenberg and Sylvester, shading their eyes with their hands, watched the Spits landing on No. 1 runway. A section streaked overhead, was lost for a moment in the sun, reappeared beyond No. 145's shed and broke up.

The first Spit came in to land. De Hemptinne probably. Undercarriage still retracted!

"Wheels," roared Offenberg, standing up. "Wheels!"

Then he fell silent, suddenly realising the futility of his warning.

The Spitfire continued its descent, overshot the runway a little to the right and landed on its belly in the grass where it zigzagged dangerously. Bits of the propeller flew into the air. It disappeared in a cloud of dust.

Offenberg ran as fast as he could across the field. The two other planes landed normally one after the other on the runway.

Offenberg kept on running. Provided nothing had happened to Baudouin! He must have tightened his belt. When the belt was not tight the body was flung forward on impact. The head hit the gunsight and that was the end.

He was the only other Belgian at Tangmere.

Offenberg was out of breath from running. His flying boots prevented him from going any faster. He must help Baudouin.

A siren wailed from the control tower. The ambulance, thought Pyker.

About fifty yards from the machine he saw the cockpit open; an elbow appeared over the side and a body was raised in the seat. Exhausted but happy, Offenberg pulled up. He was greeted by a smile from Baudouin, who slipped out on to the wing.

"She's taken a bashing, eh? The undercarriage lever got stuck. I couldn't move it."

Pyker was speechless. He tried to regain his breath, for his running had winded him.

"My dear man," said Baudouin de Hemptinne, a man of the world to his fingertips, "what a state you're in. It's lucky for you because here comes the ambulance to take you back to dispersal. I shall stay here. The C.O. will be coming and I'd better be on the spot to explain things to him."

Offenberg drove back to B Flight dispersal in the ambulance, furious and happy at the same time.

"What was wrong with your pal?"

"Oh, absolutely nothing. Lever got stuck and he couldn't get his wheels down."

"Another Spit which the Huns won't get!"

For a week the weather, which had seemed so favourable, deteriorated again. It rained for days on end and the clouds seemed to cling to the ground. From dispersal Offenberg could not even see the control tower at the other end of the field.

It seemed obvious that Fighter Command was definitely going to carry the war to the other side of the Channel and that the new hunting grounds would be over northern France.

The Germans were to be forced to keep their fighters in the west of Europe and to this end the R.A.F. invented a new war formation. A few bombers were to go each day to attack certain vital points in France, escorted by a mass of fighters, which would force the Luftwaffe to accept battle. These formations were known as circuses. It was an appropriate name – a circus performing in the skies of Europe with human cannon-balls and jugglers, with the finest plumes, the music of engines and the cymbal clashes of bombs.

A circus with acrobats hanging from their propellors and wrestlers clenching their teeth.

But there would be no one to tour the villages before the performance, no roll of drums to herald the arrival of the travelling circus.

A few vapour trails in the sky above would announce to the spectators that the show was about to start. The trapeze artistes would work without a net and there would be no cheating, no trickery. The machine-guns would be really loaded and the target would be a living one.

And the spectators down below were begged not to laugh when the artiste fell from his trapeze.

25th March 1941

About 15.30 hours Squadron Leader Leather sent for Pyker who, ensconced in an armchair in the flight room, had been reading magazines all day. It was bad weather over the Channel and the Met had announced a deterioration for the evening.

That morning the squadron had received the news. A veteran of twenty, little Langdon from New Zealand, whom Pyker had known, since they had been together for the last three months of 1940, had been brought down over Malta. He was a quiet boy whose face had not yet lost the traces of childhood.

He had been brought down far from home, defending a strip of island which he knew only from having seen it on the school maps at Wellington in his own country. He died as a pilot of twenty with 1,000 flying hours and more than 100 combats to his credit.

Pyker banished his gloomy thoughts and went to see the squadron leader.

"Yes, Sir?"

"Pyker, I need a good pilot for a co-operative exercise with the searchlight crews. Do you feel up to it? It's bad weather."

"Oh, yes, I prefer to fly in this much rather than sit here doing nothing. Okay sir, I'll have a crack."

Pyker took his helmet and gloves, knotted his old mascot scarf round his neck. He took off in a slight cross-wind and could hardly see the end of the runway. He flew south but once in the cotton-wool he could not see the coast.

At 10,000 feet he came through the muck, which had grown less dense, to discover a sea of clouds looking resplendent in the first light of the moon. Pyker was alone in this immensity and the earth below, where men were waiting for the sky to clear to resume their conflict, seemed very far away.

How right he had been to accept this mission.

The sky was all his. It belonged to him alone. It was his domain where no one would dare to venture that evening. His loneliness was complete apart from a few short waves flowing between him and the control tower where men were awake. Pyker was an archangel, and alone in the half light he performed his *haute école*. From time to time the beam of a searchlight came through a rift, like a vast golden finger pointing at Orion's belt.

At 18.00 hours, when Control ordered him back to base, he descended with regret on his given course.

But visibility was nil. The clouds enveloped him and would not open. Not a glimmer of light in this void. Pyker descended towards English soil. His pals were already in the mess drinking tea. He looked at his watch. Would he drink his tea that night or would they write finis to the chapter of his ledger? A friendly comforting voice told him to make for the sea. He banked and continued on his way down on the course received.

Provided it was the sea below him!

10,000 . . . 7,000 . . . 5,000 feet. . . .

The darkness still enveloped him.

The voice of his guide brought him towards the shore. 3,000 . . . 2,000 . . . Lights suddenly twinkled in the darkness and Pyker landed on terra firma, on the good solid soil of England.

The lone warrior had returned. . . .

****

30th March

A newcomer has arrived at Tangmere to take over command of B Flight. His name is Stevens and he has come to us from No. 17 Squadron. On first contact he does not please the pilots, who as a general rule are always distrustful of those they do not know.

However, no one will judge him yet, and we prefer to wait for a few days.

We shall give our verdict when we return from the next scrap and have seen the way he has led us over the skies of France. In the meantime Stevens is the intruder who has taken Bungey's place. The Australian left us this morning for a hospital near London where they will operate on his injured knee.

8
BADER'S CIRCUS

9th April

THE TEA WAS REVOLTING AT BREAKFAST. WITH the best will in the world I shall never get used to this hideous beverage. Sometimes I think I've managed it and then a bitter taste fills my mouth and sticks to my palate. And that's it . . . I need another fortnight's efforts to overcome my aversion. It is a vicious circle. . . .

At 10.00 hours I took off with Gundry and Turner on an interception patrol. It was a single machine flying over the Channel half way between the two coasts but whose unorthodox behaviour seemed to have disturbed Control.

We flew on course 240° after leaving the coast at Bognor and climbed at 1,500 feet per minute.

We then flew on course 180° and reached 15,000 feet.

A thick layer of cloud lay over the sea at 10,000 feet with a few gaps here and there. Nothing . . . Nothing to be seen . . .

We circled for some minutes and yet the Section insisted that we were close to the bandit.

They confirmed and I was prepared to believe them, but however hard I looked I could see nothing . . .

I made up my mind.

"Blue leader to Blue 2 and 3. Stay at this altitude above the clouds. I'm going down below to take a look."

"O.K. Blue leader."

Half roll . . . I dived vertically through a yawning gap in the clouds into a vast cauldron. My ears hurt. Below the muck visibility was not so good. I tried to spot this enemy who would not appear but lurked in the thick grey clouds.

Nothing. A voice suddenly reached me from too near. It was Turner.

"Blue leader from Blue 2. Bandit in sight. He's just passed through a clear patch. Too late. He's gone to ground again. It's a Ju 88."

"O.K. Blue 2. Blue leader on the way up."

I returned into the void. The clouds enfolded me in their grey mantle. Above the layer I found my two wingers and giving up the chase we returned in close formation to the north.

13.00 *Hours*

Stevens, the new flight commander, blackguarded me at dispersal, where I was pontificating in flying kit.

"Pyker, I think you fly too much. I think you've already done too many hours this month."

"Oh, I like flying."

"So much the better. But I like my pilots to arrange that they all do the same amount of flying. You are the one that least needs it in any case."

"What do you mean?"

"I mean that you can go and take a walk."

What a bad type this Stevens is . . . What can it matter to him if I fly more than the others. He doesn't have to pay for the juice after all . . . Anyhow, it's pointless arguing with him, to try and make him see . . . He'd never understand. . . .

****

Editor's Note—Offenberg returned to the mess, shaved, put on his "Best Blue" and went to Chichester on the 3 o'clock bus.

He visited the Lydons to have a rest in the garden where the buds were already out. He sat down on an old wooden seat and Claire, the baby of the family, came and sat beside him. He told her stories, old Belgian fairy stories which he thought he had long forgotten.

But that day he remembered all the old legends of the land of Flanders.

The little English girl listened to this tall fellow speaking.

He had forgotten his aircraft and his fighting ... forgotten the names of missing comrades posted on the board. Only a big brother at peace with himself, caressing the silky hair of a child....

****

15th April

The weather is still appalling. At dispersal it is useless looking over the sandbags which reach half way up the windows of the hut, I can see nothing but grey sky, too low, refusing to lift. A fine drizzle is falling. What a bloody life ... The stove has been re-lit and I can hear it roaring. Camplin has just put on the old gramophone, which grinds out a Bing Crosby number which nearly makes me vomit, the words are such trash. But he is listening religiously, sitting on one of the three iron beds. Perhaps he's thinking of other things ... of the village he will revisit on his next leave if an Me hasn't brought him down in the meantime. I wonder if I shall ever see Belgium again? I've been away so long now and the war seems to be interminable. I wonder how they all are in Brussels....

"Look, the rain's stopped!"

Barrister passed on his old bicycle, made his way carefully round a big puddle, using his foot on the front wheel as a brake as he came to the hut.

Odd fellow that Barrister! He will spend nights if necessary getting a Spitfire airworthy but he refuses to spend five minutes repairing that terrible old bike.

A jeep pulled up outside the window and the C.O. got out. He ran towards the door, pulling up his raincoat collar. What was up? He came inside.

"Morning, boys. Bloody awful weather, isn't it?"

"Morning, sir."

He took off his soaking raincoat, threw it on a chair and sat down near the stove.

"Camplin, still playing those dreadful old song hits. Turn it off will you, I have news for you. Wing Commander Bader has requested that I be given a rest and your new C.O. arrives tomorrow. He's a Canadian from No. 242 Squadron, who was with Bader at Coltishall ..."

"But sir, if this goes on the 242 will still be stationed at Norwich and all its fellows will be here. "A" Flight has just been given a new leader: Ian Arthur. He seems a decent type he's also from 242."

It is true that Bader has brought all his pals to Tangmere. Group Captain Woodhall, the new station commander, is one of his best friends and worked with him in Group 12. Crowley-Milling, one of the 610 flight commanders, also belonged to No. 242. I think that Bader is on the wrong tack. All the Tangmere pilots are used to each other, know each other and have learned to work as a team. How are they going to react when given new leaders? I like Leather. He's a great fellow. How many times have I played golf with him at Goodwood and Tadmerton Heath?

He's leaving. If the new chap is anything like Stevens, the man who knows all the answers, I should like to leave too ... I should prefer a transfer to 609 where there is a bunch of Belgian pilots ... Yes, if Leather goes I shall ask for a transfer to 609. I shall rejoin Dumonceau, de Spirlet and the others at Biggin Hill in the Belgian flight. After all they are better off than those here for they are flying Spitfire Mark IIIs. And besides I shall be with my own countrymen and we shall be able to gossip about home. The time won't seem so long.

"Well," Leather went on, "it's no use pulling long faces. What's done is done. What about you, Pyker? Are you glad to see the back of me? My successor may not be so good at golf but perhaps he'll let you fly more often."

"No, I'm going too. All my old pals are gone and I can't get used to all these new faces around me."

Camplin did not move from the bed where he was lying. Stevens, in his armchair on the far side of the stove, turned over the pages of a magazine and pretended not to hear.

"Well, I'll buy you a farewell drink this evening in the mess for I'm leaving early tomorrow. Don't forget to turn up. I'm counting on you, Pyker. Bye, boys."

He went out, banging the door, got into his jeep and drove

through a large puddle, which splashed the glass panes against which I had leaned my forehead.

Another fine chap leaving!

"Hmm, we shall see," said·Sylvester, stifling a yawn. "After all there must be some good types in Canada."

17th April 1941

I took breakfast in the mess with Gundry, who seemed half asleep. I was given kippers, which everyone must have smelt through the door. When I return to Belgium and tell them that I ate potatoes, fish and sausages – largely filled with sawdust – for breakfast, the good folk will never believe me. And yet I find it very enjoyable. . . .

Nobby Clarke did not seem interested in the menu . . . With a gloomy eye he followed the movements of the fair-haired WAAF who removed my plate and brought me the marmalade. It was Denise, the pretty English girl from Bristol, who refuses categorically to go out with a pilot. Many have tried and been turned down. No one has succeeded. That girl must be made of stone. And yet it would be nice to hold her in your arms, to call her "darling" and say a host of things you don't mean

Nobby, who is very romantic, must certainly be dreaming of scenes far less chaste.

"A penny for your thoughts, Nobby."

"My thoughts . . . Ah yes, you mean Denise. Don't you think she has a terrific chassis?"

"Eat your kipper."

"I can't after what happened last night." As if to banish the memory, he ran his hand through his hair and closed his eyes.

"It was on the way back from Bognor. We decided to have a drink or two there, and the one or two developed into a fantastic number. You know I'm not good at figures . . . I can't tell you how many we had. Well, if I take off today I'm sure I'll never stay in the middle of the runway. Oh! My poor head!"

Poor Nobby. It will teach him a lesson, but he might have invited me!

Denise returned to our table, slipped round Nobby as she stretched out her arm to take away the teapot, placing her attractive breasts, which could be seen through her blue overall right under his nose. Nobby closed his eyes and drummed softly on the table.

"Come on, Nobby. It's no good getting nervy. Get up if you can and let's go and get warm at dispersal."

A few hours later, Control gave us the order to take off. Bader himself led the circus over France. Above the flight door some wit had written: "*Green Bus Line. Only return tickets will be issued.*" Sometimes however there are some who do not use their return half. As soon as I was in my Spit being strapped into my harness by the mechanic, I noticed poor Nobby Clarke sadly hoisting himself into his aircraft. He turned and put two fingers up at me, a gesture which could not be more impolite. My mechanic roared with laughter. Nobby is priceless and will get out of it even if he has the thickest of thick heads.

The wing took off, climbed and set its course for Dungeness where we had a rendezvous with eighteen Blenheims and another escort wing. Over the Channel the air was teeming with aircraft. I had Spits to left and right and below me. I had never seen so many at one time. What a scrap it would be if the Jerries attacked us ... We were top cover at 30,000 feet. I made a rapid calculation ... Twelve machines per squadron plus the Biggin Hill wing, that made seventy-two fighters in the air.

Woody called Bader on the intercom. Woody is Group Captain Woodhall, the station commander and controller of the sector. He had nothing to report. The sector was quiet, I was flying Blue 1.

A few woolly clouds drifted past below us. In the distance we could see the Breton coast. As we approached land Bader called Stan Turner, our new Squadron commander, and gave him orders to fly east to see that nothing came from there, while the Blenheims were bombing Cherbourg.

Above Saint-Malo, the flak opened fire but with no results. We were too high for them to hit us and the black puffs of smoke burst widely spaced far below us.

On the radio we heard the Blenheims carry out their attack. It was useless imposing radio silence, the fellows had to say something. Moreover, it was of no importance. The Germans knew quite well we were there and what we were doing. Half closing my eyes I scanned the horizon. Not an enemy fighter to be seen in the sky.

To starboard I saw the Blenheims returning northwards. The circus was over. We turned for home. None of the others had met a single enemy. The Germans must be on holiday!

Clouds blew up from the west during the afternoon. Splendid clouds for playing hide and seek, well spaced out and handy to dodge into when things got hot and to come out at the far end.

The telephone rang; Control asked for two machines to get into the air immediately. What was happening?

I rushed forward. Gundry, who is my No. 2, was already in his Spit and shouting: "Snap to it, Pyker."

Together on the runway we took off seawards.

"Hullo, Pyker," Control called, "Beetles here. Bandits at 15,000 feet vector 130°. He's 10 miles from the shore."

"O.K., Beetles."

I climbed to 17,000 feet on course 140° to get between him and the sun and above him. The clouds were thicker here than they were at Tangmere. We should not find them in them. Gundry signalled to me from his cockpit. He too seemed to find it hopeless.

We searched for a good twenty minutes without seeing anything suspicious, despite the assurances from Control.

"Pyker here. Bandit must be in the clouds below. I can't see him. Can I return to base?"

As soon as the permission was granted, Gundry and I returned line astern, in other words one behind the other.

19th April

I slept at dispersal last night to avoid crossing the icy airfield at four o'clock in the morning. Baudouin de Hemptinne and Gundry decided to share my fate. With the three of us it is bearable. When I am alone with Baudouin we both get homesick, talking of Brussels, of other Belgians, of the war, the restrictions placed on occupied countries by the Germans and our problematical return.

"Do you think, Baudouin, that this war will ever end? I don't fancy so myself at this rate."

"Of course it will. You'll see Brussels again. You'll see . . . Can you imagine our return. They'll throw flowers at us and all the girls will kiss us. What a party that will be . . ."

"We shall have to explain why we deserted."

"Don't be ridiculous, Jean. You'll be received as a liberator, as a hero . . . Besides, they always love people who return from a far-off country."

"We've been a terribly long way off, don't you think? We're so far yet in a Spitfire I could be at home within the hour. The

102

Channel ... No, Baudouin, there is a whole world that separates us from there ... And perhaps we shall never return. There are too many battles, too many tracers in the sky, too many dangers. A damned Messerschmitt one day will get me from behind ... Do you know, Baudouin, they've never got close enough on my tail yet to fire at me. Never, do you hear ... And that can't go on. There'll be one who is quicker than I and he'll get me ..."

Baudouin tried to reassure me.

"No Jean, *mon vieux*. They won't get you. You are stronger than they. And we'll bring down some more ... Together, eh? Tomorrow morning you and I will go up over the Channel. A Ju 88 ... I've always wanted to shoot a Junkers into the sea. Just the two of us ..."

"That's it. We'll do it, just the two of us."

****

Editor's Note.—Offenberg telephoned to the sector and asked the controller if he could set out at dawn on a "rhubarb" with Baudouin over France. Surprised at such a request at midnight, the officer on duty said that he saw no earthly reason for sending him over there.

He had only to ask Group Captain Woodhall next morning. "Rhubarbs" were no concern of his. A patrol perhaps over the coast ... as soon as it grew light.

****

"What did he say?" asked Baudouin.

"He said he can't fix it for us. We are allowed to patrol along the coast, but not too far out. I didn't tell him that we were after a Ju 88 ... he wouldn't have understood. Let's get some sleep now. We take off at dawn."

"Goodnight, Baudouin."

"Goodnight, Jean. Night Gundry."

****

Editor's Note.—The three of them fell asleep on their hard mattresses, without sheets, rolled in their grey blankets. The fire had gone out and the cold seeped into the hut through the chinks in the door and the windows.

*   *   *

At dawn the two Spitfires piloted by the Belgians followed the South Coast beaches at 15,000 feet. The first gleams of dawn rose gently over the Continent, across the strip of sea which separated them from the other world where their dear ones had remained.

"Dawn, Jean."

"Yes, Baudouin. It's going to be a fine day."

****

4th May

I get more and more browned off with life in this squadron. The day we returned to Tangmere a message came through from Air Ministry transferring Eric Faure to North Weald in Essex. This must be one of Stevens' little tricks for he wants to get rid of all the veterans so that he can train the youngsters as he wants to. In this way I feel he won't have anyone to point out any errors of judgement. This is an observation that has been very frequent recently.

Of what Stevens calls "the old gang" there remains only Baudouin de Hemptinne, Mike Newling and myself.

It must infuriate him when I speak to Baudouin in French, as he doesn't understand a word of the language. However, he cannot stop me flying.

11.00 hours

Squadron patrol. Off Cherbourg we met a formation of Blenheims returning from ops. and covered them on the home journey. I was Blue 1.

It was wonderful weather aloft and the whole squadron operated at 10,000 feet. I thought it was a trifle low. But the new C.O., Turner, decided it and as a good boy I kept my place in the formation with my three youngsters behind me. . . .

We were following the French coast two or three miles off shore. It won't be long now, I thought. The Mes will pounce on us.

I looked to port and saw the outlines of the Blenheims growing fainter. Nothing happened.

"Red leader. Squadron returning to base."

The fishermen sitting on the quayside must have been looking up at the twelve Spitfires which dipped their wings and made off.

In the distance I could see the English coast.

5th May 1941

I am in readiness at 4.30 hours and rather than ride a bicycle from the mess to dispersal I preferred to spend the night here. It is relatively comfortable and the army beds do not prevent me from sleeping. Obviously the mattress leaves something to be desired. . . . It is composed of three "biscuits." I don't know what genius invented the name but it speaks volumes. One would be inclined to say army biscuits, used for iron rations. These mattresses are just as hard. . . .

At three in the morning three bombs fell at the edge of the airfield. They only managed to wake me up.

Nothing happened all the morning. I'm afraid it will be another futile day. Nothing to report. What a joke. Obviously there won't be anything to report if we sit here and wait for it. If Turner wants to do something useful he only has to organise a little raid on the other side and not at 30,000 feet.

The Messerschmitts can't get up there . . . and one risks coming home without having had a scrap.

We've only got to keep the pressure on the Luftwaffe. Their fighters must be pinned down in the west. I'm all for them remaining in the west . . . How difficult life is with Stevens. If on top of that the Messerschmitts leave that would be the end.

Thanks to my Flight commander's great heart I am allowed to fly this afternoon. All alone over Tangmere for a short period of training!

I took off at 15.10 hours in Spit 8071 which was to do its air test. I climbed slowly doing a turn, without taking my eyes off the field. My field of vision gradually grew larger. . . .

3,000 . . . 5,000 . . . 7,000 . . . I thought I could make out the French coast. That was impossible. I was too far away. 8,000 the French coast . . . the French coast . . . So much the worse. I gave up, turned south, and dived. I pulled out at 1,000 feet.

Now I was flying at 200 feet straight for the enemy coast over a green and blue-flecked sea which sped past beneath my wings.

Cherbourg lay a little to starboard. I banked to port. There was too much flak at Cherbourg. A few ships were sailing well inshore.

There . . . straight ahead of me I saw two aircraft in single file which I identified as Heinkel 60's. I went down closer to the water. If only they didn't spot me! Safety catch removed . . . my gonio was functioning. The Heinkels were at about 800 feet just north of Barfluer Point. I turned to intercept them and attack almost head on, the sun behind me as I climbed. The nearest machine fired, but too late. I pumped a burst into the leader and zoomed.

Just as I banked over the coast I caught a glimpse of the Heinkel crashing into the water . . . and what a crash! Was it the leader or the second? I couldn't tell. I passed so close that for an instant I could see the gunner slumped against his machine gun. I had no time to start an attack on the second Heinkel for a couple of Mes put in an appearance flying from the east. Their silhouettes were getting unpleasantly large. Very unhealthy . . . I had only a reduced amount of ammunition left. I was alone. Well, come what may!

I turned north. An Me followed suit and I could see the black crosses on his wings. Flying at the same height we converged on a point, almost head on.

I gave him the first burst and pulled hard on the stick to avoid a collision. Luckily the German had the bright idea of diving. I sped northwards. My good Spitfire behaved beautifully and the engine purred with a regularity which gladdened my heart. I was now being chased by the two Mes, one on each flank. In my mirror I could see that they were not more than 500 yards off.

I zoomed violently on a right hand climbing turn and the moment the first appeared in my gonio I let him have it, and then without waiting banked to the left and fired at the second from 90°.

Out of the corner of my eye I saw my Messerschmitt in a shallow dive with a trail of white smoke coming from his engine.

He disappeared below my right wing. I thought it best to get away as quickly as possible from these waters and make for home. I skimmed over the water beneath a cloudless sky.

The fight had taken place at about 1,000 feet. What a rocket I was going to get! Stevens would certainly take advantage of it to ground me. Never mind!

As soon as I landed Clarke rushed over to me as I parked the aircraft, climbed on the wing and helped me to open the hood.

"Where the Hell have you been?" he shouted. "The Sector

thought you'd gone over to the other side. What the blazes came over you?"

With a smile I took off my helmet and slipped out of the cockpit. I caught sight of Turner coming out of the Squadron hut followed by some other men. He drove up. Before he began to bawl at me I told him what had happened, where I had been and how I had fared.

His great rage seemed to evaporate in a flash. He roared with laughter and slapped me on the shoulder with his huge woodcutter's paw.

"Good show, Pyker. You're a fellow after my own heart. I must go and tell the Group Captain straight away. I don't know how he'll take it, but never mind, I think it's splendid. See you later, Pyker."

He tittered to himself as he walked off to his jeep. He drove off like a whirlwind to the control tower, waving one arm at me as he left.

Barrister, the chief mechanic, was hovering round the Spitfire with an anxious look on his face, testing the controls.

"Not a scratch on the machine," he said with a smile. "I couldn't care less what you get up to as long as you don't break anything."

Barrister is never surprised at anything. Imperturbable, he accepts the craziest stupidities. Let a pilot try the rashest stunt before his eyes, he won't raise a finger or bat an eyelid . . . as long as nothing is broken.

If an aircraft returned from ops riddled with holes he would work with his team all night without a murmur to patch them up and get them airworthy. But if, by ill luck, a pilot wrote off a plane from carelessness or rashness Barrister would pour the vials of wrath on his head. This happened to poor Flying Officer Turner – he bears the same name as the C.O., but is no relation – who managed to damage his Spitfire against a wheelbarrow which had been left at the edge of the runway by some civilian workmen employed on camouflaging the runways. He never heard the last of it.

"Good show, sir," said Barrister, walking off with a spanner under his arm.

Before leaving dispersal Turner – the Squadron commander – not Barrister's bête noire – telephoned to tell us to arrange transport for the whole squadron. Rendezvous Bognor, Hotel

Victoria, in the bar, he added, as though we did not know already. Bader came with us.

Between two drinks Turner told me that he had recommended me for the D.F.C., and that the Group Captain wants to see me tomorrow morning to give me a rocket.

Stevens looked as sick as hell.

* * *

This morning, after a rather restless night, I was summoned to Group Captain Woodhall's office. I knew that at times he could take a joke and often shut his eyes to offences committed by exuberant youths whose nerves are put to such strain. Nevertheless, I was full of apprehension as I reported to his adjutant's office. The adjutant is a "kiwi" flight lieutenant.

"The Group Captain wants to see me," I said to him. "I'm Pilot Officer Offenberg of 145 Squadron."

"Offenberg," he said, raising his head. "Ah, yes – Offenberg."

His "Ah yes" sent shivers down my spine. I was more and more convinced that Woodhall would ground me for a fortnight.

"Has he said anything? Is he annoyed?"

"My dear Offenberg, I do not allow myself to analyse the differential emotional states through which the Base Commandant passes. I have the impression, however, that he was not particularly amused by your spectacular single-handed exploit. He may have calmed down after a good night's rest, and I'll go and see if he can receive you."

The Flight Lieutenant, whom I knew only from having seen him in the Mess, disappeared behind a sliding door opening on to the save into which I had to stick my head.

A deep voice rang out from the back of the office: "Let him come in."

That meant me. Feeling particularly small, I passed in front of the adjutant who put out his left arm and held the door open. As I passed I looked at him again, trying to read something on his face. I think he wore a slight smile but I could not be sure. I was in front of Woodie who stood with one elbow on the mantelpiece watching my entrance.

"Pilot Officer Offenberg reporting, sir," I said, saluting him. I stammered a little. The Group Captain gave no sign and looked stern and tough. He left me, standing to attention, for some moments which seemed terribly long

Then he went over to the window and opened it. I suddenly noticed that his hair was turning grey. Outside, the Spitfires were taking off and the din of engines being revved up entered the room. An ashtray shivered on the glass-topped desk.

Woodie closed the window and quiet was restored.

I did not move. I was waiting for his rage to explode and to fall upon my unsuspecting shoulders.

"Offenberg," he said at last, "in this Air Force we can't do what we like and I myself am bound by rigid laws that have been written in this big book known as King's Regulations, which you know quite well. Somewhere in all the paraphernalia of things to do and not to do, there is mention of discipline and obedience. That applies to all the members of the R.A.F. . . . even to the fighter pilots. A pilot has to know how to obey exactly like an infantryman. I am well aware that you and your peers are often called upon to use your own initiative, particularly in combat. But yesterday you were guilty of a grave offence against discipline by carrying out a dangerous mission without permission, and I am obliged to reprimand you. I must also ask for your word as an officer that you will not repeat the episode."

I stammered out my word of honour in atrocious English, for words suddenly failed me. The Group Captain came over and looked me straight in the eyes.

"However," he went on, "although King's Regulations states that one must not risk damaging His Majesty's aircraft, there is no paragraph forbidding pilots to go to France and demolish the Führer's machines."

He smiled. I now thought that perhaps he would not ground me after all.

"Pilot Officer Offenberg you are a very fine pilot. You have been recommended by your Squadron commander for the D.F.C. and to be second in command of B Flight." He held out his hand. "That's all. We'll leave it at that."

"Thank you, sir."

"Don't thank me, Offenberg. The reverse would be more natural, for it is thanks to young pilots of your stamp that we have won the first round. It is I who should thank you for having joined us. Now go back to your squadron. That's all."

I saluted, turned sharply on my heels and left.

On the other side of the door the adjutant, who must have

known exactly what was going to happen, smiled and held out his hand.

"Good show, Pyker."

"Thanks."

I can't get over the fact that I got off so lightly.

At the 145 office Turner reproached me in his drawling voice, confirmed me in my command despite my protests, for I am not the senior in the Flight. He would not hear of my refusal and insisted that seniority does not count here even if it does in Belgium. He couldn't care less.

Turner is not precisely a man of refinement and hardly ever uses polite language when he utters an opinion on something. After he has drunk a few glasses he would scare off a regiment of Polish infantry. When he was with the Canadians of No. 242 Squadron, he did not hesitate to bring out his revolver in cafés and fire at glasses placed on the counter. He fought magnificently in France, where he was more or less abandoned with his pals at the debcâle. They continued to fight, stealing fuel and arming themselves with machine guns. Without ground staff or luggage, with nothing but their Hurricanes, they returned to England at the very last moment. Turner has twelve confirmed victories to his credit.

It is not easy to discuss things with him or to contradict him. So I am second in command of B Flight.

****

Editor's Note.—The Luftwaffe bombers, which now operated only at night, returned a little too frequently to Tangmere airfield, dropping their bombs at random and preventing the pilots from getting any rest.

What was more serious, they sometimes dropped their bombs right in the middle of the field. A dozen Spitfires and a Miles Magister were destroyed in this way and Wing Commander Bader considered that the joke had gone far enough.

On the 7th May he ordered 145 Squadron to move to Marston, an auxiliary airfield some miles from Tangmere. The 610 and 616 were transferred to West Hampnet.

The pilots kept their rooms in Tangmere Mess which was very comfortable, but spent the day on the smaller airfields which meant they had to drive several miles in a military truck instead of being in the air.

When they were on night readiness they slept in ramshackle huts at Marston and West Hampnet.

Plenty of draughts, no trace of comfort and meals invariably late. The men who spent the night in these dumps usually did so in flying kit. They kept on their fur-lined boots with a map slipped in a pocket above the knee, a fisherman's jersey, no collar or tie and naturally very dilapidated tunics, the top button of which was always left undone.

This undone button was a sign of the clan. Thanks to this sartorial peculiarity, the fighter boys recognised each other wherever they happened to meet.

A great rivalry existed between the fighter and the bomber pilots. The "bus drivers" were looked down upon by the lords of the chase. They did not fraternise and looked upon each other with a bleak eye.

At Marston, the aircraft were safe and although the German bombers continued their night raids they were invariably attracted by the runways of Tangmere.

Unfortunately the Spitfires had gone. One evening, however, a bomb fell on the corner of the Sergeants' Mess, demolishing a whole wall but neither killing nor wounding anyone.

The only trouble was that the Sergeant Pilots who were quartered that night in the mess were very proud of the incident and did not fail to explain and bore the officers with the details on the following day. This wretched 100 lb. bomb assumed the most extraordinary proportions. By the end of the afternoon it was already a 1,000 pounder. When evening came nobody mentioned pounds – it was a matter of tons.

On the 8th May, Bader led No. 145 over the Channel to the Pas de Calais and made the Squadron take up a formation which Pyker did not like. "It's an idiotic formation," he wrote that evening in his diary.

Fortunately no enemy fighter put in an appearance above them and the whole Squadron returned to base.

On the 10th May he took off from West Hampnet at midnight on a lone patrol inland.

For him it was the first anniversary of the war and he could not help remembering the events of that day a year ago. Jottard had come and woken him up in the pilots' quarters at Nivelles.

Poor Jottard, his old friend, whose body the sea had not disgorged.

In the untroubled sky of that May night, Offenberg patrolled

111

in the direction of London at 15,000 feet. He was in the heart of a new star. He looked for landmarks -- some searchlight down below on the coast, but the darkness furnished no signpost and for one moment he felt that the earth was no longer inhabited. The roof of his cockpit could not have been quite closed and the cold numbed his hands, seeped into his boots and through his flying suit to freeze his body.

Suddenly his Spitfire was shaken and began to vibrate. An aircraft must have crossed his path and he had been caught in the slipstream. He peered into the night but the marauder has passed protected by the darkness. For one moment he thought of calling the sector but decided that it was useless. He flew on an easterly course. There ahead to port far away in the May night fires sprang up one by one. . . .

London was burning. An immense explosion lit up the horizon. The Nazi bombers were over the capital. He would have liked to go there but it was not his sector. Everyone had to keep to his own territory and he had given his word as an officer to the Group Captain. He would not break his promise.

He took a last look at the far-off city where great walls were tumbling, and terrified children crying in a man-made inferno . . . where men were rushing about the streets searching the ruins for the dying by the ghastly light of the fires.

Offenberg banked and his wing hid the far-off gleams. He returned to Marston and parked his aircraft between two blue lights at the edge of the runway.

As he entered the hut a young Londoner asked him anxiously: "Did you see anything, Pyker?"

Out of pity for him, Offenberg merely replied: "No, I saw nothing."

A few days later Stevens grounded him for two days on the basis that he had taken off "down wind," where, the wind being nil, there had been no reason to take off in one direction more than another.

*　　*　　*

In the afternoon of 21st May, while the Squadron was returning from a patrol south of Dungeness, Flight Lieutenant Stevens of B Flight collided with his winger, Owen, over Tangmere.

Beneath Offenberg's horrified gaze the two machines spun and crashed a few yards from each other at the edge of the airfield.

112

As was only natural, Offenberg replaced Stevens as Flight commander while waiting for the promotion proposals sent through the official channels to be agreed by the higher authorities.

On the 4th June at dawn Squadron Leader Turner took Offenberg, Baudouin de Hemptinne and Flying Officer Newling for an early morning sweep over the North of France.

Before taking off Turner gave them a few vague instructions and their E.T.A. Dungeness – Cap Gris Nez – Calais – Boulogne – Beachy Head. Altitude 25,000 feet.

They took off at the crack of dawn, turned above Littlehampton and climbed following the coast. Offenberg drew in his notebook the design of the formation adopted.

*　　*　　*

They reached Dungeness Point and set their course for the French coast.

Tangmere Control called and there was a crackle in their headphones. Turner could not understand the message and asked for it to be repeated.

"Bogey at 3 o'clock. Altitude so far unknown. Keep your eyes open."

"Okay, Beetles."

Ahead they could see nothing except the coast of France growing clearer.

"Red leader to Red 3 – can you see anything?"

"No, Red leader – nothing."

There were only a few fishing boats a mile from the shore off Calais and to port some way off, the mole of Zeebrugge. Stan recalled Control, which announced: "The plot has faded." The enemy must have flown back to his base inland, out of range of the RFD.

Not an aircraft in the sky and the sector was so calm that Stan Turner proposed a little *haute ecole* to amuse themselves. On their return to Tangmere they were told that the unidentified aircraft reported was none other than a Spitfire from Tangmere flown by Flying Officer Clarke who had crossed the Channel without permission. Near Le Havre he had met a Junkers 87 Stuka which he quickly sent to the bottom with a well-placed burst before the German pilot was aware of his presence. Coming down to wave-top level he speeded for the coast and came out over an observation post which he sprayed with his cannon. He then flew about the sky over Havre at 5,000 feet and before the flak gunners had time to get their guns trained on him he took photos of the port. This is why Group Captain Woodhall found that it was "a jolly good show" and grounded Clarke for four days.

After a rapid lunch in the mess which ended as it did every day with the sacrosanct sweet, apple pie and custard, Bader called the fighters to another briefing. The Wing went to Northern France, not to escort bombers this time but out of pure bravado. The actual technique had not changed for several months. They went to provoke the Luftwaffe on its own territory, not very far inland. Occasionally fighters who got lost or excited in a battle refused to break away and pursued the enemy ruthlessly right over their airfields. These, however, were exceptional cases. The Luftwaffe had obviously lost its early aggressiveness and as a general rule the Me 109s kept their distance, waiting to pick of stragglers. Only then would they dive and attack....

That afternoon, the formation stretched out over several miles. At 15,000 feet Bader with the 616 at 18,000 feet, 610 astern and to starboard keeping watch on the sky to the south. Turner with the 145 much higher at 30,000 feet in the sun....

Offenberg leading Blue Section took off and got into formation at the head of his flight behind Turner, the whole squadron following the coast. When they arrived over Beachy Head, Turner gave orders to continue their climb in circles. The 610 arrived beneath them and carried out a similar manoeuvre. Offenberg saw three sections of four Spitfires getting their altitude. At 12,000 feet the pilots tightened their masks for the air was becoming rarified. Squadron formation is called "Fingers Four." Actually if one stretches out the hand without the thumb, the fingertips give an exact picture of the position of aircraft in a section.

1

3   2

4

The 616 arrived over Beachy Head just as the 145 reached 22,000 feet. Then the whole wing set course for the French coast.

Below, two fast launches from Newhaven ploughed wakes of foam in the calm sea. Those who would be shot down into the Channel and were still alive had a chance of being picked up.

Radio silence was imposed for it was useless to warn the Germans. At 30,000 the 145 reached the condensation zone and vapour trails began to be seen in the sky. The coast was now quite near. Turner descended 1,000 feet and the vapour trails disappeared. It was to be hoped that the observation posts on the shore had not seen these long white trails in the sky, signs which betrayed the presence of fighters. Offenberg looked skywards. Any aircraft higher than them would betray its presence. But the sky remained empty. No one in the sun. He looked below. The coast stretched north-south with the mouth of the river at Le Touquet. Silence was not unnecessary. The enemy must have spotted them.

Tangmere notified the wing leader: "Keep a look out in the direction of Saint-Omer. The 'big-boys' are climbing south-east."

The Me 109s were probably trying to outflank the formation from the south and to fall upon them from the rear, taking advantage of the position between the sun and the allied aircraft.

Pyker's cockpit began to be covered with ice.

"Red 1 from Blue 1. Icing on my windscreen'.'

"Mine too. Let's go down."

The first section descended slowly, soon followed by the others. The ice broke off from the wings. The pilots were terribly cold. Sergeant Sylvester, acting as weaver and watching the rear aircraft, reported a formation of Messerschmitts diving lower down at 2 o'clock. The Jerries had not seen 145. Offenberg saw the yellow noses and the black crosses banking below him. Turner reacted very quickly and dived behind them. He fired at 100 yards and Offenberg saw a 109 explode and spin earthwards in a cloud of black smoke.

The scrap, the infernal merry-go-round, began with aircraft diving, zooming, turning on their backs and doing tight turns. Offenberg thought he saw one Me firing at another behind him but he may have been mistaken. Two enemy fighters were climbing to starboard. When they passed beneath him he plunged after them, diving to port. He fired at the moment when his target turned over on his back and half rolled into a vertical

115

dive. On the intercom there was a cacophony of warnings, cries and oaths.

"Two aircraft below."

"Aircraft at six o'clock."

"Okay, I can see them."

"Tell me when to break, I can't see them any more."

"He nearly got you."

"Look behind you."

"I shall ram him."

"Like a bird, like a bird . . ."

"The bastard."

"Did I get him?"

And the voice of some wit imitating the high-pitched tone of a woman: "Oh do stop it, this is terrifying."

A fighter with a yellow nose dived on Pyker from port. But he had seen him. At the moment of the enemy's dive, he reduced the gas, banked violently towards the attacker, giving him a short burst, rolled over on his back and flattened out. The Me was probably hit in the midriff. He did not know. He was thinking of other things. No time to congratulate himself. A quick glance at the instrument panel . . . oil pressure fallen slightly. A trifle. Temperature okay. He noticed a Spitfire over the coast, streaming glycol. He was still at a good height and could reach the English coast.

Someone shouted: "There's a Spit steaming glycol."

The dogfight had been in progress a mere ten minutes. The Germans broke off the engagement.

The last Messerschmitt streaked past 5,000 feet lower at a hell of a speed for home. Like squires of old days who protected the knights in the tumult of battle, Offenberg's winger, Sergeant Camplin, had stuck faithfully to his side.

"Come on, Blue 2."

"Okay, Blue 1."

They dived on the Messerschmitt one behind the other. Following the usual tactics, when Pyker was at 500 yards, almost within firing range, the 109 performed a half roll and fell like a plummet. Pyker turned his Spitfire over and followed him down in a giddy dive. He had started his half roll too soon and lost sight of the Messerschmitt. When he pulled out he felt as though his eardrums would burst. It was terribly painful. Centrifugal force had distorted his face, making him look for a moment like a terrifying mask. He was on the point of blacking

116

out. The Spit came out of the dive. Where were the others? The sky was empty. Only Camplin remained, waiting for him.

On landing, when he returned to dispersal, Pyker took off his muffler. He noticed that it was wringing wet with sweat.

The Tangmere wing had no losses but a pilot of 610 – the man Offenberg had seen while he was flying over the French coast streaming glycol – had baled out near Dover.

On the 16th June the Base Adjutant telephoned to No. 145 Squadron office to say that Pilot Officers Offenberg and de Hemptinne, both of Belgian nationality, had been granted their transfer to No. 609 at Biggin Hill, south of London. Biggin Hill – No. 1 fighter aerodrome, the best known, the most famous in the world. They were to report to their new squadron on the following day. That evening, in accordance with the old squadron custom, their departure was celebrated in the mess by all the boys. Everyone turned up. Bader, Turner, Ian Arthur, the amiable flight lieutenant from A Flight and Sylvester ... Pyker, whom everyone was sorry to lose, had carried out 230 operational flights since joining the squadron.

9

BIGGIN HILL

THE PARTICIPATION OF BELGIAN FIGHTER PILOTS in the war in the air was soon numerically important enough to allow Fighter Command to form a Belgian group in the bosom of a British unit. Replying favourably to a wish expressed by the Belgian authorities, the Air Ministry did them the honour of appointing one of its most famous squadrons to welcome the Belgian pilots. In this way, on the 11th February 1941 began a partnership between the Belgians and the "West Riding Squadron," usually known in fighter circles by its number 609, a partnership which would continue until V day.

The unit originally included seven Belgian pilots whose names are worthy of recording: François de Spirlet, killed on active service over Duxford at dawn on the 26th June 1942 piloting one of the first Typhoons of No. 609; Eugène Seghers, D.F.C., killed on the 26th July 1944 over Uckfield while attacking a V1, against which he exploded; Vicky Ortmans, D.F.C., a born scrapper and first class pilot, brought down five times in the course of his career, shot down in the Channel on the 21st October 1941 and taken prisoner after achieving six confirmed victories. He was to die as an airman after the war piloting a training aircraft; R. Wilmet, arrived at Biggin Hill on the 17th April 1941, died in an accident in Nigeria while serving with the 349 Belgian Squadron in 1943; Roger Malengrau, survivor of the Battle of Britain, arrived at 609 on the 15th May 1941. Major Malengrau is today Belgian Consul in Lagos; the oldest of them, Willy van Lierde, reported to 609 on the 15th April 1941 is still alive today, and Count Yvan Du Monceau de Bergendael, D.F.C., Croix de Guerre with eight palms, one of our great fighters, with eight confirmed victories, today a colonel in the Belgian Air Force. These were soon joined by Second Lieutenant R. de Hemricourt de Grunne, a fine fighter with fourteen victories against the Russian Ratas during the Spanish civil war, three more during the Battle of Britain, shot down in flames by the enemy fighters on the 18th August 1940 when serving with No. 32 Squadron. Rodolphe de Grunne joined 609 almost before his dreadful burns were healed. He was shot down again over the Channel on the 21st May 1941. Taking off from Biggin Hill with the famous "Sailor" Malan, the squadron met a formation of Me 109s off Dungeness. His body was never washed up and the grey North Sea serves as his shroud. On the 17th June, de Hemptinne and Offenberg arrived together at the guardroom of Biggin Hill station, having come from Tangmere via London. As soon as they arrived they learned that their Belgian pals could not welcome them. They were about to take off for France and hardly had time to greet them. They merely got a slap on the shoulder.

"See you soon. We shall be back for dinner."

"Eh, Pyker – leave something for us."

A few minutes later the Spitfires took off with a roar in a cloud of dust. Pyker and Baudouin's new squadron was off on a mission.

Offenberg waited impatiently for their return. An hour passed and the time seemed to pass terribly slowly. Where could they be?

He searched the sky, cocked an ear for the drone of an aircraft and suddenly noticed black specks above the horizon. A few minutes later the formation broke up, the Spitfires glided down and landed in pairs.

They were all back. De Spirlet was the first to open his hood. Pyker saw him hoist himself up on his seat, take off his helmet and straighten his white muffler.

"Hullo, François. Had a scrap?"

"Yes, I got one of the bastards nearly half way between Le Touquet and Dungeness."

"Confirmed?"

An extremely young-looking squadron leader came up. He had also been on the mission for he was in flying kit and was sponging his forehead with a handkerchief. He held out his hand before Offenberg had time to salute.

"Flying Officer Offenberg."

"I'm Robinson, in command of 609 Squadron. Happy to have you with us. You know, with all these Belgians here, I've often heard about you, so you're not really a stranger. Besides, the Belgians are pretty good fighter pilots aren't they, François?" he said, turning to de Spirlet with a laugh. "You know," he went on, "your friend François sent one to the bottom less than half an hour ago. I saw the Jerry disappear into the water with a terrific splash."

"Yes," said de Spirlet, "there was a huge greener patch of water. Nothing came out. Only a darker patch against the green."

"Come on boys. No time for sentiment. There's a war on. See you later." He walked off with his Mae West still round him and his old helmet in his hand.

* * *

The day after their arrival they were sent on patrol over the south-east of England and Baudouin de Hemptinne became involved in a violent combat against twenty Me 109s, in the course of which a British pilot, Flying Officer Hill, was brought down and killed.

The same day, Offenberg received official notification that His Majesty of England had been pleased to award him the Distinguished Flying Cross. He was the first Belgian to receive this decoration.

The award of this medal well earnt in combat created various reactions in governmental circles, for Fighter Command, in its enthusiasm, had forgotten to ask the approval of the Belgian authorities. This was arranged, however, as soon as the British attaché had sent a letter of apology from his government and asked for the official approbation of the Belgian authorities.

On the 29th July 1941 Mr. Gutt, Minister for National Defence, gave his consent and on the 4th August sent his personal congratulations to Offenberg.

Pyker was literally bombarded with letters from all quarters. Colonel Wouters, Military Attaché at the Belgian Embassy, commanding the Belgian Air Force in Great Britain, issued an order of the day addressed to all C.O.s of Belgian units informing them of the great honour bestowed upon Offenberg. The Commander-in-Chief Belgian Land Forces announced it to his troops.

Offenberg went on with his war. In his diary entry of the 18th July he merely wrote, "I've been awarded the D.F.C. I don't think I deserve it." And the following morning in his Spitfire Mark V with six other aircraft he was escorting a Lysander off Dover.

****

21st June

Second show of the day. We took off about 17.00 hours for a sweep whose route was Dover-Calais-Bois de Guines-Boulogne. Several squadrons participated.

We climbed to 16,000 feet. I could see several ships in Dover Harbour as I passed over it. We had hardly crossed the French coast when black specks appeared in the distance above the land. The Luftwaffe. They had been very quick today. I counted about a score bearing down on us at a fairly good height. We had the benefit of the sun in our backs.

They attacked a squadron which was circling higher than ours.

A kind of grandoise ballet began to unfold beneath our eyes as we climbed up to join it. It must never be said that the 609 was left out of the dance. An Me 109 shot like a meteor south of Boulogne, a little below us. The squadron leader saw it and detached my section.

I dived at once after checking my weapons. The Me did a half roll on top of a loop and dived at full speed. I pursued him to ground level without being able to catch him. I was still between 600 and 700 yards away. Although I was flat out I could only maintain the distance.

If only I could have had a little extra power! Tired of it, I fired all the same. I knew that I was much too far away but it only needed a lucky shot and the loss of a shell. No luck. Missiles wasted. Nothing doing. I turned to the north. The German pilot had spotted my manoeuvre and followed. Oh, no. No one's going to fire at me from behind. I banked to the left and made for him. A fraction of a second later we were heading for each other, with our cannon spitting fire. What was he going to do? I pulled the stick, my Spit reacted immediately and climbed. Ugh! I must have missed him by a couple of feet. As I had no ammunition left I returned northwards and set my course for England. Off Dover on my own I noticed away to the right two miles from shore a white parachute opening and two seconds later a huge waterspout where a Spitfire had crashed into the sea. I had to send help to that white flower swaying in its descent above the water.

I headed for Dover. I could do no more for I already saw a launch making for him at full speed. The pilot would get away with an enforced bath. Returned to Biggin Hill where several Spits had already landed.

I had two bullets in my right wing which seemed to have been fired from astern. I do not remember having seen a Hun on my tail. Very odd.

At the debriefing – that is, the moment when the pilots give an account of the battle – I learned that the results obtained by 609 were far from being insignificant.

Flying Officer Ogilvie and Sergeant Boyd had each shot down a German fighter and Vicky had damaged a third.

I had hardly had time to watch the various battles taking place around me. I caught hold of Vicky as he left.

"Hi, Vicky! How did you bring down your Boche? You were in yellow section, weren't you?"

"Yes, No. 3. You were far too quick when you dived on that Me near Boulogne."

"Come, come, it was Robinson who detached our section to pursue that feller. I couldn't catch him up at first but we damn nearly collided later."

"I stayed at 16,000 feet with the others and we took the brunt of the attack. Above Le Touquet four aircraft flew beneath us in line on the same course as ourselves. It did not take me long to see that they were Jerries. In the preliminary tangle I thought they were Spits. They seemed to be after our blood and got ready to attack, turning to starboard in a slight dive. I can tell you we were waiting for them!

"Baudouin, who was leading the section, banked to port to attack the second Me in the line. At that moment I lost him from sight. I was already on number one when I noticed that one of his pals was on my tail. I turned as tight as a drum. By the time I managed to shake him off I was at 5,000 feet, ten miles west of Le Touquet over the water. I was just thinking it would be better to get over the land as I hadn't brought my bathing suit when I noticed a Spit and an Me having a merry-go-round a mile to port. I took the opportunity of getting on the beam of the 109 and giving him a two-second burst."

"Did you get him?"

"No, since he went on flying."

Vicky brought out a comb from his jacket and tidied his hair. "And then?"

"Then I went in a second time. I don't know what he was up to but I remember that he was upside down when I fired. Lucky, for when I stopped firing I was about twenty yards away. In that position he couldn't climb. I almost shaved his belly and said 'Excuse me' as I passed."

"You missed him?"

"Not quite. I banked to take a look and he was speeding down at forty-five degrees with black smoke coming from his engine."

"To be quite certain I followed him down and sprayed him for the last time from 220 yards. Then I had a feeling I was being followed. I banked to port to find out. There was no one but I had lost sight of my Me."

Vicky shrugged his shoulders and shook his head like a young horse. He took off his Mae West. Great type Vicky!

22nd June

The 609, led by Squadron Leader Robinson, took off a quarter of an hour after Mass, which I attended in the little chapel at Biggin Hill. I was No. 2 in Red section behind the C.O. We described circles about three miles south-west of Dunkirk at 20,000 feet when some Me 109Fs attacked us. Red 1 did a left hand climbing turn. I followed him for a moment, then banked to the right, losing Red 1 because I caught sight of an Me 109F climbing 4,000 feet below me. I banked and dived on him but just as I was in a good position to fire I took a look behind.

Another Messerschmitt with a yellow nose was behind me a little lower down. He fired. Tracers passed my left wing at the moment I banked violently to starboard. His aim was very bad. He did not follow me. A glance at my altimeter – 12,000 feet. Heavens, how easy it was to lose height in a battle. I had to get back in formation, but I could not see a friendly plane in the vicinity. Oh yes, down there. Those black specks. A dozen or so black specks which seemed to be over Dunkirk. Perhaps they were Spits. Perhaps. Well, let's go and find out. If they're not Spits then it'll be the bloody Luftwaffe. Yes, but ten to one. Can't be helped. I made for them and as I drew near saw that they were Me 109Fs. Bad, bad! It was better to get inland. But where were the others?

So there were only Messerschmitts in the air today. Two 109s were flying westward at the same altitude as myself but they were well spaced out. Tally-ho! I got in position and attacked the right hand machine from behind. He saw me and dived to port. I was 400 yards behind him.

What was the other one doing? He did not attempt to follow me. What a bind!

I closed in to 300 yards and gave him a few short bursts. It was very difficult to aim for we were diving at a crazy speed. I did not manage to get any closer and when he headed for land I decided to leave him to his fate and to fly northwards.

At the moment I was very low – only about 1,200 feet. Since I was approaching Gravelines I thought it wise to avoid the town and make a slight detour to starboard. Suddenly I was surrounded by flak tracers. They climbed up towards me but the gunners were wildly inaccurate. As I approached the shore I could hardly believe my eyes.

An Me 109E was in front of me hedgehopping over the dunes. What that cretin was doing was terribly dangerous in these waters. I set off in hot pursuit and easily caught him up. I must be calm. My mask irritated me and I tore it from my face. 500 yards ... 300 ... 200 ... I gave him a short burst. I was terribly busy in that cockpit for with my left hand I was obliged to wipe my windscreen, which was covered with ice, while keeping my eye on an Me 109F who was cavorting about inland rather higher than ourselves. I broke away to the left to 100 yards and immediately got on to his tail again. At 100 yards I opened fire ... I was almost on top of him. I broke away, perhaps at twenty yards ... Glycol streamed from the Me and covered my windscreen as I flew seaward at altitude zero. I had noticed the other Me making in my direction. Now he was on my tail. At 1,000 feet perhaps, I did a gentle left bank to watch him out of the corner of my eye. He dived on my tail. I let him approach. I bet that Hun was singing his paean of victory over the radio. When he was at 300 yards I banked violently to the left ... My wing almost touched the water. He tried to follow me, firing as he went. My turn was too tight for him ever to get me. I saw his wings vibrating. In a moment he would be in a spin.

I went on banking until I found myself facing north. Then I streaked away in a straight line a few feet above the water; this gives one an extraordinary sense of speed and power. The water passed beneath me at a giddy speed. The Me did not follow; he must have lost his nerve. I turned east-north-east, reduced gas and looked behind me. At last, away to starboard, I saw some Spitfires. I decided to join them. There were six. Spits ... As I drew closer my eyes nearly popped out of my head. No – not more Mes!

And yet they were. Yellow noses, black crosses, very unhealthy. I probably had not enough ammunition left to fire a really decent burst, so I veered towards the white cliffs of Dover. The Messerschmitts were a mile away to starboard at 12,000 feet.

Immediately on landing at Biggin Hill I inspected my machine. Not a scratch. It was almost miraculous, but God, how tired I was!

****

Editor's Note.—Other combats took place that day along the French Coast between Calais and Berck-Plage. Sergeant Pilot Rigler, a fat good-humoured fellow who had gone prematurely bald, shot down two Me 109Es and one Me 109F.

François de Spirlet was shot down; direct hit by a cannon shell in his engine. As this occurred over the Pas-de-Calais, he turned on his back and baled out. An Air Sea Rescue launch fished him out of the sea. He was reported to be slightly wounded in the leg and head and was evacuated to Ramsgate Hospital.

The following morning at dawn, Offenberg and his flight were once more at 25,000 feet on the route Calais-Béthune-Boulogne-Le Touquet. The other wing accompanied the Biggin

Hill boys but the Luftwaffe, who had lost on the previous day, refused to play. Not even the flak greeted them as they flew over.

After a snappy lunch and a short briefing the wing took off again for a sweep over the ground covered that morning but in reverse. Not a German showed his nose. Offenberg, bored with the proceedings, took Spitfire 3117 and threw it about the peaceful sky, south of London.

On June 24th another circus was organised by Wing Commander Malan, the South African fighter ace.

All the Belgians of 609 with the exception of de Spirlet took off in the Biggin Hill formation. Twenty-four Blenheims flew below them in impeccable formation. Nothing happened on the outward journey. From time to time the engine of Offenberg's Spit vibrated, making the fuselage rattle. Then it ran smoothly again. Pyker thought of leaving the party and making for home, but changed his mind. Perhaps it was nothing. The 609 flew over Dunkirk and turned for Commines. Robinson, the C.O., ordered Blue section, in which Offenberg was flying No. 3 to disengage.

The four aircraft flew north in combat formation. Offenberg's engine was firing smoothly and the oil pressure was normal.

Suddenly, Sergeant Pilot Rigler called on the intercom:

"Blue 1. Bandits at 11 o'clock. At least fifteen Jerries."

"O.K. Blue section. I can see the bastards."

Four against fifteen, the odds were unequal. They looked like Me 109Fs in open formation. Blue section went into the attack. While the first pair – Bisdee, the B Flight commander and Rigler – attacked two Messerschmitts, Offenberg kept his eye on the main body of the enemy. Tracers ... An Me 109 was attacking him from below to stern.

He did a left hand turn, kicked hard on the rudder and went into a spin. "I was hot under the collar," he wrote, "for I could see him close on my tail and his aim seemed horribly accurate." Just as he straightened out the vibrations started again, more serious this time. No ... his engine wasn't going to let him down over France. That would really be too absurd.

Suddenly the usual cacophony which accompanied a dogfight ceased. He tried to call but there was no reply. His radio was out of action. So he made for home praying that the engine would not conk before he reached the coast.

He would try and make Biggin Hill. The vibrations grew

worse. A few splutters. But there ahead of him he could see the British coast. He gave up thinking, glided slowly with one eye on his mirror. He was sweating profusely and the straps of his harness cut into his shoulders. His face beneath the mask was covered with sweat. There ahead lay an airfield. It was Hawkinge. He could not call them up because his radio was dead. So he flew low over the field and dipped his wings. Near the tower a green flare rose into the air. Permission to land . . . He landed "on his bats" with a spluttering engine.

He telephoned at once to Biggin Hill but no one was available to fetch him. Not until the following day did his flight commander Bisdee pick him up in a Leopard Moth and fly him back to Biggin Hill, just in time to jump into another Spitfire and take off in a sweep over Nazebrouck.

Twice that day he returned to Biggin Hill and took off again for France where he engaged with enemy fighters. He realised that he had not even had time to eat a decent meal. Until the end of the month he would sally forth two or three times a day on ops. He fulminated and wrote in his diary after one mission: "I'm livid because I've taken part in sixteen sweeps since June 1941 and haven't had a chance to bring down a single Boche . . . Or rather I did have one chance and I missed him like a fool."

****

26th June

On 26th June, on return from my second patrol, I found de Spirlet ensconced in one of the mess armchairs.

"And where have you come from, pray?"

"Out of the drink via Ramsgate Hospital. The last time we saw each other was somewhere near Dunkirk. Well, you might at least look pleased to see me."

"I am pleased," I said, shaking him by the hand. "But what happened to you?"

"You very nearly lost the best pilot in the squadron," he replied, with a grin. "What do you expect, I didn't see him arrive. Or rather I did see him but I was a little late. Then, after my graceful descent hanging by my shoulders from the parachute, I slipped gently into the waters of the Channel. I think I swallowed half the sea."

"Did you manage to blow up your dinghy and get into it?"

"It's as easy as pie to blow it up, but I had a hell of a

job getting into it. At last I managed to lie down inside. Some Spits flew over me and dipped their wings. Each time I struggled up to wave to them, but the cockleshell rocked like mad and I found myself with my face in the water. I fell in three times ... No more sea bathing for me."

"You must have been wounded or they wouldn't have kept you so long at Ramsgate."

François stood up, put his hands in his pockets, planted himself firmly on both feet and explained what had happened.

"No, not even a scratch. I was obviously soaking wet but the water wasn't cold and I was more or less certain that I should be rescued. I'm not the first to have fallen into the drink: Vicky's had some experience. So that the Spits should spot me easily. I poured that famous chemical into the sea ... You know, the little yellow bag in the dinghy which colours the water. I was surrounded by a splendid yellow patch in the middle of the Channel. It was later that when I waved I fell into the water three times. After about half an hour I saw two ships making towards me, one coming from the south and a smaller one from the north ..."

I could not help interrupting François to ask him the question that sprang to my lips.

"A German and an R.A.F., eh?"

"No. I thought so for a long time but when they drew closer I saw that it was a naval corvette and a fast Air Sea Rescue launch."

"What happened? I suppose the launch fished you out first?"

"Not a bit of it. They both drew up, one on each side of me. They rocked on the waves. A sailor flung me a line and so did the R.A.F. fellow. I managed to catch both of them, but I couldn't make up my mind which to choose ... R.A.F. or R.N. I was on the horns of a dilemma, particularly as the two skippers began to yell at each other through their megaphones.

" 'I saw him first,' roared the sailor.

" 'I know,' said the chap in the launch, 'but he's an airman, and therefore it's up to us to fish him out.'

"The argument continued for several minutes while I was still bobbing about in my dinghy in the water.

"I finally decided to abandon the Royal Navy and to cling on to the line which the R.A.F. type had thrown me.

"I was hoisted aboard to an accompaniment of oaths, insults and shouts of victory."

"Okay, but I can't understand your absence of six days. You've had time to walk back and visit all the pubs on the way."

"Oh, my story's not finished yet. Wait a bit . . . Despite all my remonstrances I was taken to Ramsgate Hospital. The doctor there was convinced I was suffering from an attack of jaundice."

I could not help roaring with laughter at the thought of poor François being treated for jaundice when there was nothing wrong with him except a rather yellow skin from the colouring he had poured into the water.

"All right, my dear fellow. You can laugh. But I swear to you that next time you won't find me playing the surrealist painter in the middle of the Channel. If I had my way I'd send all those quacks to do a course with the Air Sea Rescue." On this remark I left him.

Our aristocratic François de Spirlet was not at all pleased with the R.A.F. medical services.

21st June 1941

I slept badly and on waking up at dawn wandered round the camp to find the place where the Catholic priest said Mass. I managed to find it after about a quarter of an hour and entered half way through the service. It was cold this morning and I shivered in spite of the pullover I wore under my tunic. I felt very tired. Only two soldiers had the courage to come to Mass this morning in the little hut which is not even a chapel. But does one need chapels in which to pray?

I returned to the squadron. Nothing happened until 13.00 hours. With the squadron commander's permission I telephoned to the crew room to ask if I could take a youngster with me and carry out a patrol over the coast. My request was refused because something serious was being hatched. It depressed me profoundly, for there is nothing worse for a pilot's morale than to remain on the ground. I voiced my opinion to Bisdee.

"I agree," he said. "It's very bad to stick on the floor. But you shouldn't grumble. How many hours' flying have you had this month?"

"I don't know. Wait."

I took my log book, made a rapid calculation and said triumphantly: "Exactly forty-one hours."

"And when was the last time you flew?"

"Yesterday. I did two sweeps over France but no combats."

"No combats, eh? So Monsieur wants to fly but it doesn't count unless there's a scrap. Forty-one operational hours in a fighter is far too much. You'll have to bring your total down next month."

Sergeant Pilot Hughes-Rees, who was present at the conversation, nearly split his sides.

"What's eating you?" I asked.

"Nothing. Absolutely nothing. But next time I advise you not to grouse. I'm beginning to get sick of flying. Biggin Hill – Gravelines, Biggin Hill – Lille ... rhubarbs ... rhubarbs, circuses and all the bag of tricks. It isn't very exciting. So this afternoon I'm going to ask for eight days' leave and go home."

"Home, eh? You see, Rees, the difference between us is that I've no longer a home, so I want to get on with the job and finish the war as quickly as possible. I've no time to lose, and if in a combat the squadron doesn't shoot down any planes I consider it's a damned waste of time. Each time we go up we ought to shoot down as many as possible. The more we do, the quicker I shall return home. That's why I should like to fly all day, and if I were allowed to, all night."

"How bloodthirsty you foreigners are."

"You're telling me. If Pyker had his own way he'd only come back here to fill up and grab a couple of sandwiches."

We were called to a briefing. It was for a big show.

Two hours later we were above Sens at 20,000 feet without having been intercepted. We had hardly set course for home when I noticed some 109s diving towards us. They were not aggressive and passed beneath us on a southerly course. The whole squadron went down in pursuit of them. The German pilots were in very open formation and flew in pairs ahead of us and slightly below.

"Yellow 1 here. Some Messerschmitts above us. Shall I climb up and have a look?"

"Okay, Yellow 1."

I suddenly thought of Ortmans, who was No. 2 in that section. We broke off our pursuit because the distance was increasing, and it was useless burning up juice to no good purpose.

To port, Squadron Commander Robinson's section made contact with a German pair and hung on to their tails. The Germans made as tight turns as they could but Robinson was tighter and fired a burst which put one of the Mes out of action with the accompanying tail of black smoke. Much higher than us, Vicky Ortmans followed Hugh Rees in his attack. The two Mes tried to carry out a climbing turn but they got separated. Hugh Rees dived on the left-hand one, Ortmans chased the other and got dangerously near at 200 yards without aiming. The German did a 45° dive to starboard but Ortmans did not leave him and opened fire at 400 yards.

The German pilot did a vertical turn to avoid being hit, then made a superb half roll. Ortmans followed suit and remained in the same axis as the Me. At 100 yards he opened fire and decreased the distance to 30 yards.

He gave a slight correction to his firing when the Me reached the red spot in the centre of his gonio he stopped firing. Pieces broke from the right wing of the German and red flames suddenly appeared under the cabin.

Ortmans dived vertically at 500 m.p.h. to 2,000 feet. The German crashed. In his mad descent Vicky had difficulty in pulling out, but helped by his speed he zoomed to 10,000 feet in a few seconds. The whole of this time a German was attacking me, and each time I banked towards him he missed me and I missed him. I had already fired my 120 cannon shells and my two remaining machine-gun bursts would not enable me to bring down the Me except from terribly close. So we gave a display of aerobatics, but let no one be deceived: the first one to get the other in his gonio would not hesitate to fire. My enemy was a crack pilot. However much I tried I could not get into a good position. Nor could he, incidentally. It is a pity we could not have spoken to each other over the intercom. I wondered what he was thinking to himself.

Once when I crossed him at about thirty yards, I was under the impression that he waved to me. Just when we might have become friends a Spitfire appeared from somewhere and dived on him. He broke away and dived inland. I left them, for two other enemy aircraft were overhead.

I returned on my own to Biggin Hill, taking great care not to get spotted on the way. In any case it was a good day for 609. Everyone returned to the fold. On the other side of the Channel the Luftwaffe must have been sending telegrams to Berlin to ask for replenishments.

6th July

This morning the squadron escorted three Blenheims which

130

had been ordered to attack some German E-boats near the coast north of Gravelines.

We took off about 07.30 hours and joined the bombers over Manston, where they seemed to be waiting for us. As soon as we arrived they turned and set course for Gravelines at floor level.

They formed a magnificent V below us. Their three shadows sped over the water and the shadows of our machines cut and re-cut them. We were at 5,000 feet and I was Blue section leader.

I went on ahead of them with my section but could see nothing along the French coast. Off Dunkirk the flak fired at us and a few black smoke puffs burst here and there. I broke away.

As there were no more E-boats on the sea than in the palm of my hand, we returned to Tangmere and the Blenheims kept their bombs for another time.

Afternoon. The weather was now magnificent. We were given a second escort mission. It was a raid on Lille carried out by six Stirlings. We were to provide cover with three other squadrons.

This was not the first time I had escorted Stirlings to Lille. At the beginning of the year with No. 145 I carried out exactly the same mission.

We flew to 25,000 feet and Malengrau was No. 2 in my section. On the outward journey everything went perfectly. The flak fired on us and as usual their aim was bad. Not a bomber was hit.

At my altitude they could have gone on firing at me all day.

On the return journey, just as we were passing the coast above Gravelines, I noticed a Messerschmitt diving on us from behind, trying to get on Malengrau's tail.

"Blue 2, disengage. Bandit behind you."

Malengrau broke off immediately, while I did a left hand turn to attack the Jerry.

My turn was too tight and I went down in a spin.

The coast began to turn. What a fool I was!

I came out of the spin, only to see the Me 109 diving like a meteor earthwards. Malengrau's crate had been hit. I must have warned him too late. He was streaming glycol and his engine had stopped.

We were over the French coast.

"Blue leader here. Try to glide as far as England. We'll cover you. Stick it out, Roger."

With another section I followed him down, keeping 3,000 feet above him.

He glided slowly and drew near the English coast. Would he manage to make it?

The squadron leader notified Control and the rescue launches set out immediately. The shore drew closer, then the cliffs ... Malengrau crossed them at 3,000 feet and landed in a field.

"Good show, Roger."

As soon as I landed I took the Miles Magister N.3829 and flew it to Manston to pick him up and bring him back to Biggin Hill.

We celebrated this little adventure in the *White Hart* with several pints of beer.

7th July (8.30)

We escorted four Stirlings to Albert, near Amiens. The raid was carried out without incident and we did not meet the least opposition. It was almost kid glove warfare. But I was certain that it would not continue like this and that sooner or later a cloud would disclose a swarm of Messerschmitts. For a good hour we had been frolicking with impunity above their territory and nothing had happened.

I was Blue 1, and all went well until we got over Le Touquet, when I noticed an Me 109 attacking my No. 4.

"Blue 4, break immediately. Break, break ..."

He broke off and I banked to port without getting excited. Yesterday in the same manoeuvre I had only managed to go down in a spin. Gently ...

The Bosche dived below me. I did a roll on the way down. I followed suit and we both dived almost vertically.

I must get him ... I must get him. ...

He had seen me and continued in his breath-taking dive.

The water rushed up towards me and I was suddenly afraid. I no longer dared to look at my air speed indicator.

I was following him at 400 yards exactly on a line with him. We should both break our necks if we went on at that speed. The water drew dangerously close and I was afraid of a black-out. I pulled on the stick, flattened out and then for a second I saw nothing. I really had blacked out ... It was the end. I have no idea how long I was in this state.

As soon as I could see again I noticed an enormous splash in the centre of a fleet of a dozen fishing boats some miles from the French coast.

The Me, in his crazy dive, had not been able to pull out and had crashed at 500 m.p.h. into the sea.

I had not fired a single bullet, but Sergeant Evans, my No. 4, was missing. I did not think that the Messerschmitt was in a good firing position when I first spotted him.

We hardly had time to snatch a bite before we received orders to take off on a sweep: Gravelines-Béthune-Forêt d'Hardelot, to clean up the sector. We flew for an hour and a half without seeing anything and without being attacked. And yet, very high in the sun, I saw a formation of Mes. Yellow-livered swine!

About 15.00 hours the Prime Minister, Winston Churchill, paid a visit to the squadron.

The group captain introduced me and almost made me blush when, in front of me, he described the morning's combat.

8th July

Worn out by the events of yesterday and by the excitement, I had to recuperate and slept like a log until 9 o'clock. The squadron leader had told my orderly not to wake me. The dirty dogs seized the opportunity to take off without me. They made a sweep over Sens, during which one of the Stirlings which we were protecting was brought down by flak. After all, that wasn't our fault.

Well rested and my nerves in good order, I took off in the afternoon for a show in the usual Gravelines-Calais sector.

It's about time the Group changed the record. I'm going to know that region if things go on like this.

Visibility was extraordinarily good. At 28,000 feet above Gravelines I could see the Zuider Zee. Pity I couldn't work over Belgium. What would I not give to make a landing outside Brussels!

In the evening we received a visit from Vicky Ortmans' brother, Christian, who has just got his wings.

9th July

And the round continues. This afternoon we carried out a sweep in the region of Béthune after crossing the English coast at Dungeness Point.

Above Béthune a fool of a German fighter dived on the formation but did not fire, broke away downstairs and flew beneath us. I followed him for a moment and fired a burst just as he carried out a masterly half roll ending in a vertical dive. That was the hand of a master.

I rejoined the formation with my No. 2 and took my place at 25,000 feet. It was useless risking getting shot down by leaving the squadron.

A few moments later over Le Touquet we saw far below some Me 109s which did not seem to have noticed our presence.

We dived. I picked one of them and he flew right through my tracers when I strained every nerve to fire a lovely deflection shot.

No effect at all, although I fired from terribly close range. They must be pretty solid, those Messerschmitts.

Although it was a good day it brought little result and only Bisdee, who commands B Flight and whose nickname is "the Bishop," managed to shoot an Me 109 into the drink.

10th July

I have been given seven days' official leave.

This is the first time I'm pleased, and these few days of rest are welcome for I feel extremely tired. Obviously the others will take advantage of this and go out on sortie after sortie, and when I return they will turn the knife round in the wound, explaining endlessly what happened.

What shall I do? Well, I can go and spend a few days with the Lydons at Chichester and then go to London to hear the news and see if the war is still going on at Eaton Square.

Before leaving Biggin Hill I met an intelligence officer who buttonholed me in great excitement and to my great surprise told me the most marvellous true stories. The intelligence officers always have wonderful stories to tell, but this one is worth while relating.

Donnet, my old pal who got his wings along with me, my best pal in the 77th, has arrived in England with Divoy in a little training plane which they pinched right under the noses of the Germans.

Never mind about Chichester. I would cadge a lift to London and go to the Embassy. I had to see Donnet.

At Eaton Square I was given their address and found both of them at the Sun Court Hotel in Earls Court, where they were waiting for a posting.

I was really delighted to see these old friends. Donnet told me his story. They had worked for three months getting an SV.4 serviceable for flying. The plane belonged to a Captain d'Huart and was under seals in a hangar at Terblock. They worked miracles to get fuel and reasonable instruments. On the night of the 4th/5th July, with the help of Michel Janssens – someone had to start the prop – they took the plane out of its shed, started the engine and took off without waiting for it to heat up. They grazed a few trees at the edge of the field.

At dawn, after being fired on by the light flak in Belgium, they landed at The Thyrse in East Anglia with one engine conking badly.

These two "cracks" had gone so far as to put on their Belgian Air Force uniforms and to crown the exploit they had brought with them a lot of information.

Fine types!

We had to celebrate this peacefully with some good beer, sitting at the bar. We ended up in an old pub in the city when an old moustached Englishman noticed, first of all, that I was wearing British uniform which did not prevent me from jabbering a foreign language, in reality only bad French, and secondly, that I was wearing the blue and white striped ribbon of the D.F.C. After collecting the habitues and admiring the rare animal I was taken to be, the old man was delighted when I told him where Donnet had come from and how he got here.

"Good show, sir."

"That's a couple of good boys!"

"Imagine a Belgian with the D.F.C."

And the conversation ended with the inevitable remark: "Let me buy you a drink."

In order not to offend their excellent sentiments Donnet and I accepted and as the scene was repeated in all the pubs we entered we were pretty drunk when we eventually got to the Ritz Bar. We hoped that in such a smart place the scene would not be repeated, but unfortunately we were spotted and invited – almost forced – to drink. I gave up the struggle about midnight to get sober at the Grosvenor Hotel near Victoria where I had booked a room.

There was apparently a raid that night, but I wouldn't know. And the Germans still think they are going to undermine the morale of the Londoners. They're barking up the wrong tree, those boys.

As soon as I looked out of the window this morning I felt in tremendous form. Marvellous weather to carry out a "rhubarb" on the Continent. Perfect visibility and the sun shining brightly through dispersed clouds. Absolutely what the doctor ordered. When things got to hot you showed a clean pair of heels and disappeared into the first cumulus. You had to be careful, however, leaving it. I put on a jumper and my battledress tunic, on which I had sewn my bright ribbon, and my operational cap.

Life is wonderful. My seven days' leave at Chichester have completely restored me. Now back to work.

In front of the Nissen hut which served as dispersal I found Sergeant Pilots Rigler and Boyd sitting in wicker chairs. Boyd, in his shirt sleeves, his Mae West round his neck, was combing the wavy hair of which he is so proud. Vicky Ortmans was chasing Pilot Officer Billy Goat, D.F.C., who had just been awarded the Belgian Croix de Guerre without palm by the Belgians of 609 Squadron. Billy Goat, of course, was the gentle whimsical goat which had been adopted as the squadron mascot. She wandered among the pilots without paying the least attention to rank, attacked all the dogs in the neighbourhood, sat in the armchairs and generally managed to make herself entirely useless. Flying Officer MacKenzie, a tall fairhaired fellow, his jacket opened to the waist over a pale blue open-necked shirt which had nothing regulation about it, sprawled in an armchair, his two long legs on the back of another. His hair had long since exceeded regulation length.

"Have you seen Bisdee?"

"Oh, yes, he's somewhere about."

I found him in the flight office pretending to read through some files.

"Hallo, Pyker. Glad to see you. How about a little trip to France before lunch?"

"I was about to suggest it."

"Fine. I'll be with you in ten minutes. Put on your Mae West and I'll be there."

Bisdee might have been inviting me to take a walk by the stream. A few minutes later we took off together and climbed a south-westerly direction. I stuck to his wing and from time to time he turned round to wave at me. When we got to Dover, still in formation, he suggested we should split up. He would fly further south and I would try to make Calais.

No sooner said than done. I pulled back my throttle, slipped beneath his machine and flew off towards the French coast, taking advantage of the clouds. The sea below looked very cold for the month of July and I wondered if it were cold in the water. In the old days we went sea bathing at this time of the year with the whole family. How far away all that seems now. Better not to think of it for the moment.

Hmm, Calais. No, it was Dunkirk. It was so close to Belgium. Over the coast north of Dunkirk I turned and made my way towards Nieuport. How wonderful it must be on that yellow sand down there. I passed over Nieuport at 10,000 feet and saw the mole pointing like a reproaching finger towards England. I would go as far as Ostend.

Why not go into Belgium?

There to my right was the Dixmude Railway ... and there was the town. The clouds were terribly thin here if I were attacked and soon I should not be able to find a woolly hiding place. I had better return home.

The sky was entirely clear and the visibility was good enough for me to see Roulers ahead of me. Yes, it was useless taking risks. I followed the railway line and returned to Nieuport, where the flak sent a few desultory shells which burst far too low. Flying towards Gravelines I saw a big ship some miles off the coast, sailing east. It was strange that there was no aerial umbrella protecting it. No luck. I returned to North Foreland, followed the Thames Estuary for a while before returning to Biggin Hill.

Bisdee, already at dispersal, had returned in disgust. He had flown with impunity from Marquise to the Forest of Watten without meeting a single enemy plane.

"I felt like going and shooting up Galland's headquarters at Saint-Omer," he growled.

We were almost the only ones at Biggin Hill for the squadron had been given orders to escort three Blenheims which were off to attack a ship off Gravelines ... My ship! Had I not made my detour to North Foreland I should have met them.

****

Editor's Note.—A few minutes later the 609 returned to Biggin Hill. All the pilots looked sour and conversation was in whispers. This was unusual for usually when they returned from ops there were shouts, laughter and a lot of horseplay. In all their exuberance of youth they relaxed by recapitulating their exploits of the day. What was the matter? Ritchie explained to Offenberg.

"The Mes came in very low over the coast and the three poor Blenheims were shot down in a few seconds. We were too high. By the time we appeared on the scene they had already taken a powder. The bastards were fleeing in the distance. It's a very bad show, Pyker."

Offenberg suddenly thought of those young fellows in the wheezy, old Blenheims who had probably left full of good cheer. They had already made appointments for the afternoon. Some of them perhaps were off on leave next day, returning home for a well earned rest. And now nothing remained of them. Empty chairs in the mess ... Rooms where the beds were unmade ... A photograph smiling on a bedside table ... An unfinished letter left open on the desk and a shoe trailing under the chest of drawers with the laces still knotted.

Tomorrow, telegrams would go to various lost villages and trembling hands would open these official missives with slow gestures – the gestures of weeping mothers. . . .

Yes, it was a very bad show.

The following afternoon Offenberg flew as No. 4 in Blue section on a sweep Gravelines-Lille escorting a squadron of Stirlings which were to attack the important railway junctions round that town. But they were not allowed to penetrate so far into occupied territory with impunity and hardly had the squadron turned for home than it was intecepted by a score of Messerschmitts.

"Beauty leader – bandits at 10 o'clock below."

"Okay boys, take your choice. Going down."

He was just going to obey when four Mes passed in formation above the section. No one had spotted the Germans and they could have been shot down like rabbits. Offenberg wondered why they had flown over without attacking. But there was no time for reflection. He must act quickly. He raised the nose of his aircraft and sent a short burst into No. 4 of the German section. He pulled too violently on the stick, the nose shot up and he stalled. Just as the Spitfire began to spin, he had time to see a cloud of white smoke round the German's rudder at which he had just fired in so unorthodox a manner. Now he was spinning fast. He was alone and did not know whether the others had spotted the white smoke. The Me would not be credited to him, to even as a probable for there were no witnesses. His section had dived to the attack just as he had caught sight of the Messerschmitts and climbed. Slowly he pulled his Spitfire out of the spin. What did it matter if it were not entered in his squadron log. Offenberg knew that the German fighter had been hit by his shells. He straightened out and cast a rapid glance at his instrument panel. Then he scanned the sky. On the intercome he heard that the squadron leader had just damaged one.

But where were they? He climbed to 25,000 feet, above the layer of cloud. The reflection of the sun's rays on the cumulus blinded him for a moment. He lowered his goggles. About two miles away to starboard a Spitfire was chasing an Me, which was trying to do tight turns. Red tracers scarred the white clouds and the two fighters disappeared. Ahead a fighter with black crosses was flying eastwards. He was hardly a mile away, skimming the cumulus . . . He, too, had seen the lone Spitfire but he merely disappeared into the cotton wool as if by magic. It was useless hunting for him in these clouds for the moment he was spotted he would disappear again. Pyker returned alone to England. In the distance voices rallied the scattered squadron. The circus was over. They would do better next time.

On the 21st July 1941, the day of the Belgian national holiday, B Flight of 609 went to London, led by Robinson, who it was rumoured was about to leave the squadron to be promoted wing commander.

On the parade ground of Wellington Barracks nine airmen were called one by one before Mr. Gutt, Belgian Minister of National Defence, to receive the Croix de Guerre at his hands. Including Squadron Leader Robinson, they were: Offenberg, de Spirlet, Leroy du Vivier, León Prévot, Baudouin de Hemptinne, Vicky Ortmans, Séghers and Gonnay. . . .

These medals had been earned the hard way. They represented for each of them hundreds of fights, long monotonous patrols in the enemy sky, dangerous flights in Hurricanes, Spitfires or Blenheims when the Luftwaffe fought over England. They had taken part in the toughest battle and they belonged to that little band which had aroused the admiration of the world. They were survivors of the Battle of Britain and they did not yet know that only two of them would one day return home – two wing commanders, two colonels, not yet thirty – Leroy du

Vivier and Prévot. All the others would die as pilots as they had all probably foreseen.

****

24th July

Biggin Hill sector detailed 609 to escort some bombers off the French coast where a reconnaissance aircraft had sighted the presence of a tanker escorted by three flak ships. They were sailing the direction of Le Havre, and we should find them off Fécamp. The sky was overcast and we received orders to join the bombers above the clouds at Manston. Twelve Spitfires took off from Biggin Hill and after a slight detour which brought us above Dunsfold, we set course for Manston. I was leader of Yellow section on the left flank with Rigler as my No. 2. I felt extremely relieved at having such a fellow behind me. If we met the Luftwaffe I should hardly have to bother about what went on behind me.

At Manston the bombers headed for sea in formation. We joined them in a flash. They were six Beauforts. No. 92 Squadron was top cover. We took our place in very spread out formation at 500 feet, slightly to stern of the Beauforts, which flew at sea level.

After twenty minutes flying – the French coast was now very close – the squadron leader sent my section of four aircraft on ahead with orders to silence the flak ship. I pushed my throttle forward leaving the others near the bombers, and climbed to about 1,200 feet so as to enlarge my field of vision. Ahead we could make out the coast. A few more minutes and we should come out over the land. We had not yet seen a ship.

"Yellow leader. Can you see anything, Yellow 2?"

"No, we must be too far north."

I decided to turn out to sea. A mile offshore we followed the coast south. This was the first time I had been sent to attack ships. The attack had to be delivered so low that if we were hit we should not even have time to bale out. It would mean a ducking.

I forced myself not to think of these low altitude attacks which terrified me. I had grown so used to fighting Messerschmitts between 25 and 30,000 feet that I felt I was going to lose my nerve.

"Ships on the starboard bow," called Rigler.

140

I counted four of them. They were our targets. We must hurry up and attack them before the arrival of the bombers. We had already lost precious time by coming out too far north of our position. We must press on.

"Yellow section – line ahead."

"Okay, Yellow leader."

One by one we dived on the flak ship which lay to stern. The tracers left my guns. I had only one thought ... I must dive in the tracers. They're going to bring me down.

I got the ship in my gonio and opened fire at 1,000 yards with both cannon and machine-guns. My aircraft vibrated. The target approached at an appalling speed. I disengaged on a climbing turn towards the shore. Our four aircraft dived into the gunfire from the ships and came through unscathed. I watched them out of the corner of my eye. As though out of the blue another Spitfire section plunged in turn in Indian file on the second ship.

My section re-formed.

"Yellow leader. We'll attack the third ship in line. Remain at sea level after the attack."

"Okay."

I made a left hand turn, did a shallow but fast dive from 1,000 feet so as to fly across the ship. I opened fire rather late at about 500 yards. A short burst and then a second ... I thought I saw a man on the deck waving his arms. I passed fifteen feet over the vessel and this time did not make the mistake of climbing. I remained close to the waves. I was so near the water that I was scared. There was a strong swell and I thought that a wave taller than the others might touch my fuselage. I pulled her nose up a little. . . .

In my mirror I saw two Spits following me.

Where was No. 4?

"Yellow leader – are you okay, Yellow 4?"

"Okay, leader."

Ugh! Once more they had not hit us.

We re-formed over the coast.

I recognised the voice of Rigler, who seemed to be talking to himself: "This is bloody dangerous!"

As I turned again towards the ships I saw to my horror a Spit spinning down like a comet with a black tail. It exploded in the sea, throwing up a huge spray of foam.

"They've got one of our Spits." My gorge rose but I forced myself to remain calm.

"Yellow leader. Section attack."

We flew in at a terrific speed just above the water towards the flak ship. I fired. My shells must have found their mark. But I had fired too soon. Small sprays of water rose ahead of the vessel. I pulled her nose up and this time I was certain that my shells lashed the target.

The bombers, a mile offshore from my position, attacked the tanker while Robinson rallied the flock. It was time to return home. I had hardly any ammunition left. One burst perhaps or two at the most. There was half an hour's flying still to be done before we were back in the fold.

We followed the bombers at 1,000 feet. They did not sink the tanker. At dispersal, Joe Atkinson summed up the whole affair as he sponged his forehead. "It was a pretty hot show."

*　　*　　*

During the afternoon I flew with the whole squadron over the Channel, bound for enemy territory. The itinerary this time was Dunkirk-Nieppe Forest. We crossed the coast slightly north of Dunkirk; this was extremely reasonable, I think, for the gentlemen who momentarily occupy this ancient fort are extremely discourteous and each time we condescend to pay them a visit they send us raspberries in all directions and particularly into the air. The excitement was tense. Voices called on the radio. A Spit in formation in front of me left his leader for a moment, righted himself and side slipped back into place. Was he going to have a collision? No – no collision, but his prop certainly must have passed a few inches away from the leader's tail unit.

"That was a near miss, boy!"

A voice called on the intercom. somewhere in the sector.

"My oil temperature's down, Red leader. What shall I do?"

Complete silence.

Then the voice rang out again, this time more insistently. "My oil temperature's very low, Red leader."

I looked at my instruments and took a glance below. From 25,000 feet the world seems quite different. The men down there look strangely like ants, small black specks. A car driving along the narrow ribbon of a road was probably going hell for leather; from that height it did not appear to be moving. And all those tiny black specks which were men were probably thinking of us up in the air. Their thoughts were probably different according to the locality where the man had been born. For the black specks who came from beyond the Rhine, we were common pirates who had to be brought down. For those born to the west, we were doubtless liberators and heroes. How ridiculous it all was!

The same voice interrupted my train of thought.

"My oil temperature's even lower. Should I leave the formation?"

A far-off voice in a broad Scottish accent broke the golden rule of silence.

"Go back to flying school, laddie, and get dry behind the ears."

There was no reply. Some humorist, however, pressed the transmission button of his radio for a brief second – just long enough for all the pilots of the Biggin Hill squadron operating in the sector to enjoy a boisterous "Ha, ha, ha!"

The calm reigning over the north of France boded no good. We had been across the coast now for ten minutes and nothing had appeared.

I was in line abreast with Red 1, Yellow 1 slightly to port – perhaps at 400 yards – was between us and the sun.

Two Me 109s sped past to starboard, lower than us, flying east.

Robinson made for them. At the same moment the enemy formation turned leisurely southwards and made a great circle from south to north. They did not seem to have spotted our Spitfires.

"Red 1 to Yellow 1, take care, those chaps are probably there to lead us into a trap."

I saw that Yellow 1 had probably taken in the set up, for without waiting for my warning he had made off about a mile to port. If our section were attacked, the Yellow section would come out of the sun on to the tails of the 109s.

The Germans continued their port course. We were now 800 yards from them and gaining speed.

"Yellow 1, I am going in to attack."

He was in an excellent position in the sun and dived on the nearest 109, holding his fire, doubtless hoping to surprise the German and to shoot him down from close range. The German pilots must have spotted him at 300 yards for he did a vertical turn and broke away.

Some tracers passed my cockpit. A German was following me. He must have fired from a long way off for I had heard nothing. I dived away to starboard.

I had a glimpse of a Messerschmitt speeding like a whirlwind above me. Ugh! I pulled out. There were aircraft all over the sky. A second Me attacked me from three-quarters to stern. No you don't, my lad. I turned on him this time and opened fire just as he began his attack. Then I had to take quick avoiding action for another arrived on my tail. When I looked closer I saw that it was a Spitfire. In the meanwhile I had lost sight of the 109.

A glance at the shore to get my bearings ... I was ten miles from Calais, inland.

But to hell with navigation! A 109, perhaps the same one, fired again.

I reduced throttle, banked to the left and the idiot shot past me at full speed. I climbed into the sun. The Me 109 did not seem to fancy his chances and dived for home.

I rejoined a section of three Spitfires making their way up the coast and together we climbed to 18,000 feet.

We returned to Biggin Hill where I landed safely at 15.20 hours.

Robinson and Rigler had each shot down a 109. Good show. We had no casualties.

Ziegler amused us for a moment by showing us a report from H.Q. Fighter Command. A pilot from 92 Squadron had apparently asked for confirmation of a 109 shot down in flames by his first burst. Now the film of his combat showed that his first and second bursts were fired at a Spitfire and his third at a Messerschmitt.

With an extremely British sense of humour, an Intelligence Officer had written in his report: "One must make no mistake. This side only fires on black crosses, fasces or rising suns."

10

GRAVESEND

Editor's Note.—On Sunday, 27th July, Offenberg got up early. A very devout Catholic, he never failed to go to Mass on

Sunday and to take Communion. If death were to surprise him he would be ready.... On his last leave in Chichester he had asked good Mrs. Lydon to look after all his belongings. He also asked his squadron commander to send the few pounds that remained in the bank to Chichester should he be shot down. At the end of the war he wanted everything sent home to his mother.

That afternoon the whole squadron took off for Gravesend airfield south of the Thames. The pilots were quartered in an old castle dating from Queen Elizabeth. The natives insisted, however, that there were no ghosts within its old walls. In any case, Offenberg remarked the beds looked like a reformatory.

At the inaugural dinner in Cobham Hall Squadron Leader Robinson, D.S.O., D.F.C., made a speech to thank his pilots. They had fought well and he was proud of having such men under his command. But the authorities had decided to promote him. The next day he would be a Wing Commander and in this capacity he could no longer remain in command of No. 609.

So Mike Robinson was leaving them! Everyone was very distressed.

And there was other news. Flight Lieutenant Bisdee, B Flight commander, was going for a rest. He had earned this respite for he had taken part in operations with 609 since November 1939.

Then Robinson turned to the Belgian section. "And I have a particularly good piece of news for you. Pyker will take over B Flight instead of Bisdee."

There was a great shout of applause.

"Good old Pyker."

"You've deserved it."

"I'm very pleased."

"Would you credit it? A flight lieutenant!"

It was true. Pyker became Flight Lieutenant J. Offenberg, D.F.C. They drank his health; there was laughter; tall stories were exchanged in corners. They drank more and the stories began to get more licentious. They drank another glass, the best one, followed by the last one and one for the road.

Someone remarked that the last one was not really necessary since they were all quartered in the house, but others overruled this, saying that since the corridors were very long, one for the road was amply justified.

The following day the bad weather grounded the Squadron. The new C.O., Squadron Leader Gilroy, D.F.C., arrived and introduced himself to the pilots. He looked very shy but at the same time very sympathetic.

****

31st July

609 was available, which meant that if the controller of Biggin Hill sector decided to send them on patrol, we had exactly half an hour to get ready and take off. Everyone stood by in more or less unorthodox flying kit. Even the boots were not regulation. It was a beautiful day and Tidswell, the gay squadron adjutant, left his papers and joined us to gossip in the warm sun. As the sector is very calm, too calm for my liking, I took the opportunity of going to the workshop to fetch a new Mae West. The old corporal who gave it to me spoke an English I found difficult to understand.

"What part do you come from?" I asked.

"From Yorkshire, sir."

"Do they all speak the same way in Yorkshire?"

"No, some of them speak much better."

"When I have time I'll go up there and study the language so that I shall be able to understand you."

A great smile lit up the corporal's face.

"Yes. You do that. It's the finest county in England. You'll see."

On my new Mae West, a brilliant orange-yellow, someone had stencilled Flight Lieutenant Offenberg, D.F.C.

"Why didn't they write Pyker as they did on my old one?"

"Well you see, sir, the workshop boys wondered how a Christian could have such a name and personally I thought that what was written on the one you're holding was far more suitable."

"Do you think so?"

"Aye," he replied in his inimitable accent. "And besides, we ground wallahs never know what you are. Sergeant pilot or squadron commander look so much alike in their flying kit that we never know how to behave. Like that," he said, pointing to my Mae West, "you can't make a mistake."

On my return to the Flight, Joe Atkinson was the first to catch sight of me. He raised his arms in the air and gurgled with pleasure: loud enough to alarm all the Messerschmitts hunting off Dover.

"Come and have a look. A great white Chief has arrived. If

146

the Jerries shoot you down now they'll have to pay you the honours due to your rank. No more economical bursts of machine-gun fire. You must be brought down by cannon. Nothing smaller than a cannon!"

Boyd and Sergeant Rigler – who is known as "Hairwave" because he is quite bald – hearing the laughter, wandered over while Jimmy Baraldi, a flower in his button-hole, put his head out of the hut window.

"Gee, what a handsome guy!"

One can never be serious with these fellows. They're incredible. They risk their necks two or three times a day, look upon it as a fine routine, and haven't a care in the world.

After placing my precious belt in safety I telephoned the Controller on duty who gave us permission to go and lunch, advising us not to tax our stomachs and not to eat any beans. "They're very bad for the intestines at high altitude because of the decompression," he added, hanging up.

We had hardly had time to eat in the mess and to get back than the squadron was placed in readiness. I fetched my new Mae West, put my helmet within reach and sat down in one of the leather armchairs facing the airfield.

I was comfortably installed when a few shapes rushed past like a whirlwind.

Paul Ritchie, a flight commander, shouted as he passed.

"Hurry up, Pyker, we're off."

I leaped up. "Where are we going?"

"Oh, nothing very exciting. Some minesweepers to strafe on the other side of the Channel."

Nothing exciting! He's got a nerve. Ritchie. I've already done a similar job but my old interception fighter habits make me feel home-sick for dog fights at a great height, single combat.

Squadron Leader Gilroy led the formation.

We hedgehopped. The villages fled past beneath my wings in quick succession. All these English villages look alike. From time to time when I looked below I saw an arm waving from a window. The four leading aircraft were ahead of me, one slightly lower. That was real hedgehopping!

The coast came in view, Dover and then the sea gleaming in the sunlight.

We discovered the four minesweepers north of Cap Gris Nez, sailing without escort two miles from the shore.

The first section led by Gilroy immediately attacked from south-west to north east. The ships' guns replied.

Gilroy called me.

"Blue 1 from Beauty leader. Attack now."

"Okay, Beauty leader."

The first section had hardly disengaged to port when I led Blue Section on an almost opposite course in a lightning dive on a minesweeper. In this way the machine-gunners would have to change their angle of fire by 180° and would not have time to get their new aim. The sea sped past my Spitfire at a giddy rate. At 500 yards I opened fire with both cannons and machine-guns. I turned on a level with the smoke stack of the first sweeper and no one had fired on me. My shells lashed the vessel.

The third section went in to attack from another direction, immediately followed by Gilroy's section which I saw streaking over the waves straight for the ship. The sailors abandoned one of the sweepers and were busy getting into a dinghy they had lowered. Had we made another attack they would all have been killed in the open.

Gilroy must have spotted this for he called to his sections.

"Okay, Beauty aircraft. That's enough for today."

We reformed above the coast, gaining height. One of the minesweepers was on fire with a thick cloud of black smoke belching from its bows.

Suddenly: "Beauty leader – two bandits at three o'clock upstairs."

I looked. Two Mes were above Dunkirk about 8,000 feet higher than us. Had they just arrived or had they been present during the whole attack without intervening? 609 turned in their direction. They dipped their wings, turned about and fled inland.

Gilroy called "Binto," the code name of Biggin Hill Control. "Mission ended. All aircraft returning to base."

****

Editor's Note.—The Biggin Hill wing continued its raids over northern France and the Channel, escorting Blenheims, Stirlings and Beauforts which attacked important targets in enemy territory. The favourites were Amiens, Lille, Albert and the airfields of Abbeville and Saint-Omer.

The German fighter arm had been reduced to a minimum in

the West, for pressing needs were beginning to be felt on the Russian front. The night blitz of the Luftwaffe on the English towns died a natural death and Bomber Command started its great offensive, trying to dislocate the enemy's systems of communication and to destroy the morale of the civilian population.

The fighters from Gravesend airfield, now flying Spitfire Mark VBs, armed with 220 mm cannon and four 303 machine-guns, had not sufficient range to escort the heavy bombers over German territory. Equipped with reserve tanks of only thirty gallons they had to be content to operate within a reduced radius. As a general rule Biggin Hill Wing operated over northern France and patrolled the Pas de Calais. The British fighters had carried the battle beyond their sea-girt island. At first, in small numbers, a few fighters carried out light raids on their own, known as "rhubarbs"; then in force escorting a few bombers in operations called "circuses."

The fighters gave the enemy no respite. Their targets were as numerous as they were diverse. They had to shoot down German aircraft, to destroy them on the ground, to bomb and machine-gun airfields, ports and lines of communication. But, above all, to force the Third Reich to keep important air forces in the West.

Belgians came each day to swell the ranks of their country's section in the R.A.F.

The Belgian Government, installed in stately houses in Eaton Square, had ordered a general mobilisation of all Belgians abroad and young men now arrived from countries as far afield as China, South Africa and the two Americas. The majority of the recruits, however, who disembarked on English soil did not come from these free countries. A long and perilous voyage brought them to Lisbon and Gibraltar, from Belgium via unoccupied France – the zone No-No – the Pyrenees and Spain whose pro-German sentiments, developed under Franco's regime, were hardly favourable to the Belgians who tried to join the Free Forces.

Most of the foreigners arrested in Spain arrived in London after experiencing the horrors of Spanish prisons and concentration camps. Most of these volunteers, filled with admiration for the R.A.F., expressed a wish to serve as airmen, and each week news reached the Belgians of 609 giving the names of those who had arrived and those who were on their way. A few new figures joined Offenberg's Belgian flight: Muller and

Nitelet, who had just got their wings. On the 4th August 1941 two new pilots reported to 609, Jean Morai and the Battle of Britain veteran, Giovanni Dieu, a Blenheim pilot from No 236 who had finally been transferred to a fighter squadron. Other echoes reached them that their Government was having talks with the Air Ministry with a view to creating the first entirely Belgian squadron within the framework of the R.A.F. Those from 609, all seasoned pilots would be posted to this new unit and Offenberg would become squadron leader, having thus been promoted from second lieutenant to squadron commander in less than a year.

Offenberg, a sincere and honest man, paid little heed to all these rumours. He was not eager for either promotion or "gongs." He only wanted one thing -- to fly. Let them give him a well-armed Spitfire so that he could continue the good work and he asked for nothing better. He was glad at the success of others and never felt in the least bit jealous. On his return from a mission he never bothered to see if a new kill would be added to his score. What did it matter to him? What was the difference whether he or someone else got the additional palm to their Croix de Guerre? An enemy aircraft had been shot down in flames and that was enough. He wrote his combat reports in a few words, often claiming nothing, neither a confirmation, a probable, an aircraft destroyed or damaged. He left it to others, to those who had time to bother about such things, to estimate whether he were the victor or not. But without seeking it, he was the best and everyone admitted it.

* * *

On Wednesday, 6th August, Squadron Leader Gilroy, who valued and admired Offenberg's calm courage, called him into his office. The day was drawing to a close and the last Spitfires from Gravesend landed in the dying light of the setting sun.

"What are you doing this evening, Pyker?"

"Nothing in particular. Why?"

"What do you say to a trip up to London with me? We can go in my car. I have a date with Group Captain Crerar, the Commandant of Dyce in Scotland. Do you know him."

"Yes, vaguely. I met him when I was up there with No. 145 and I once drank champagne with him."

"Well, will you come?"

"Yes, I'd like to see him again."

They left together for London and arrived about nine o'clock in the evening. They met Crerar at the Piccadilly Hotel.

"Let's go and dine in Soho."

"Good idea!"

They drove up Shaftesbury Avenue, turned off to the narrow streets where the prostitutes plied their trade but where, too, the foreign restaurants offered the best food in London. They went to "Rose's," a little Belgian restaurant in Greek Street where Offenberg had on several occasions eaten their inevitable horse steak and chips. They found the small restaurant almost entirely monopolised by French sailors.

"All right. Let's go somewhere else," said Offenberg.

They eventually finished at *Isola Bella* in Frith Street, where they found a table on the first floor. Italian food and Chianti ... The group captain, who did not know this picturesque corner of London, found the food splendid and, thanks to the wine, recovered the exuberance of his Celtic ancestors.

"Let's go and have a drink somewhere else."

"But, sir, we're on duty tomorrow at six o'clock."

"Never mind," said Gilroy. "It's only midnight. We needn't start worrying about that now. Let's go and have a drink with the Groupie."

Gilroy and Offenberg did not get back to Gravesend until five in the morning. It was not worth while going to bed. They exchanged their collar and tie for a polka dot scarf, put on a flying suit and were ready to take off.

7th August. It was not quite seven o'clock when Pyker took off from Gravesend with twelve aircraft from 609. Mission – to escort a Lysander of Air Sea Rescue over the Channel along the English coast. They flew in very open formation over Dover on course 100°. All eyes scanned the sea looking for a sign, the yellow patch of a rescue launch, a man hanging in his rubber dinghy, being buffeted by the waves. They saw nothing. The sea was a vast expanse and the water looked very cold in the grey morning light. The cliffs of Dover struck by the sun's rays seemed whiter than usual. The white cliffs of Dover....

This was the first time that Offenberg had had time to admire them. Beyond stretched the green meadows of England, the vast English countryside which had grown so familiar. This land which he had defended so unswervingly, was now in part his country – a second country where he did not feel in the least foreign. He checked his weapons, glanced at the gonio and saw the luminous circle. All was well. He was leading his section, his No. 2 was close to his wings, a little above him. He could see the pilot's head when he turned round.

Suddenly Gilroy called on the intercom. "Beauty leader – four bandits at three o'clock."

Four Messerschmitts were flying in from the east out of the sun. They were slightly lower – 2,000 feet perhaps – and still some distance off.

Blue Section climbed to the south.

Offenberg turned, gave full gas, climbed with his section on the course received, banking slightly to keep an eye on the enemy formation. Me 109s making straight for them ... They were trying to shoot down the Lysander which was close to the water. A Messerschmitt broke away and dived on the reconnaissance plane, whose machine-gunner opened fire. Tracers flew.... Red 1, Gilroy, attacked another 109 from very close quarters but missed it. His No. 2, Choron, who had remained behind the squadron commander, opened fire in turn on the tail of the German fighter. He almost rammed it. Pieces of the enemy aircraft broke off. It dived almost vertically and Offenberg saw it crash into the sea. A great patch of oil appeared at the place where it had hit.

Choron was French and Pyker could not help congratulating him: "Bravo, la France."

Pyker, at 5,000 feet in position with the sun behind, dived into the fray. He chose a Messerschmitt, approached at a terrific speed and took careful aim. 500 yards ... 300 ... He fired. His machine-gun spat a long burst but his cannon jammed. The machine-gun bullets seemed to rake the Me 109 without having hit it in its vitals. He broke away to port and returned. From some distance he fired a very long burst with all his ammunition. He could no longer fire, although he still had 120 shells in his wings. Nevertheless he continued to fight, dived on one of the Messerschmitts, which broke and fled to France.

Pyker pursued him for fun. The German pilot was fleeing for his life before an unarmed Spitfire. Had he known for a moment that the man behind him was quite harmless even if he came within fifty yards of his tail, he would have shot him down. But the Luftwaffe pilot knew nothing and thought he was saving his own skin. Off Calais Offenberg gave up the chase, set his course for the Thames estuary and reached Gravesend.

In his combat report he used the term once employed by Bader, his wing commander at Tangmere, stating coldly: "Put the breeze up an Me 109F."

At 13.00 hours 609 had become top cover for some Blenheims attacking the airfield of Saint-Omer. The Spitfires flew at 25,000 feet, crossing the English coast north of Dover and reaching France at Gravelines. Attacked by a group of Mes, they defended themselves furiously. Offenberg was machine-gunned from the rear but his winger was Sergeant Rigler, a fighter pilot with a deadly eye. He brought the German down.

On his return to Biggin Hill Pyker put on a uniform, jumped in a small Tiger Moth and flew to Tangmere, where he landed at 17.00 hours. He would take a few days' rest with the Lydons in Chichester.

Adopted by these good folk, he was always welcome and this was now his second family. Sheila, the pretty little English girl, received with open arms this big brother who had come back from the war. For a few days he was at peace and his nerves relaxed. He was happy. He played every day in the garden with the younger sister Clair and bought her a white rabbit. When the Spitfires from Tangmere streaked low over the town he forced himself not to look and pretended not to hear them.

14th August, 1941. After five days' leave at Chichester Offenberg was a new man. He felt extremely fit and ready to start fighting again. He was in a hurry to return over France to have a crack at the pilots from Abbeville or Saint-Omer. He had thought more than once that it would be a good thing to organise a kind of cocktail party for everyone. A party for those on both sides of the Channel where the pilots could meet, discuss flying tactics and get to know each other. For the moment you only met a Messerschmitt and then another a few minutes later. It might be the same one. You never had time to wave as you passed between two bursts of machine-gun fire. And yet they knew each other well. For months now they had met over the same places. The R.A.F. could quote most of the names of the Abbeville boys and those of Saint-Omer knew the names of the pilots from Biggin Hill.

It had become a sort of fraternity. A friendly association of war pilots. Besides, was it not almost in the nature of a private war which they fought each day?

They were the only ones fighting in the west. No army of imposing infantry battalions ... The gunners had not fired a shot for months. Only the fighters were in combat. They had all adopted certain habits and they each knew what the others were doing, their techniques, their cunning and their traps. When Offenberg left the territory for a few days he was quite happy. But then he began to long for his pals, his squadron and his Spitfire, "M for Monkey." And then he began to miss the Germans. When he woke up and looked at his watch in the little bedroom Mrs. Lydon always kept for him, he could not help thinking of the two Spitfires which visited the French coast – those early morning reconnaissance aircraft who were so punctual that the Germans called them "the milk round."

And at dawn did not the Luftwaffe regularly send a few young pilots to intercept them, to get their hand in? As a general rule the milk round did not turn out badly.

Five days was the maximum that Offenberg could remain away from his aircraft. Then he packed his suitcase, said good-bye, jumped into the first train for London and rejoined his squadron. This time, too, he had returned before the end of his leave. He arrived about 10.30 at Gravesend but was too late to take part in the first mission, which was nearly over. The first person he met at dispersal was his friend Baudouin de Hemptinne, having a slanging match with the others. They were all in flying kit.

Baudouin de Hemptinne, his Mae West round his shoulders and his face hunched in his collar, which was still attached by the back stud. The knot of his tie hung lamentably beneath his Adam's apple. How many times had Offenberg seen Baudouin dressed like this? An aristocrat of the old school, Captain de Hemptinne insisted on flying in a collar and tie. But as soon as his Spitfire reached 25,000 feet and things began to get hot he tore the collar off on one side. One could be certain that he would tear the other as soon as the scrap began. The performance never changed. And immediately he got out of his cockpit he would advance aggressively on the other pilots, announcing in a theatrical fashion. "It's all over. It's the last time I'll fly with you." And there would be a chorus of "And I'll never come back."

This did not prevent Baudouin from being the first at the controls of his aircraft at the next "scramble."

Offenberg went over to Choron. Maurice Choron was a rare bird in the 609 for he was French. A cheerful, good-natured fellow who liked running after the skirts if he had a chance, he was quite a character. A former instructor at the Bastia Aero-club, he had one day met a British officer on holiday there. This was in 1939, a few months before the "phoney war." The young airman made friends with the stocky little Corsican, the pro-fessional pilot, and in this way a magnificent fighter team was born. Mike Robinson found Choron in England after the débâcle and took him into his squadron. He had been his winger ever since. When Robinson, the lord of the manor – his parents had just paid for the Spitfire he flew on ops – took over the command of 609, he brought Choron with him. The French-man was happy to find a whole bunch of Belgian pilots with whom he immediately got on well. He was in B Flight under Offenberg's orders but nearly always flew as Robinson's No. 2 in Red section.

"Good morning, Maurice," said Offenberg. "What's happened since I've been away? Are the Abbeville boys just as aggressive?"

"Don't mention them, old man. If they go on firing at me I shall begin to get worried. As you know . . ."

Offenberg knew. The fighters had been told to go to France to provoke the Luftwaffe into the air.

"But, above all," they had been told, "don't fight with them. As soon as you see them take off, don't linger in the neighbour-hood. You can, of course, if you get an opportunity, shoot down one or two but not too many. We want Mr. Göring to keep his fighters where they are. They will dig their own graves with-out you risking your necks. We have to take into account Ger-mans who break their necks taxi-ing over an airfield, those who crash on force landings, the engines of Messerschmitts kept running and getting worn out, hastening their despatch to the overhaul bench, etc., etc. Finally, as you see, the war is to be limited to trips in the French sky."

And this is precisely what happened until the Luftwaffe real-ised the new R.A.F. technique and began to ignore the British fighters. Fighter Command despatched swarms of aircraft but the Germans remained on the ground. The German pilots, lying in their deck chairs, warmed themselves in the sun, counting the number of aircraft that flew over.

This was the period when Offenberg called the Germans "yellow-livered incompetents" when they met Messerschmitts who refused to fight. Then the R.A.F. wanted to intensify things. Ah, so you won't take off? All right then, we'll bomb you. And they sent a few wretched, fairly inoffensive Blenheims,

155

protected by an armada of Spitfires. This time the boys at Abbeville, Saint-Omer and elsewhere were obliged to take off even if only to try and destroy the bombers. That is how things stood on the 14th August, 1941, when Jean Offenberg returned to Gravesend.

"You know – they're good types, the Abbeville boys," said Choron. "They know their stuff."

Offenberg hardly had time to shake all the outstretched hands than 609 received orders to take off for a trip over the Channel between Dungeness and Boulogne. They went, saw nothing and returned to Gravesend, to repeat the performance after lunch.

That evening Choron summed up the position in a few words: "It's no good going over there any more unless we push a little further inland. At the moment these trips aren't as dangerous as riding a horse."

Horse riding was the C.O.'s favourite pastime. As soon as he arrived anywhere he would invariably discover a stable where he could hire horses. Then he would lead 609, which had a few good horsemen such as Dumonceau and de Hemptinne. The others had a pronounced aversion to this type of locomotion.

These outings on Gilroy's orders usually finished lamentably for most of the pilots. More than one of them returned hanging on to his horse's neck ready to expire. Some spectacular falls resulted in a few days' rest on the orders of Dr. Lawrence. This began to disturb the wing commander. When the pilots approached the horses to choose their mounts in a way which would have horrified a real horseman, they immediately picked those with long manes.

"You see," said Choron, "then at least you've got something to cling on to. The fellow whose horse has the longest mane will stick on longer than the others."

And thus, after a wasted day, half the squadron went in the few cars available at Gravesend to join the pilots of 92 at Biggin Hill, making as their excuse some unimportant anniversary which had to be celebrated.

16th August 1941. It was of no avail that Flying Officer Atkinson -- Joey to his friends – a philosophy student from Oxford – pleaded the English week-end, the Controller of Operations at Biggin Hill sent his regrets and made the 609 take off at dawn on a raid, itinerary Nieuport-Dunkirk-Saint-Omer. Another wing was detailed to patrol the neighbourhood of Abbeville. On its arrival over Nieuport the 609 turned and followed the coast. As usual not an enemy to be seen. Sergeant Palmer, who loved machine-gunning ships, noticed a little boat off Calais.

"Beauty leader, a vessel to starboard. Can I attack it?"

"Permission refused. Blue 4, remain where you are."

Palmer adored skimming over the waves – it gives a tremendous impression of speed – and firing his shells at the ships when they came in his sights. Whenever he saw one he asked permission to go down, and his request was automatically refused by Gilroy, who had more to do than to gratify Sergeant Pilot Palmer's whims.

The squadron arrived over Saint-Omer airfield without incident. Gilroy circled the field. The Messerschmitts seemed to be taxi-ing out on to the runway. They were taking off ... There was a whole squadron of them, if not more.

Gilroy warned Biggin Hill.

"Binto, from Beauty leader. The Saint-Omer boys are taking off."

The reply came back immediately.

"Thank you, Beauty leader. Keep them busy for a bit."

Offenberg, leading Blue section, laughed up his sleeve. They would keep these good Jerries busy, and when they had used up enough juice the Controller would send some Blenheims, scheduled to arrive just as the Luftwaffe had to land unless they wished to run out of fuel. If the Abbeville boys had also taken off the Blenheims would meet with no serious opposition over the target.

The R.A.F. fighters kept the Germans under observation as they climbed towards the south. What were they cooking now? What did it matter anyway, so long as they had left their airfield? Suddenly the sky was empty and the Mes had disappeared in the distance. It was now time to return, for there were often "bogies" waiting for them as they left the coast. The Germans let the formation through without intercepting it on the outward journey, but took care to send a few fighters on their tails on the way back.

Above Le Touquet Offenberg noticed four Mes about to attack his section.

Just before they were in firing position he gave the order to break and the Germans streaked above them, their shots going very wide.

Blue section re-formed and took up its place again in the formation. Their enemies were now far away. Before they reached the British coast, Control called them.

"Beauty aircraft, land at Biggin Hill. I repeat: land at Biggin Hill."

That meant that another raid was in preparation. Joe Atkinson did not fail to remark over his intercom that the R.A.F. ought to institute the English week-end.

At this juncture Palmer saw a boat.

"Ship ahead."

"It's one of ours."

"I'm not so sure."

"Oh, go to hell. Why don't you join the Marines?"

Palmer fell silent, grumbling to himself about squadron commanders who had no sense for combined air-sea operations.

Biggin lay ahead. They landed. They were almost at home at Biggin Hill. Even though they had come from Gravesend, in their heart of hearts they all belonged to the R.A.F. No. 1 Fighter Station.

A hasty bite, a rapid briefing and they took off in wing formation.

Moustier-Gravelines-Saint-Omer. The Germans were caught napping and took off once more.

Wing leader "Sailor" Malan warned Binto and deployed his squadrons. The 609 flew northwards at 25,000 feet. Offenberg took as winger a newcomer, Muller, who flew No. 2 in Blue section.

There had hardly been time to explain the operation before take-off, but Offenberg was content to follow Gilroy's manoeuvres, hoping that the Mes would soon put in an appearance. Muller stuck like grim death to Pyker.

Blue and Yellow sections weaved above their leader, Red section. All the pilots were scanning the sky, but no enemy appeared. Everyone, however, was sure that the Jerries would be at the rendezvous along the coast, waiting to shoot down stragglers.

The coup was classic by now.

609 flew on towards the coast, still at 25,000 feet.

Ten miles from Gravelines, Gilroy called that he could see Messerschmitts below. The Germans had tried to get into position but they were too slow and their fighters were not yet in place. They were far too low and 609 had the advantage of height.

Gilroy despatched Offenberg's Blue section, which dived on them. The German fighters were lower than he had estimated.

They split in two, slipped below a cloud and he lost sight of them. Pyker did a left-hand climbing turn but only his No. 2, Muller, had followed him.

"We missed them."

A quick look round. Somewhat higher, Spitfires and Messerschmitts were engaged in a dog-fight. Offenberg and Muller were now at 1,000 feet. If they tried to join in the scrap they would arrive too late. Useless to insist. Besides, their fuel was getting low and it was advisable to make for home.

They left France at 1,000 feet and began to climb towards England. Some Spitfires flew over them on the opposite course.

The Germans had probably not thought of that. The Mes were watching the tired squadrons, damaged by the dogfight. They did not expect to find another R.A.F. wing which had come direct from England on their tails.

The Germans, therefore, already tired from their first fight, could not stand up to this new attack, which literally fell on them out of the blue.

They landed at Gravesend. No one missing. . . .

Sergeant Pilot Nash had damaged a Messerschmitt. It was a paltry sheet for such an arduous day.

Joe Atkinson would have liked to leave for the week-end but was refused permission. On the contrary, the pilots were warned that there would be a third raid.

"A fine business for a Saturday," said Choron. "I have a date this evening and I shall miss it with all these scraps."

"Don't worry. If you can't get there we'll take your place. We're not exactly Communists but ... What's her telephone number?"

"Nothing doing. I don't share my addresses. You must find your own."

"Oh, shut up, you sex maniacs," said Roger Malengrau. "If that's your only subject of conversation it's time to change the record. They never think of anything else," he said, turning to Offenberg.

"Not for long, they won't. There's something cooking. Why can't you all be serious? I'm going to have a bit of training. Are you coming, Palmer?"

Recalled by Control, Pyker landed at once with his sergeant pilot.

They had to return to France as bomber escorts. The Luftwaffe was to be given no respite that day. From dawn to dusk the raids followed in swift succession, one formation penetrating occupied territory before the other had left. As soon as a German squadron took the air to intercept it, a new British formation appeared. The German controllers must have been tearing their hair. It was too much. The Nazi pilots could not take this punishment.

And yet when the Biggin Hill wing escorted some bombers to Saint-Omer they found Messerschmitts once more as they left.

Baudouin was leading Yellow section and his No. 3 called him on the intercom.

"Yellow 1 from Yellow 3. Can you reduce speed?"

"What's wrong, Yellow 3?"

"I don't know. Even with full gas I can't keep up."

Baudouin reduced throttle and after a minute or two found his section behind the squadron. No one had spotted a few Mes higher up, following on their tails. No. 4 of his section was attacked and shouted on the intercom: "Yellow 1, bandit on my tail." Baudoin turned and dived. He noticed a Spit going down in a cloud of black smoke. It was Craffer, his No. 4. A furious dog-fight developed.

Baudouin rallied the other sections with the words: "I'm in a dog-fight right behind you."

Dog-fight: the favourite term used by the R.A.F. to define those mad "free-for-alls" where, firing on the turn, and wading in savagely, one risked a collision at every moment.

Baudouin had no time to give any further details. Two 109s were ahead of him, one diving, the other climbing to the northwest.

Offenberg had turned over the sea and arrived like a whirlwind over the mêlée with his section. Gilroy had done the same and was at the same height a little to the north.

At 150 yards Baudouin opened fire on the nearest German fighter, which seemed to disintegrate before his eyes.

Offenberg had seen the scrap and dived on two Mes, who fled inland.

Dusk fell over the sea. They headed for home. . . .

Sunday, 17th August. The pilots were called at 06.30 hours. It was early after the strain of the previous day but the war had to go on and there was no respite, even on the Lord's day.

An hour later, in the silent countryside, twelve pilots from 609 started up their engines, let them warm up for a few minutes, and took off into the wind which was blowing from the Thames.

A slight early morning mist covered the river, and the people in the houses below must have woken with a start as the squadron flew overhead. They were only flying to Biggin Hill and so it was not worth while gaining height.

On their arrival they were told that the raid was off. The pilots were furious. To wake them up at that grizzly hour and to bring them here when they were dog-tired, only to tell them there was nothing doing!

Choron naturally groused more than anyone else. He had missed everything, including his previous evening's date. It wasn't fair!

Offenberg wanted to go to Mass since it was Sunday.

He took off immediately for Gravesend and arrived in time for Mass.

The loudspeakers announced that Pilot Officer Smith, the New Zealander, had been detailed to march the troops to church – an old-fashioned English church parade.

In the R.A.F., everyone was forced to fall in and go to church whatever his religion. No one was forced to go and pray but they had to march there all the same. A few moments later the loudspeakers called for Dieu at the crew room.

Although this meant God in French it was only a call for Flying Officer Giovanni Dieu, and the coincidence caused some ribald comments among the Belgians.

Pilot Officer Smith, who knew little French, knew what Dieu meant. He telephoned the base adjutant and protested that it was useless going to church since God had been called somewhere else. His wisecrack must have earned him a pretty substantial rocket, by the way he held the receiver six inches from his ear.

He hung up with an air of disgust and said: "That bloody fool can never take a joke."

As a whole, the station adjutants did not appreciate the 609, and in particular Billy Goat, whom the pilots took everywhere with them, for their mascot spent its days destroying the flower beds and snapping at any stranger who came within reach.

Pilot Officer Smith went off to church, mumbling under his breath.

In the afternoon the sky became overcast and a fine rain started to fall. Most of the pilots had returned to Cobham Hall, waiting for dusk. Some of them employed the time to put their affairs in order and write some letters, but the majority retired to bed to be fresh for the evening.

Wing Commander Malan, D.S.O. and bar, D.F.C. and bar, was leaving Biggin Hill and handing over his command to Wing Commander Robinson, the former 609 Squadron commander.

This was an excellent excuse for a party. All the pilots were invited and no one failed to turn up.

Transport was laid on to take this boisterous crowd to their lost paradise, where beer flowed freely in huge pewter tankards.

In the car with Offenberg and Dieu, Joe Atkinson related the end of Pilot Officer Smith's adventures on parade that morning. Forced to go to church, the New Zealander had cut an excellent figure.

The padre had noticed him and, flattered to see a native from the Antipodes, called out to him in the mess: "Well, Pilot Officer Smith, I'm glad to see you've joined the flock. I saw you in church this morning, didn't I?"

"Quite so, quite so, you saw me at church, but I saw you first."

Leaving the good padre nonplussed by this remark, Pilot Officer Smith went to get some rest to be fit for the evening.

*　　*　　*

About two o'clock in the morning, the pathfinders reached Cobham Hall in open cars, singing lusty songs which had little in common with the Gregorian chant.

18th August 1941. The day did not begin too well. 609, which had left to carry out a sweep betwen Gravelines and Lille, was intercepted. Red section was attacked by a couple of Mes over Calais on the return trip, but having used up their ammunition the pilots found it unhealthy to linger in those waters.

Towards 18.00 hours, the 609 and two squadrons from Biggin Hill received orders to take off again. Wing Commander Douglas Bader had been shot down by the Germans and had broken one of his artificial legs. He was apparently with Galland on Saint-Omer airfield. The Tangmere wing was ordered to fly over a spare leg for Bader. They would do this while Biggin Hill was bombing the German base and take the opportunity of dropping the parcel for this glorious prisoner-of-war.

The 609 crossed the French coast south of Boulogne and had hardly penetrated inland when, at 09.00 hours, a good 10,000 feet below, a section of four Messerschmitts passed on a southerly course. Dumonceau, Red 2, spotted them first.

"Beauty leader, bandits at 9 o'clock below."

"Okay, Red section, let them have it."

Red section dived into the attack.

Gilroy, the squadron leader, attacked No. 4 of the German formation, and Yvan Dumonceau manoeuvred to come out on the tail of No. 3.

Almost together, they fired on their respective targets. Dumonceau opened fire with his cannon from a long distance and missed the target. The Messerschmitt he had chosen dived and, so as not to get in his leader's way, he did a terribly tight turn to get in position to attack No. 2. The turn was too tight and he blacked out. When he came to his senses he seemed to be alone in an empty sky. No, to his left was a lone Spitfire. Dumonceau joined him. He read the letters on the fuselage, PR – X. It was his No. 4. Good show.

Gilroy also missed his Messerschmitt. Offenberg, Yellow section leader, had remained at 25,000 feet, watching the fight from above. What a pity Dumonceau had missed his prey.

To port from below, a section of 109s climbed up to the formation.

"Look out! Bandits at ten o'clock below."

"Okay, Yellow 1. We've seen them."

"All right. In we go."

The scrap suddenly developed; a violent, merciless dog-fight, spangled with the scarlet sparks of the tracers.

Offenberg's No. 2, Vicky Ortmans, found himself on the tail of a 109. He held his fire until he was at 100 yards. The plane was hit and began to emit long red flames and black smoke.

Offenberg followed this flaming torch as it spun down. No one baled out. The pilot must have been killed. No time to get soft-hearted. He was looking for the others. Where were they? Since none of his squadron was with him, he joined a formation flying several thousand feet higher. They were the Tangmere boys.

Dumonceau also found himself alone. He noticed the formation of five machines well above him. A strange formation, he thought.

Like Offenberg, he considered it rash to remain alone in such dangerous regions and zoomed up towards them. The leading plane was at least half a mile ahead of its comrades. As he approached he suddenly saw that No. 2 had a large yellow circle under its engine and that Nos. 3 and 4 were painted in the same colour from nose to tail. Black crosses. They were Me 109s chasing a Spitfire. A glance at his compass showed 300°. They were flying towards England. Dumonceau pushed his throttle forward and got behind the Germans, 500 feet above them and a mile to stern. In the middle of the Channel the leading German broke off and attacked the Spitfire, which did not seem to realise that it had four Jerries on its tail.

Dumonceau attacked and did a left-hand turn towards the three other Germans. They spotted him and did a climbing turn to break away. At this moment Dumonceau banked to the right and attacked No. 1, who had not spotted him. Too late: he too had seen the approach of the Spitfire. He broke off, pursued by Dumonceau. They both dived towards the French coast. Calais lay ahead. 20,000 feet ... 15,000 ... 12,000 ... Dumonceau was gaining on him. His wings would not stand this speed for long. He persisted and did not pull out yet. At 10,000 feet he opened fire at 400 yards with cannon and machine-guns. Black smoke and red flames came from the Messerschmitt. At 100 yards he stopped firing and broke away to port. He thought he had not enough ammunition left to begin another combat. At 8,000 feet he scanned the sky, looking for some trace, some sign. Two miles off Calais black smoke rose from the sea.

Dusk was falling. One by one the fighters returned to their stations, called in by the controllers. The Biggin Hill squadrons reached more peaceful skies. Offenberg was depressed but the day had been saved because Dumonceau and Vicky Ortmans had both shot down an enemy fighter.

19th August 1941. Gilroy was absent that day and Pyker led the 609 into battle. This was the first time that a Belgian airman had commanded a British squadron even as a deputy. Offenberg had been the first to be awarded the D.F.C. and he would be the first to lead a British squadron into action.

Between Boulogne and Dunkirk, they were intercepted by German fighters and a long battle ensued. The formations broke up, the aircraft twisted and turned, rolled and dived ... Tracer bullets pencilled thin red lines of fire against the clouds.

Offenberg dived on an Me. In Indian file the hunter and the hunted performed their rolls. The Belgian fired short bursts each time his deflection was good. In this way they descended from 25,000 to 15,000 feet. A layer of cloud below made a magnificent background for Offenberg; it showed up the black silhouette of the Messerschmitt which became yellow when he turned on his back. For one moment the tracers framed the enemy. Was he hit? No smoke came from his tail. Offenberg continued. The German pilot, on his back, glided into the clouds, which closed behind him. Further south, Yellow section (de Hemptinne flying No. 1 with Sergeant Pilot Pollard) each damaged one of the enemy planes.

The 609 tried to re-form but there were so many Spits and Mes in the air that a hen could not have found her chicks. As soon as an R.A.F. plane left a German fighter, he was fired on by another. The radio was a madhouse. Over the Channel, Ortmans, fighting like a fiend, waded into a section of four Mes. A born fighter, obstinate as a bull, he had not Offenberg's coolheadedness in a fight. He was too aggressive and had no sense of danger. He never thought of the possible consequences. There was only one goal, one thought in his head ... He had to and would bring down that German aircraft, even if he went down with it. Strange to relate, this type of fighting suited him perfectly. He had been shot down twice, had seven victories to his credit and was in the best of health.

But that day Ortmans did not see the Me 109 which came out of a magnificent curve on his tail. While he was firing, a second Me damaged his left aileron. Ortmans made for the English coast. His Spitfire VB was difficult to fly. Another enemy plane loomed up on his tail and began to fire. His machine would not answer to the controls. The Germans hit his glycol tank and the cockpit was flooded. ...

Over the Channel, Ortmans called out: "Yellow 3 baling out."

Opening his hood, he released his harness, turned over on his back and left the machine. Offenberg saw the white silk descending towards the sea. Vicky was swaying in the breeze. He looked around him. He was not in the least afraid. He knew he was going to get wet again and would probably catch a terrible cold. The doc would probably ground him for a day or two. What a life! Offenberg remained upstairs. Ortmans reached the water and Pyker saw him a moment later getting into his rubber dinghy. He went down to 1,000 feet, trying to attract the attention of the air sea rescue launches. A Lysander relayed him. His fuel was dangerously low. He flew over Vicky at fifty feet, dipped his wings. Vicky, lying down in his yellow rubber dinghy, seemed to smile at him. He waved.

The first airfield over the coast was Manston. Pyker landed and taxied to the end of the runway; as he turned on to the taxi track his motor conked for lack of fuel. He had been flying for two hours and a quarter, which was the limit of the Spit VB's endurance.

He refuelled and returned to Gravesend, where he found that everyone had landed. Vicky had been shot down for the third time and had just been fished out.

At 18.30 hours, Pyker took 609 over France in company with the Biggin Hill circus. The wing commander took his squadrons to Boulogne and the 609 circled at 25,000 feet. No. 92 Squadron was slightly to port, at about 10,000 feet. At twenty-five miles from Biggin Hill, when it would have been intelligent to keep silent because perhaps the Jerries did not yet know that the R.A.F. was on the way, a voice called out:

"Beauty leader from Blue 1. I have engine trouble. I'm returning to base."

"Okay."

Dumonceau took his place. To the east of Calais they saw another wing of Spitfires making for them.

Binto (the Biggin Hill controller) could not explain what was going on. Dumonceau and his winger lost sight of Offenberg – Beauty leader – and waited until things had calmed down a little before joining a squadron. There were masses of Spitfires in the sky. . . .

Offenberg led 609 – or rather what remained of it – in the direction of Guines Forest. His No. 2 warned him that he could see vapour trails very high preceded by small black dots whose outlines he could not distinguish. There was no doubt about it: they were German fighters. Beauty leader ordered Yellow 1 (de Hemptinne) to keep an eye on them and warn him if they looked like attacking. Above the Channel Yvan Dumonceau decided to climb into the sun. He reached 30,000 feet. He noticed that his No. 2 had not followed him.

The long white trails lengthened in the sky. He dived out of the sun towards Boulogne, turned for Calais and returned to 30,000 feet over the Channel into the sun.

Offenberg was curious to know what had happened to his Blue 1 but could not contact him although he called repeatedly on the intercom. He had better watch the sky. Dumonceau knew how to take care of himself. His winger was with him and they had probably joined up with another squadron.

"Those bandits don't look very aggressive."

"You're telling me!"

Dumonceau was all alone over the sea. When he climbed into the sun for the second time he noticed five aircraft in single file, thought they were Spits and reduced his gas. They were Me 109Es. Well, it could not be helped. He attacked and opened fire from 600 yards with his cannon on No. 5 of the formation, the Tail-end-Charlie. He achieved no results, broke off and climbed to the west. On reaching 20,000 feet he noticed four Mes diving on him from the direction of Le Touquet. Ah, no ... He turned and came face to face with four more in echelon to port. Dumonceau flew towards the oncoming machines from three-quarters, opened fire with cannon and machine-guns and passed them at 150 yards. He missed them all in succession.

Still flying to port with an eye on the German section he called on the radio:

"Cretins at 12,000 feet over Boulogne."

This call heard by his R.A.F. pals would bring them to the spot towards which he was flying.

Thirty miles away, Offenberg and the 609 continued to patrol, watching the Mes which had still not attacked. Dumonceau was attacked by four Mes. He defended himself vigorously, giving them several one-second bursts. One of the Germans passed in his gonio at less than fifty yards just as he was firing. The hit machine dived into the sea with a long black trail of smoke pouring from it.

Since the remaining three Mes seemed intent on bringing him down he had no time to observe the end of his victim. Was it his engine that had been hit? Never mind.

Dumonceau did not understand what had happened, but for no good reason two of the three attackers suddenly broke off the combat. One remained and carried out five attacks between Boulogne and a point ten miles from Dover. Dumonceau climbed towards him each time he attacked and the two men fired almost head on.

Calm and collected he noticed that the German aimed too high and had no time to correct his aim because the approach speed was more than 800 m.p.h. Young Dumonceau did not waver and each time made straight for the Hun who was always the first to break off in a zoom.

On the radio Dumonceau called: "There's a Messerschmitt

here in the middle of the Channel which is simply asking to be shot down."

By common consent they broke off the engagement. Dumonceau had no ammunition left. He landed on the first airfield he saw: Hawkinge near Dover.

Ortmans returned to Biggin Hill that evening in excellent fettle. He had not even caught a cold.

"The water was quite warm," he said. "The chaps in the launch were old friends. They'd fished me out once before. The skipper said as soon as he saw me: "Oh, not you again?"

21st August. Flying at 30,000 feet with two squadrons above and to stern the 609 on a course for Gravelines turned above Manston, passing the squadron of Blenheims they were protecting. Offenberg was once more leading the squadron. It was midday. Above Gravelines thirty Mes were patrolling 2,000 feet lower and a mile to port.

Pyker called:

"Yellow Section from Beauty leader."

"Yellow 1."

"Attack those bastards to port."

Yellow Section (de Hemptinne) broke off while the Wing continued on towards Saint-Omer, remaining above the bombers to protect them until they reached the target. On arriving over Saint-Omer, the Biggin Hill Wing split their formation into sections of four aircraft.

It was in very spread out groups, therefore, that the Wing arrived over Gravelines on the homeward journey.

The coast was barely in sight when Offenberg – Red 1 – glanced back at his wingers, Red 3 and 4, both of whom were on his port wing. He caught sight of a lone Me about to attack them from the rear. Two other Jerries were lurking higher up. "Nos 3 and 4. Break, quick."

He himself banked to port while his two mates dived to starboard. Offenberg was now facing the German, who was surprised by the speed of the manoeuvre. A moment before he had been firing as he pleased at the two Spits and was now in a very tricky position. The tables had been turned!

Offenberg opened fire turning towards the German who broke away from this highly dangerous spot. Offenberg's No. 2 had not left his side and returned to wing tip formation.

No. 4 Red Section called to the leader: "I've been slightly hit.

I'm O.K. Thanks for the warning ... I should have been a goner ..."

Offenberg was anxious. He hoped that his No. 3, Sergeant Pollard, had had time to break before being hit by the Me's shells.

"Red 3. Can you hear me?"

No reply. But in view of the turmoil on the waves at this hour perhaps he had not heard. He had probably returned to Biggin Hill. Unless the other two Mes had followed him down in his dive ... Red 3 still did not reply to his calls. With his remaining winger he gained height.

Binto announced that enemy aircraft were concentrated above Gravelines and seemed to be waiting. On hearing this news, Pyker changed on to course 180°, returned to the spot indicated by the controller, and found himself below a formation of about twenty enemy fighters circling 1,500 feet above him.

Like a flight of vultures the Mes lurked down one after the other in a dive which they continued after the attack.

At each new dive Offenberg replied by turning into the attacker and giving him short burst from head on.

The odds, however, were very unequal.

"Red 2. We're disengaging now."

"Yes. It's getting unhealthy."

"Good; when I give the order after the next attack go into a spin. A power dive's no use. The Me with its supercharger could catch us. Understood?"

"Okay."

A Messerschmitt attacked.

Pyker turned into him for the fourth time, gave a burst, pulled back his throttle, pulled on the stick and kicked his staller and went into a fast spin.

After three complete turns he straightened out and saw two Mes in line ahead of 2,000 feet over Gravelines beach. He did not hesitate. He attacked the two aircraft and broke away seawards. The spot was more than unhealthy.

He had practically no ammunition left and he might have quite a few arguments with the Luftwaffe before he reached Biggin Hill.

While Jean Offenberg was having this little skirmish with the Führer's personnel, Yellow Section had attacked the four first Mes they had spotted near Calais and had dived on an enemy formation below them, flying south.

De Hemptinne was busy pursuing the Huns when his No. 2

announced quite calmly that there were five Mes slightly to stern of those he was already chasing.

It was too late to change now. De Hemptinne pressed home his attack, chose the rear Me, came in from three-quarters and gave him a short burst. The Me rolled on his back and dived.

At the same moment his No. 2, Sergeant Van Schaick, attacked the next in line from stern, arriving within 250 yards of his tail ... He held his fire until the distance had decreased to 100 yards. The Me turned on its back with black and white smoke pouring from its engine. It went down in a vertical dive. Van Schaick saw that he did not pull out. A dozen Mes continued to attack them and the dog fight lasted nearly half an hour.

De Hemptinne had torn off his collar. The sweat was making his clothes stick to his body. At last he gave the order to break.

Excited by his kill, Van Schaick went down to ground level, pulled out, flew north of Cap Gris Nez and shot up an E-boat about a mile off the coast. The vessel caught fire. Van Schaick returned to Gravesend skimming across the Channel at wave-top level.

*　　*　　*

The German Fighter Arm must have been exceedingly weary. The raids from Biggin Hill Wing continued and were strangely alike in pattern. François de Spirlet was made a flight commander and Paul Ritchie, who had been promoted in rank, left to command the third Squadron on the Wing – No. 74. Baudouin was given a flight in No. 131 Squadron at Turnhill.

On Sunday, 24th August, the three Squadrons, the 609, 82 and 74, spent part of the afternoon over Saint-Omer. The boys below ignored them and did not take off.

Wing Commander Robinson detached the 609 and sent it to Berck Plage with orders to continue north. If the Mes intercepted the two other squadrons on the return journey, the 609 would fall on them from the rear.

Control at Biggin Hill had nothing to report. No enemy aircraft appeared on the radar screens. The 609 reached Berck Plage and flew steadily north.

Spirlet's Yellow Section and Offenberg's Blue Section made graceful circles above the third section without forgetting to keep a weather eye open.

Suddenly Red 4 called. It was Palmer.

"Beauty leader. A ship at three o'clock."

According to the clock system three o'clock would have meant inland. Sergeant Palmer had made a mistake: he should have said nine o'clock.

Squadron Leader Gilroy had not caught the beginning of the phrase.

"Upstairs or below?" he asked.

Palmer, excited by the presence of his favourite target, was a trifle perplexed by such a question.

"Below, obviously."

Gilroy, who saw nothing below at three o'clock, asked for further information when Offenberg broke in before Palmer got any more involved.

"He's talking about a ship off Le Touquet."

The squadron commander realised at once what had happened. The waves burnt up with his magisterial "rocket," and Palmer felt very small in his cockpit. That evening poor Palmer was not seen in the Sergeants' mess; he was hiding in shame in his hut.

29th August, 1941. At seven in the morning, the Wing assembled and took off for France. Gilroy led them: Offenberg was in his favourite position at the head of Blue Section. The leader of Yellow Section was a newcomer to the Squadron, Christian, Vicky Ortmans' brother, a tall fellow with pitch black hair. He looked very determined and wore a small Adolf Hitler moustache. He had arrived three days before and this was his second operational flight.

The sea was extraordinarily calm. The aircraft crossed the coast at 15,000 feet south of Cap Gris Nez and turned for Hardelot. Above them at about 25,000 feet No. 92 Squadron was top cover. Hardelot-Hazebrouck . . . Nothing to report. The German fighters must still have been asleep.

At ten miles from Dunkirk on the return journey, Binto announced an enemy formation bearing down on them, descending the coast.

Over the intercom. Offenberg heard that 92 Squadron was already in a dog-fight elsewhere. Things were going to get hot . . . He had hardly checked his gonio before a dozen black crosses passed several thousand feet overhead in a very shallow dive.

The Germans had not yet seen them.

"Section, attack."

"O.K., Blue leader."

Offenberg backed in pursuit of the Germans. Too late, he had been spotted. The Mes disengaged and a terrific dog-fight ensued. Offenberg with his throttle full out streaked almost head on towards an Me. The outline of the German aircraft swiftly grew larger. At 1,000 yards he fired his cannon. M for Monkey vibrated and the recoil of his guns slowed down its speed. He broke away in a dive just as he caught sight of an Me on his tail in the mirror. Christian Ortmans to port saw two Mes speeding past him. As Christian said to the Intelligence Officer who interrogated him later:

"Then I cut my corners and turned so tight that I risked going into a spin. I don't know how it happened but I suddenly found myself on the tail of one of them at less than twenty yards in a good position to make an attack from three-quarters astern. I fired a two-second burst. At that moment I saw some clouds lower down and I thought I could not reach him before he disappeared into the protective covering. I left the field clear for my winger, Sergeant Palmer, who followed him for a few minutes firing from a long distance.

"I noticed nothing but Palmer insists that the Messerschmitt dived inland leaving a trail of smoke."

Offenberg, too, beyond Dunkirk, was chasing a Messerschmitt which he did not manage to catch in spite of all his efforts. Tired of the struggle, he gave a long salvo with all his machine-guns from 500 yards. A piece broke off the enemy plane. Had he hit it? A thin trail of black smoke came from the left side of the fighter which went down in an almost vertical dive. He did not seem to be out of control but to be flying normally. An old season fighter, Offenberg remembered the Battle of Britain. It was never right to follow a fighter down on to his own territory. He pulled on the stick, opened his throttle and zoomed eastwards into the sun. He lowered his dark windscreen so as not to be blinded by the glare. The turmoil on the radio died down a little. Above the disturbance he heard a strident voice cry: "That's one less for the Luftwaffe."

Instinctively he looked at his watch. It was 07.31 hours.

The leader reformed his section above Cap Gris Nez.

"Beauty Leader – I am north of Cap Gris Nez at 10,000 feet. Come and join me."

Offenberg heard, set his course and descended to 10,000 feet. "I'm coming, Blue 1."

"Yellow 1, O.K."

Then he called again: "Is everything okay, Christian?"

"Fine, Pyker."

A quarter of an hour later they landed at Gravesend. It was François de Spirlet who had brought down a Messerschmitt at 07.31 hours. The German had done a half roll under his nose on a level with Gravelines. He dived after him. The German did not even try to break. François opened fire at 400 yards and the Me continued to dive straight ahead at 45°. He saw him crash two miles inland from Gravelines.

Since the German had not even tried to break at the moment of attack François imagined that he had already been wounded in the course of a preceding combat.

II

FURIOUS AUTUMN

ON THE 24TH SEPTEMBER 609 SQUADRON IN FULL complement under Squadron Commander Gilroy and Belgian flight commanders returned to their old quarters at Biggin Hill. The pilots abandoned the ancient walls and discomfort of Cobham Hall to others. They were happy to be returning to the old familiar place among known faces and to the prestige attaching to those who lived on the most famous fighter station in Great Britain. Two new pilots were posted to Jean Offenberg's B Flight. One was the New Zealander, Pilot Officer Smith, and the other Sergeant Greenfield. The evening before they left, 609 foregathered in camp round the bar where oysters were served free. A little Alsatian wine had appeared from somewhere and was a good appetiser. In the dining room later that evening they sat down to a magnificent feast. They were all there round the huge refectory tables. Tomorrow they would take off again with the same smile on their lips, but today they were celebrating a new departure and despite their pleasure at returning to Biggin Hill they felt a little nostalgic at leaving this camp where they had made so many new friends. Besides, nothing could be truer than the old French proverb, "*partir est mourir un peu,*" and life was made up of departures. Wherever they went they left for the great unknown, the fascination of the hostile sky. When they left with a handshake they knew that perhaps it was for the last time. Buffeted by unfavourable winds, this handful of youths, this glorious band of sky gypsies, had nothing in the world, no family, no homes to which they could return. Their only bonds were the camps, the airfields, their new friends and their slender pay. All they possessed would easily go into a suitcase . . . and they asked for nothing better.

What did it matter to them if others were rich and lived in stately dwellings? They needed nothing, for their wealth could not be counted in gold coins or bank notes. Their youth, enthusiasm, aggression, fearlessness, joy and sometimes their grief could neither be bought nor sold. These friends who had saved their life – and had not each of them saved the life of another – were they not more precious than all the gold in the world? And if they were to be offered three times as much they would return to the combat all the same. The foreigners here were not mercenaries; they did not fly and fight for the British, they flew with them.

And that evening at Cobham Hall, as dusk fell over the Thames, in the great hall of honour where they dined, they sat close to each other at the table. There was no need to give them lectures on *espirit de corps*. They had acquired that team spirit which cannot be learned from books, in the school of combat.

It was a hard school where there was no place for weaklings. You had to learn quickly and there was no chance of sitting for your exams again. When a gap was made in their ranks they hardly had time to grieve before the ranks were closed again.

War is always a bitter thing, an implacable game where one cannot always win. Tomorrow it would be their turn. Tomorrow if they foregathered some faces would no longer be there and some voices would have been silenced. So that evening they made the best of life and enjoyed themselves, drowning in noise and laughter the sadness which they were never prepared to admit.

On the morning of the 24th they took off as a squadron from Gravesend and got into formation above the clouds. Gilroy called them on the radio.

"Beauty aircraft from Red 1. Go down and say goodbye to them."

Wing to wing, they dived through the clouds and roared across the Gravesend airfield.

A figure below waved in reply to the fighters' salute, to this goodbye which for many would be a farewell.

27th September. The Under Secretary of State for Air, Sir Archibald Sinclair, paid a visit to the legendary pilots of Biggin Hill. In order to show him how a fighter wing worked, the ops office organised a raid over France in his honour. A raid, a classic sweep in which nothing had been left to chance. Not a raid conceived on the spur of the moment – no, everything had been prepared, calculated and weighed.

The illustrious visitor was told that the wing would operate in his honour (forgetting to tell him that if he had not come they would have carried it out all the same). The pilots were briefed down to the smallest details – the E.T.A., the cloud, the enemy fighters, the flak positions, all of which in actual fact they knew by heart. They emptied their pockets and checked their escape pack. If they were shot down and taken prisoner they were only to reply three things to the enemy intelligence officers: their name, rank and service number.

They took off for another circus performance and this time they worked at the top of the tent at 27,000 feet. They were the high cover wing, 609 was leader and took off first. Offenberg was flying his usual Blue 1 with Dumonceau as his winger. The first change of course on their route was Mardyck, south of Dunkirk. They reached the course at the point indicated and turned. A few Blenheims were below them, escorted by Spitfires which weaved around them like sheepdogs.

The 609 reached a point some fifteen miles inland. At that moment a score of Mes dived on them and passed 2,000 feet at three o'clock. Other Mes still lower were flying south.

Gilroy gave the familiar cry. "Tally-ho, bandits below."

"Okay, Beauty, Red 1."

Red Section dived and the dog-fight was on. At that moment Offenberg saw three German fighters to starboard in line formation. He dived on them with his section. Attacking the nearest Me, he fired a short burst from some way off. Thick black smoke came from the Me 109 which did a half roll to escape this dangerous adversary. Offenberg had foreseen the German manoeuvre, did a half roll in turn and dived. But he blacked out. He straightened up by instinct, rejoined Dumonceau and made for the coast.

In this merry-go-round which was taking place before his eyes, Offenberg behaved as though on a training flight. He never lost his head. His eyesight was phenomenal. He had the eye of an eagle and there was only one pilot with him that day who was his equal, and that was Dumonceau de Bergendael. They formed a dangerous team and the Luftwaffe should have steered clear of them.

They flew for the shore, reached Mardyck and were attacked by a stray Messerschmitt who was soon joined by one of his mates. At two to one it had been easy. Now the game was more even. The Germans hesitated. . . .

Each time they made as though to attack, the Spits flew towards them. The Luftwaffe pilots must have realised that they were no novices piloting the two Spits.

At ten miles off Dunkirk they were still hanging on and showed no intention of giving up. The Germans must have arranged a little combination on their intercom. One tried to climb into the sun while the other gained height between the Spits and the French coast.

Cunning did not always work with Offenberg and Dumonceau, who was usually known as "the Duke." The latter zoomed, following the German who was doing a climbing turn. Offenberg watched the other Me out of the corner of his eye. The moment the Me entered the sun Dumonceau aimed and fired his cannon at 300 yards.

The enemy was not hit. Yes – suddenly he seemed to stall and dive to the right. The Duke, calmed by the presence of Offenberg, immediately dived in pursuit. It was a giddy power dive. At 350 yards he fired his cannon. He would get him . . . He had sworn to get him. He continued his dive. The German passed over the vertical and disappeared into a cloud at 3,000 feet. Dumonceau pulled out slowly and blacked out.

His Spitfire impelled by the enormous speed acquired in the dive, he regained his height on the zoom. Offenberg was waiting for him. While his winger had been fighting, he had made two attacks on the Me, who finally abandoned the struggle. They reached 28,000 feet. The Blenheims below were flying over Le Touquet on the way home. There were no more enemy fighters in the sky. Then together, wing to wing, they turned into the blinding sunlight.

Only on landing did they learn that Giovanni Dieu had been in a scrap with three of the enemy and damaged one of them.

"Where's Vicky?" Offenberg asked suddenly.

"Vicky's in the drink."

"Not again – it's impossible."

"Dead?"

"Vicky dead? No – they've just telephoned to say that he's been fished out again. He only ran out of juice."

Everyone laughed, delighted that no one was missing and that the fantastic Ortmans had not gone for a Burton.

"You'll see," said Choron, "that if Vicky pulls that stunt again the Air Sea Rescue boys will refuse to pick him up. He's overdoing it, you know."

Sir Archibald Sinclair was introduced to the pilots. He shook hands which were sometimes calloused and workmanlike. Congratulated these youngsters whose faces bore the traces of the hard battle they had just fought.

The VIP was happy. The dividends were good. . . .

28th September. The Squadron commander having the previous evening ordered a new permanent readiness, B Flight was told to set the ball rolling. It had rained during the night. Nothing is more detestable than to get up before dawn and go down to the field. Eyes were still heavy with sleep and no one felt inclined to go for a flip in this sticky early morning mist.

Damp grass, sad-looking deserted Spitfires whose paint had peeled and the flag flapping pathetically.

Pyker recalled one of Max Elskamp's poems, the words of which he could not remember but which described the melancholy of rain falling on wet flags. It was a perfect description that morning. An infinite melancholy had settled on the airfield which reminded him a little of Bruges-la-Morte.

An impressive silence reigned. Only the creak of flying boots on the tarmac broke the monotony. Nobody felt like talking. The slightest raised voice would have broken the charm and would have sounded shrill.

It was cold in the crew room. Winter would soon be here. It would be the second winter of their exile. It was certain that none of these aliens would return home for Christmas.

An orderly lit the stove which began to roar in the centre of the room. Choron, with a black scowl on his face and his hands in his pockets, walked up and down to get warm. He was the first to break the silence.

"What a lousy day. They can keep their bloody England. I sometimes wonder why Napoleon wanted to take it. If Hitler spent a week over here in the autumn, I bet you my ticket that he wouldn't be keen on invading us."

The noise of an engine was suddenly heard at the far end of the airfield. The six pilots of B Flight, hands in their pockets, went over to the window and looked at the sky, broken here and there by the grey roofs of the sheds.

"Probably one of 92's crates," suggested Offenberg.

"They're not going to take off in this, are they?"

"No – they won't take off – probably the mechanics are doing their daily inspection."

The field telephone rang. Pyker picked up the receiver.

"Flight Lieutenant Offenberg ... Who ... ? Yes ... Only two ... Are they many ... Yes, at once ..."

Without giving any details to the pilots who had listened to this monologue, Pyker rushed outside and called one of the mechanics

"Get the engines started up. M and B. ... And let them warm up."

He returned and explained to the others in a few words that an unidentified aircraft was flying towards the English coast and it had to be intercepted.

"Choron, come with me," he ordered.

Vicky thought that everyone should go.

"We've nothing else to do," he said, "in this damned weather. If we all go together, we're bound to shoot down the bastard."

Although Pyker was the best comrade in the world he would never allow anyone to contradict his orders when it was a question of a combat. He would allow any familiarity, go out with the sergeants and behave like one of the boys on any occasion. But here he was responsible.

"I said Choron," he said with unusual curtness.

Outside, the engines of the two Spits had been started. Life returned to the almost deserted airfield. Mechanics rushed round the machines making the last tests.

Offenberg pulled down his black woollen socks, wrapped his trouser legs round his ankles and pulled the socks over them. This was a habit of his. It was his first gesture each time he left and on his return he often forgot and would walk about all day in this unorthodox rig. Since everyone knew this at Biggin Hill, no one paid any attention.

"Are you coming, Maurice? Let's get going."

They ran to their aircraft. Pyker's thoughts returned to a few months before. Then it had been the Battle of Britain. Each day he scrambled to the Hurricanes with Dunning-White, Boyd and the others. Those were the good old days of 145 Squadron. He had always longed for interception. That was real fighters' work.

And now he was on the ball once more in his cockpit. One of the mechanics helped him to adjust his harness. Pyker recognised him. It was Phillips, the first man he had ever had to punish for a trifling infraction which he had actually forgotten.

"Good morning, Phillips," he said, raising his voice so that he could be heard above the noise of the engine. "How are you getting on now?"

"All right, sir."

"Good. Just fix that left shoulder strap."

"Yes, sir. Where are you off to?"

Offenberg could not help laughing.

"I don't know yet. Somewhere near Dover, I think. Now the right one. Thank you."

Phillips helped him to close the cockpit and Offenberg adjusted his helmet and his oxygen mask.

Two minutes later the Spitfires took off together. Undercarriage retracted, they flew low for a moment, put on speed and climbed eastwards.

Control called and gave them their courses. Visibility was bad near the ground. A slight layer of mist lay over the countryside, hiding the towns and villages.

Pyker called control.

"Beauty Blue 1. Have you still got the bandit?"

"Yes – he's turning near Hastings. Course 100° now."

Offenberg was reassured. The controller must know his job and would lead them between the enemy aircraft and the French coast. He reported that they had just reached 20,000 feet, the height given them on departure. He could make out the coast. They were over the sea. Now they changed their course to 150°. In another few minutes they would be in position. The controller for interception spoke to them, gave them the enemy position and instructed them to follow his courses.

"We shall miss him," said Pyker in French. "It's taking too long and we lost too much time before we took off."

"Maybe he'll wait for us," replied Choron.

Then reverting calmly to English, Offenberg reported that the French coast was covered with low cloud. An overcast sky to the south.

Control suddenly called: "The Hun's making for home. "He's ten miles ahead of you now, probably at 15,000 feet."

Ahead there were only a few clouds and here and there a strip of sea visible below.

"Putain de malheur," said Choron, "we shall miss him."

The French and Belgians in the R.A.F. often talked to each other in a highly picturesque French which would have made the little WAAFS in the operations rooms blush had they really known the meaning of the expressions.

"I think so too," replied Offenberg.

The controller confirmed that the plot had faded out. The German had got beyond their radar and it was therefore useless to continue the hunt. Or else he had dived to sea level where the short waves could not reach him.

"Blue 1, going down."

Offenberg, always clear-headed, had just taken a decision.

He pulled out at 1,000 feet and Choron took up his place at his side. Visibility was very bad – two miles at the maximum. They searched for a moment and then decided to return home.

Contrary to the Met forecast the sky remained overcast the whole morning. As a result of his fruitless trip Offenberg missed Mass. At 14.00 hours, since there was no improvement in the weather, Gilroy relieved the squadron from duty.

*   *   *

The sky remained overcast for the first three weeks of October. A few unimportant raids were arranged haphazardly as soon as the sky cleared over the Channel. Kills were rare and losses insignificant for 609 had not been intercepted for a long time. No. 92 Squadron was not so lucky. On the 2nd October during a raid over Abbeville it lost a flight commander and two sergeants shot down in combat. The following day Biggin Hill wing took off again to escort Blenheims to Nieuport and Ostend. 609 flew at 25,000 feet out of range of the German flak. They were greeted over the Belgian coast by a few shells which burst not far from the section but without causing any damage. The 609 only heard on the radio that 92 had been attacked by Messerschmitts. Offenberg could almost follow the outcome of the dog-fight by listening to the shouts on the intercom.

"Huns on my tail."

"Break."

"Spitfire in a spin trailing smoke."

"They're Focke-Wulfs."

"I can't see them."

"Hullo, Blue 2. Can you hear me?"

"Like a bird."

"Can you see where we are?"

Below them, as if on manoeuvres, the Blenheims destroyed the Ostend power station without bothering about the furious battle which was going on over the coast.

Offenberg called: "Beauty leader, can I go down?"

"Okay, Blue 1."

Offenberg led his section down in a half roll. The four 609 pilots jettisoned their reserve tanks. The concert continued over the intercom.

"Jackie's in the drink."

"Blue 2. Blue 2. Can you hear me?"

"They've scarpered."

"That was good shooting."

"I got the blighter."

The Focke-Wulfs had disappeared. No. 92 had lost two pilots but one of the sergeants had shot down a German fighter. Pyker had arrived too late. The battle was over and they could return home.

Three new Belgians joined 609 on the 30th September – Van Aerenbergh, de Selys Longchamps and Sergeant Lallemand, who had just got his wings and as yet had no idea that two years later he would be in command of 609. Squadron Commander Gilroy took several days' leave and Offenberg was in command. He received the new arrivals.

They had arranged that when Gilroy returned he would go for a few days' rest to Chichester.

In the meantime he took the newcomers up, gave them advice, answered the innumerable questions that came into the office each day, signed notes and papers, more often than not handing all the red tape to the flight sergeant because he had not enough time to bother with all this office work.

As a squadron commander, Pyker was very popular. He left each man his own responsibilities. He made no fuss and never behaved like a barrack-room sergeant.

"Until I find out the contrary," he used to say, "everyone is a good man in my eyes."

When one of the kiwis from the base insisted that an example was to be made of thirteen of his men, Offenberg called them into his office and after an interrogation decided that only

181

one was to blame. He refused to punish the other twelve despite a host of spectacular rockets from the kiwi.

"I'm in command here and as long as I am in command I refuse to punish these men. I'm certain they're not to blame and my conscience will not allow me to do so."

The soldiers were never punished but Offenberg had increased his popularity among the "bods."

The pilots were, of course, his brothers. The young ones who had just come from flying school were given his best tips.

Highly aggressive himself, he had never hesitated to shoot down a German aircraft but, on the other hand, he never took unnecessary risks.

"In the course of a raid," he told them, "the important thing is to provoke the Jerries and to make their life impossible. It's useless getting yourself killed for the pleasure of shooting down one."

"Never attack before you are quite certain that you'll come through. Ah," he added, "if we had the invasion behind us we should see it from another angle, I'm sure. It would be quite different. It's better to miss one today and shoot down two tomorrow."

Having noticed that one young pilot seemed unsure of himself in formation flying, he decided to take him in hand. Each of the old hands was to do formation flight with him as winger. When it was Choron's turn, the Frenchman carried out his orders most unwillingly.

Returning to the squadron office an hour later and delighted to be still alive, Maurice rushed up to Offenberg.

"I did the flight and I have witnesses. I insist that you record it somewhere and sign it. You see," he went on, turning to another pilot, "everyone's got to have a turn and I don't want to make a habit of that."

The newcomer never flew up to scratch despite all Offenberg's efforts. He took him up personally, swore at him and spoke with encouragement. Nothing doing. Each trip finished the same way. A very uneasy Offenberg diving as fast as he could and roaring into the intercom. to his winger: "Climb, climb."

For the security of the squadron, No. 2 Group H.Q. decided that it was better to get rid of such a dangerous fellow.

"It's a pity," said Choron, "a great pity. He was coming on and I'm sure that he'd have shot one down later on."

"That boy shoot down a Messerschmitt!"

"No – a Spitfire!"

****

12th October

Ahead of me Biggin Hill, its runways gleaming from the fine rain which has been falling since last night. Behind me, the eleven Spitfires in formation must look to the spectators below like a flight of wild homing geese ... Biggin Hill is the fold, the lair to which you return after the hunt, where you can stretch your tired limbs and warm your numb fingers. Today it was bad hunting, we could not put up any game and we did not fire a shot. . . .

I called Control.

"Beauty squadron, permission to land."

"Okay, Beauty squadron, come in."

I gave orders to the formation to disperse over the runways, breaking away myself first. The runway approached. I was too fast and had to throttle down. I was all right ... I flattened out ... gently. I was taxi-ing among the puddles on the wet tarmac. The Spitfire's tail sank and the engine hid my horizon. I thought of those racehorses which run in blinkers. They cannot see in front of them. I could only see to each side. The buildings sped past as if I were in the centre of a slow motion film. In my mirror I saw my winger Red 2 coming down. I turned away at the end of the ribbon.

"Runway clear. Red 1 out."

The others followed immediately.

"Red 2, runway clear."

"Red 3, runway clear."

Through a window I saw someone waving to me. I turned, then kicked the rudder to brake the aircraft and stop. The Spitfire went on gliding and would not stop; it seemed as though it were being pushed by an immense hand. The prop broke against the wall. The aircraft finally came to a stop and I switched off the engine.

I was furious with myself, with the wretched machine and the slippery tarmac.

A mechanic in greasy overalls helped me open the cockpit and unfasten the straps which had bound me to my seat for the past two hours.

The man was saying something for I could see his lips moving. I pulled off my helmet which held my head as in a vice. I could not clear my eardrums and get used to everyday sounds.

The noise of the engine still rang in my ears until finally it stopped.

"It was the gremlins, sir," said the mechanic.

"The gremlins?"

"Which pushed you against the wall. You'd better not take off again today, but wait."

The gremlins. One of those fantastic superstitions which originated in the imagination of some pilots, superstitions which made them take off with a hare's foot in their pockets or a silk stocking belonging to some vague girl friend. Not to light three cigarettes from the same match. If they did not subscribe to this humbug, some of them had a feeling that they would be shot down if they took off. It was disastrous to fly with someone else's parachute. There were some – no names mentioned – who considered that to paint a swastika on the side of the plane for each German machine shot down was the best way of attracting bad luck. And now it was the gremlins! They were cunning, ill-natured gnomes who automatically took responsibility for anything that could not be explained. An engine conked in the air and the station engineer could not find the origin of the fault: it was the gremlins. Everything was their fault. They mixed the maps, blocked the shutter of your camera, swallowed your glycol and cut the aileron cables. There are some which even rode on sea gulls and led them straight at you; the moment when a collision was inevitable they abandoned the gull, hid in the clouds and returned to base. Folk lore specialists went so far as to determine the sex of the gremlins by their particular pranks. A sergeant explained to me quite seriously a few weeks ago that some of them were sexless and those are the most dangerous. Even the Air Ministry mildly recognises the existence of these outrageous creatures. One must never take off with a gremlinised aircraft. It would be catastrophic.

And this superstition grows and has penetrated to all the airfields like the wave of some incredible ocean drowning all reason. The gremlin is king. No one has even seen one of these malicious little sprites but there are some who can sense their presence. They know the charms to use ... and the others simply get killed.

How ridiculous it all is. And yet perhaps not so ridiculous. I have heard that Lord Dowding, the Chief of Fighter Command while I was at Tangmere with the 145, was a fervent spiritualist. He maintains quite seriously that the pilots who die return and still fly aircraft. They warn you, make you turn your head towards the Me which you have not seen, help you perhaps during a fight. Whisper advice into your subconscious when things are going badly and make you recognise in a flash that you are risking your neck.

Sometimes I wonder whether they are all mad or if it is I who am crazy.

****

Editor's Note.—Offenberg was not superstitious for he was too religious. But, in order to be like the others, although in reality he was so different, he carried in his Spitfire "M for Monkey" a crucifix some inches long, slipped in one of the breast pockets of his battledress.

13th October. It was not precisely bad weather that morning but a north-westerly gale blew the Spits off the ground before their engines were revved up. About 10 o'clock the wind fell a little and Offenberg sent two of the newcomers – de Selys and Van Aerenbergh to carry out a training flight near the base.

After making two or three crossings of the airfield wing to wing, the two Belgians began a mock air battle which was quite successful. Jean de Selys beat Aerenbergh several times and Offenberg watched the battle with interest.

Suddenly one of the machines seemed to collide with the other. It was learned that Van Aerenbergh touched de Sely's right wing with his propeller, cutting off his aileron and wing tip.

Offenberg rushed to an aircraft, did not bother to strap himself in, started the engine and took off. He would escort Selys's Spitfire and give him advice over the intercom. Together they reached West Malling airfield and after two vain attempts de Selys landed at 140 m.p.h. With his prop stopped, Van Aerenbergh landed safely at Biggin Hill.

The wind had not yet fallen when, at about 2 o'clock in the afternoon, a raid was announced.

The pilots were not particularly pleased to make a trip over France in such a high wind. Would it be Lille? Everyone hoped it would not be so far. Obviously, with a following wind the

Spits would arrive over their goal in a flash. Then they would have a dog-fight and return home into wind. That would complicate matters for they would only make very slow headway – so slow that half the wing would run out of fuel a long way from the field.

It was by no means with the serenity of the knights of old that the pilots reported to the briefings. Most of them were swearing at the Germans in general and at the wind in particular. The big map was open in the ops room and the general plan explained. Biggin Hill squadron was to carry out a diversionary raid. While the German fighters came up to intercept them, the R.A.F. would make a second raiding party to Amiens. The route was Gravelines-Marzingarbe-Le Touquet. And in order not to get out of practice, 609 would be top cover at 20,000 feet. The officer who brought the latest Met news gave them the synoptic view of the situation – the fronts, the centres of depression and the wind.

In an attempt to reassure the pilots, Wing Commander Rankin, who replaced Robinson on the 8th September, stated that obviously the wind was rather strong but the sea was quite calm.

Offenberg, who did not see things from the same angle, took the liberty of saying that it would make a very bad impression to see a Spitfire wing transformed into a long convoy of Mae Wests.

The orders having been given, Group Captain Barwell, commanding Biggin Hill, said simply: "Make a good show of it," and left.

609 was swiftly airborne. They set course for Manston and flew to Gravelines at record speed. Pyker led the squadron. They reached Marzingarbe with no incident and turned for Le Touquet. If the German fighters did not appear, the squadron would get away with a long trip and would not run short of fuel. Le Touquet appeared beneath their wings. Unfortunately for 609, the Germans were waiting for them on the way back and two machines, which Offenberg for a moment mistook for Hurricanes, dived in front of him. The Me 109Fs were difficult to distinguish from Hurricanes, particularly from the stern. Since, in any case, it was too late to despatch a section on their tails, Offenberg made a wide circle out to sea.

Blue 2, Sergeant Lang, reported four Mes preparing to dive. Actually two were already diving when Offenberg spotted them.

186

They missed Red section and, flying at 400 m.p.h., passed 300 yards ahead.

"I'll teach you how to dive, my friend," muttered Pyker, doing a half roll. He pushed his nose down and as soon as his deflection was perfect fired a burst. Hearing a host of warnings on the radio, he imagined that another Me was chasing him. He straightened out, did a right hand climbing turn, pushing the throttle right forward. There was no one behind him and he privately cursed all these panic merchants roaring on the intercom, preventing him from going on with his pursuit.

"Blue 2 here. Did you get that bastard?"

"Yes, I got him."

"Yes, I saw the tracers go right into him."

Since no one had seen the machine crash on land or in the sea, the Me would only rank as a possible. Joe Atkinson had undoubtedly damaged a second aircraft, but Sergeant Nash was the star turn of the day. A Messerschmitt passing within firing range, he gave him a long burst in the engine. The German had time to bale out and his machine exploded in the sea.

All these combats took place within the space of a few seconds. It was now time to return to the English coast.

"Beauty leader, from Yellow 3 – I'm short of fuel."

Ah, now it had started. Yellow 3 was Dieu and the squadron was still over the French coast. With his engine stopped, Dieu's Spitfire glided slowly towards the other coast. Offenberg remained with his section above him as cover and sent the others back to Biggin Hill. The coast was still a long way off.

"Do you think you can make it?"

"I don't know yet. I'm gliding almost on stalling point."

The coast drew near and Dieu was at 6,000 feet. He would be all right if he could land on an airfield or he could always crashland on an airfield or he could at worst crashland in a field.

Dieu reached Hawkinge, side-slipped, lost sufficient height and with a stopped prop landed on the field. Ugh!

* * *

Offenberg returned to Biggin Hill, having added an hour and fifty minutes to his total flying time.

Winter was approaching and the pilots were not sorry to have a little respite after the hard summer season. There was a rumour that the squadron would be sent to rest in the north, to No. 12 Group.

The 7th September would come to be known in history as "the sergeants' outing." Flying that day at 26,000 feet towards Saint-Omer, the 609 was intercepted by Focke-Wulf 109s and a section of Me 109s. In the course of different combats at altitude over France, Sergeant Nash, flying as Offenberg's winger, shot down a 109F and a few seconds later, getting separated from Blue section, saw a Focke-Wulf 200 yards ahead. He got it in his sights, made a slight correction and fired. The Focke-Wulf exploded in the air.

A little to the north, Red section spotted four Me 109Es at the same height.

"Each one take a Boche. Wade in."

The moment Gilroy began his attack, Sergeant van Schaick was on the tail of an Me, which turned over on its back and dived earthwards. He followed the manoeuvre and came down almost vertically. His giddy speed made aiming very difficult. At 250 yards he pressed the firing button for three seconds. Black smoke came from the German machine. Determined to get a confirmed victory, Van Schaick, who had already won the D.F.M., followed the Me down and did not break away westwards until he had seen the machine crash in the open countryside.

Finding himself alone, Van Schaick reached the coast at ground level and a few minutes later landed at Biggin Hill without a scratch.

Squadron Leader Gilroy occasionally obtained time off for his squadron. Happy at hearing the news, the pilots rubbed their hands and made plans to visit the cinema, to go to London or to dance-halls in the neighbourhood. But Gilroy had other ideas which clashed slightly with those of the pilots.

"What you lack," he said to them, "is physical training. Since my riding sesssions brought no results, and the pilots who are bad horsemen are a disgrace to the squadron since they cannot sit on the back of such a noble animal, I shall abandon you to your sad fate."

There was more rubbing of hands and a return to their original ideas. "But," he added, "you are now going to participate in organised games."

Faces grew longer.

Here is an actual extract from Offenberg's diary as to how these games were organised in 609 Squadron.

****

Thursday, 6th November 1941

This afternoon the squadron was given time off to play organised games. The squadron commander and four officers went riding. Two or three types went to London. The sergeants played cards or billiards. I played the gramophone. Lallemand flew to Heston to see Big Lambotte. The latter crashed on landing and his crate caught fire.

He was killed.

This evening I went to see Hall Tidswell, the squadron adjutant, in Orpington Hospital. He had banged his head and had slight concussion. Later, I went to London with Joe Atkinson to see a show and we returned early after dining at the Wellington Club.

****

Editor's Note.—21st October. While Pyker was on leave in Chichester, from where he would not return until the following day, 609 took off at 11.15 hours from Biggin Hill to carry out a raid over France.

Squadron Leader Gilroy led Blue section, which was in the following formation.

1
Gilroy

3   2
Vicky Ortmans   Christian Ortmans
4
Sergeant Palmer

Biggin Hill wing was rear cover at 26,000 feet for the bombers flying some miles ahead. The pilots could not even see them. When the formation approached the French coast, Gilroy announced over the intercom that he could see aircraft far to the west. He asked and obtained permission to go and have a look. Blue section was detached from the squadron. They turned south-west and spotted two Me 109s flying above some Spitfires to the west of Le Touquet.

As soon as they saw Gilroy and his section, the Mes, who were 1,000 feet higher, dived coastwards unashamed. Since other unidentified aircraft could be seen in the distance over Northern France, Gilroy did not pursue them.

A pair of German fighters dived in front of them but as Gilroy was not exactly born yesterday, he resisted the temptation and kept his eye on fifteen others which seemed to be taking far too keen an interest in his section. They were in too great a number.

He called "There are too many about here. Blue section go down."

He dived seawards, reducing his throttle. His section did not follow him so he regained height and rejoined Palmer and the Ortmans brothers. The Mes were now much nearer and in position for attack. When they dived, Gilroy turned towards them but not being able to aim correctly did not fire and crossed them. He glanced behind him. A Spit, probably one of his section was spinning down shrouded in black smoke. Christian was once more at his side. Gilroy went down to the damaged Spitfire, keeping a watch on his tail. The aircraft finally straightened out and set course for home. Gilroy remained above him like a good watchdog. Two Mes were in position for attack. When Gilroy turned towards them, they dived and fled. Then he drew near the Spitfire to see its identification number. It was PR – K, his No. 4 – Palmer. The machine was flying slowly losing height, then its prop stopped and the smoke ceased. Gilroy drew closer to him so that he should know that he was not alone. Together they descended to 2,000 feet.

Gilroy called on the intercom "Palmer, bale out. Do you hear me, Palmer? Bale out."

The sergeant did not reply. Perhaps his radio did not function or he could not jump. Perhaps he was wounded. Christian Ortmans joined Gilroy at the moment the Spit landed tail down in the water, sinking immediately and leaving nothing but a dark sinister patch on the surface of the water.

"It's my brother," cried Christian. "It's my brother!"

Gilroy replied that it was Palmer. He was certain that he had read the letters correctly. But Christian stuck to his intuition. He did not believe the squadron leader. For a quarter of an hour they continued to fly over the spot, where they saw nothing except the oil slowly spreading on the sea. Gilroy called on the radio to make sure.

"Beauty to Blue 3."

There was no reply. Vicky did not reply.

With just time to re-arm and to re-fuel, No. 609 Squadron, joined by Wing Commander Rankin, took off again.

This time they were not seeking a scrap with the Luftwaffe over the Pas de Calais. They were merely looking for Vicky Ortmans, who was probably in his little dinghy somewhere in the Channel, bobbing on the waves. For two hours, flying in zig-zags, they scanned the horizon, looking for some trace, some sign. But the sea, which was as smooth as a plaque of grey marble, revealed nothing and, all hope lost, the fighters returned to Biggin Hill. Dusk was falling, Maurice Choron, who piloted Offenberg's aircraft "M for Monkey," announced that he had run short of juice just as the formation crossed the English coast. He crash-landed somewhere in the country. That evening at the squadron Gilroy posted Vicky missing. Palmer was also on the list but Gilroy added on the report the three small sinister words: "Killed in combat."

* * *

In actual fact, Vicky had been shot down once more in the Channel, but a long way further south than they had imagined. Wounded by an explosive bullet in his left shouder, he had managed by sheer will power to inflate his dinghy and get into it. Night fell. Alone in the cold night, soaked to the skin and losing blood, he fainted from the pain.

Three days later, his dinghy was washed up on the beach north of Dieppe and when Vicky recovered consciousness he was in a German hospital.

At Biggin Hill, for another three months, his comrades thought he was dead, and his young brother Christian, grieving at the death of his much admired elder brother, applied for a transfer to a squadron going to the Far East.

Christian was killed in India.

The pilots took Vicky's car, the little Morris 8 he had baptised Caroline and which had so often served to transport Billygoat, the squadron mascot. Incidentally, Billygoat had now been promoted to flight lieutenant with a palm to his Croix de Guerre!

****

At dawn the mist wreathed the soil and I thought that we should not take off in such unpropitious weather. Apparently, however, the Channel was clear and the enemy coast without a cloud. So we were airborne after a hasty briefing with a visibility of about 800 yards at ground level. The route was Nieuport-Bergues-Gravelines, a triangle in the department of the north, too near to Saint-Omer for the Me 109s, provoked by our presence, to resist intercepting us on the way home. We reached the Belgian coast flying at 20,000 feet without the slightest incident. Even Choron, who was No. 2 in my Blue section, remained silent in his cockpit, probably nursing a few old resentments. He has not yet recovered from his adventures three weeks ago when, in company with Vicky Ortmans, he intercepted a few 109s over Calais. In the middle of the scrap, two aircraft of unknown mark passed a mile away. Choron returned in great excitement to Biggin Hill.

"It's disgusting," he roared, his coarse hair still tousled. "The British are using new crates and haven't even told us about them."

Ortmans thought that they must be Bloch 151s – French machines being used by the Germans. Taking a pencil stub, Maurice drew a rapid sketch of an aircraft with a kind of radial engine and a stocky body, which no one had yet seen.

It did not long remain a mystery. The machine was the new Luftwaffe fighter, the Focke-Wulf 190. The Germans are not yet using them in squadrons but, from time to time, they slip a couple of them in the Messerschmitt formations. To add to the confusion they have painted a big circle round their black crosses. Hence Choron's trouble. This great French pilot is brooding on an exemplary vengeance and will not forgive the German pilots for having caused him to make a mistake in identification for the first time in his career.

As I had foreseen before we took off, the Luftwaffe attacked before 609 had reached Bergues and fell on us from the east.

Away to starboard, two Focke-Wulfs, gleaming in the dawn sunshine, glided among the few cloud patches over the Franco-Belgian frontier.

I must have had the same thought as Maurice, for when the attack began I broke to starboard in the direction of the Focke-Wulfs. Choron, higher than myself and in the sun, followed about 100 yards to stern. With his infallible Corsican mountaineer's eye, he was the first to spot one of the Focke-Wulfs climbing to the south. His Spitfire was already diving on the German fighter, who increased his speed. Tracers ... The German banked to the right, pieces broke off his wing and he went down in a spin. Choron pulled on his stick and zoomed like a bullet launched from a giant spring. He said nothing. I was waiting for his victory cry on the intercom. But nothing came.

The vendetta was finished. Choron had got his Focke-Wulf.

Together we took our place in the merry-go-round. In one part of the sky the Spitfires had formed a defensive circle. I dived on the first Me to arrive and sprayed him from 300 yards with a long burst before losing sight of my victim in a zoom.

On return from the mission we noticed by some miracle no one was missing and that only Pilot Officer Smith had a dozen bullets in his fuselage. Gilroy had obtained two victories, confirmed by Flight Lieutenant Demozay of 92 Squadron, who had been present at both combats.

I did not see Choron the whole evening.

****

Editor's Note.—17th November. Offenberg, having spent a week's leave at Chichester, returned to Biggin Hill in the early afternoon. Without bothering to go to his hut, he left his suitcase in the guardroom and rushed to the squadron office.

The faces were all familiar. Everyone seemed to be there. Gilroy was signing reports. There were Barnham, Dieu, de Selys, Van Schaick, and the others ... The last time he had left 609, Vicky Ortmans had been brought down and today he had a feeling that another would be missing at roll call. Choron. He had not seen Choron.

"Where's Maurice?"

"Oh, he's left us."

"Killed?"

"Maurice killed! No. He's been invalided and is now an instructor at the Heston Fighting School."

Pyker heaved a sigh of relief, although with Choron gone things would not be so gay. He could imagine the way Maurice would have greeted the news of his transfer and smiled as he thought of it.

"Well, now we haven't a representative of the Third Republic.

He was quite a figure, Maurice. Gilroy should have tried to keep him with us."

"Gilroy did all he could. He spent a whole day phoning to all the top brass of Fighter Command. But he couldn't do a thing."

After all, Heston wasn't Peru. It was only a few minutes in a Spit. Offenberg decided that he would pay him a visit at the earliest opportunity.

Did someone guess his thoughts?

"Oh, don't worry. We shall be seeing him. I bet he'll be more often here than at Heston."

Pyker questioned everyone about the activities of the past week and learned that the squadron had made only two raids over France; there had been no results, but Lang had been shot down over the French coast in a dog-fight.

It was Gilroy who announced the great news: "We're being moved the day after tomorrow. The squadron's posted to Digby."

At first Offenberg hardly dared to credit this, because the station in question was so far away from their present scene of activity.

"But Digby's in Group 12, isn't it? There won't be any fighting there. They might just as well have sent us to Australia or to the Belgian Congo."

"You're exaggerating, Pyker, No. 12 Group is obviously farther north, but you'll see, there'll be plenty of Jerries who will venture over and who will never get back home."

Offenberg remained unconvinced. It was all very well the C.O. dangling a few fights before his eyes, he knew what this transfer meant. No. 12 Group was still Fighter Command, but its territory was too far removed from the main battlefield. Tangmere, Biggin Hill ... those were the air defence stations of the London approaches. Digby, in the south of Lincolnshire, was a deadly quiet sector.

It meant that Pyker would no longer lead Blue section over Saint-Omer, Calais and Abbeville to put up the fighters. No more take-offs at dawn and flights over the Channel. . . .

The German Fighter Arm had grown more aggressive since it had been given Focke-Wulfs and accepted battle more readily. And now they were leaving for Digby, and Gilroy announced it as calmly as if they had been going down to have a drink at the "White Hart." These English were quite remarkable. Offenberg knew that, although Gilroy seemed to take it in his stride, that in his heart of hearts he too was just as disappointed.

"Before we leave, the squadron is invited by Air Commodore Peake to dinner at the Savoy Hotel."

"Who is Peake?"

"Peake, my dear fellow, is an old gentleman who was flying when aeroplanes were made of bamboo and tied up with string. But I don't think he taught Blériot to fly!"

Offenberg tried to interrupt, but Gilroy went on: "What is more, this old gentleman has the honour of having been the first C.O. of 609 and that's why he's invited you tomorrow night. He is celebrating our departure from the sector."

"It's not a celebration, it's a funeral," said someone.

There was only one piece of good news. Alex Nitelet, a young Belgian who had joined 609 in August and had been shot down over France on his first trip, was reported safe and sound.

"How do they know?" asked Pyker.

"Because he's just written to say that he is temporarily in Spain. There's one fellow at least who knows how to get by."

The following morning, 609 was top cover for some Hurri-bombers and their furthest turning point was Hesdin. Since it was the last raid before they left and Hesdin was half-way between Saint-Omer and Abbeville, Offenberg hoped at least to shoot down a Focke-Wulf as a gesture of farewell. A Focke-Wulf to sign off a long record of combat. . . .

The Spitfires took off and climbed at once to 2,000 feet, crossing Sevenoaks and flying over the Weald of Kent. Landmarks were few for there was too much cloud. To port was Dungeness Point where they were to meet the bombers. These old faithful fighters had been loaded with a few bombs and re-baptised Hurri-bombers. Apparently they had done splendid work in the Middle East supporting the 8th Army. The squadron turned for Hardelot, gaining height. At 8,000 feet there was no cloud. Once more Offenberg was amazed at suddenly discovering a new and unsuspected world. Down below it was raining and dreary; a deadly boredom lay over the lethargic countryside and then suddenly, as though a veil had been drawn aside, there was nothing except a vast carpet of snowy cotton wool with a few darker hollows, and here and there yawning abysses, holes that would allow the pilots to get back to that other world. . . .

The bombers and the lower escort were down there near the earth. They flew towards the sun . . . The layer of cloud thinned out and now they could see large patches of sea. With 15,000 registering on the altimeter, the Germans had already spotted their arrival and were in all probability taking off. Unless they had decided to remain with their arms folded as they had done at the beginning of the summer, Jean thought of the six American volunteer pilots of Eagle Squadron who had flown low over Saint-Omer airfield in broad daylight and had not managed to make the Luftwaffe take off. Then they had split into two sections of three – to port and starboard. . . .

At 12,000 feet with the flak firing at them they began a mock combat. No one ever learned the reactions of the Saint-Omer boys who watched this free display, but the man who had forbidden them to take off must have thought he heard church bells ringing in his ears!

The 609 reached 20,000 feet.

Gilroy announced that he had spotted the bombers a few miles to port. Above Red Section, Offenberg and Spirlet leading their respective sections weaved, scanning the sky. Not a Messerschmitt in sight.

A voice called: "The bastards aren't showing up."

"Hold your horses, we're not through yet."

Then a long silence suddenly followed by a hideous cacophony in the headphones. A dog-fight was in progress somewhere else. Probably the bombers were being attacked. They headed north. It would not be long now.

Offenberg glanced round his cockpit, checked the gonio and saw that his weapons were ready to fire.

"Drop your babies."

Gilroy had just given the order to jettison the reserve fuel tanks. And then the Mes arrived. A savage dog-fight began. The formation split up and there were cries, warnings and oaths on the intercom.

"Blue 1. Messerschmitt at six o'clock."

If you said that to a fighter pilot even if he were riding a bicycle he would begin to carry out the most violent manoeuvres one after the other.

Pyker did not hesitate; he banked vertically and dived to port. An Me dived on him but he streaked past having missed him. He could see a second German fighter slightly above him. He gave full gas and attacked it on a climbing turn. The 109 was most vulnerable under the belly and this was why such an attack was always feared by the German pilots. Offenberg had been unable to get enough speed. The Jerry who had seen him or been warned by one of his mates rolled on to his back and dived. Offenberg fired his four machine guns, but too late.

The combat was over. The 609 would leave for Digby without having registered another kill in the golden book. 401 Squadron was luckier and scored two probables.

That evening the Savoy Hotel welcomed the officers of 609. Air Commodore Peake was in the hall. He was younger than Offenberg had imagined from Gilroy's humorous description of him. Leigh Mallory, O.C. 11 Group, had turned up. Group Captain Barwell, commanding Biggin Hill, and Wing Commanders Robinson and Rankin were punctual. Ladies in evening dress and gentlemen in dinner jackets crossed them in the hall as they came. Pyker felt that the Londoners no longer realised ... It was so far away here from their war.

That evening these people would read in their newspapers that seventy-five R.A.F. fighters had escorted a few bombers over northern France. That was all. Since the end of the Blitz, they had known nothing of the tough fights, the sweat, blood, tears and sudden death. These people belonged to another world and perhaps that was all to the good. ...

The women looked at these childish prematurely aged faces, at hands frozen by the cold at high altitudes, the frank smiling eyes which had momentarily lost their aggressiveness. Introductions were made and the squadron went into the restuaurant. Barwell brought the speeches to an end. He regretted, he said, the departure of one of the most famous squadrons of Fighter Command. He had always considered it a great honour to command them. If they returned to Biggin Hill after a rest, they would be very welcome. Referring to their whimsical goat which had given the Station adjutant so many grey hairs, he said amidst laughter: "Yes, you will be welcome even if you return with Billygoat."

Two days later, after two false starts, 609 left Biggin Hill by Sections and headed north.

SOMETIMES UNSEEN

THE SNOW ARRIVED.

Digby possessed neither the comfort nor the reputation of Biggin Hill. A little lost at the outset, the pilots of 609 felt that they lost something which they could not quite define. They felt lonely. Transplanted into unfamiliar surroundings, they were rather like children who had been sent to another school in term time and find strange faces in the playground during the breaks.

Fortunately, in this case, the whole class had been transferred, Gilroy, Offenberg and de Spirlet were there and the orders broadcast into the propeller streams had not changed.

Voices retained their familiar intonations and the laughter rang out just as gay and carefree. The pilots sensed that they belonged to one great family. If the countryside had changed, if other squadrons like warrior tribes camped with them round the airfield, the 609 was self-contained and the pilots were closer than they had ever been before.

Brothers in arms, they belonged to the same clan and the friendship that united them was a bond more solid than blood ties. They had time to realise this now for the first time. Back at Biggin Hill in the South the squadrons all knew each other and they had not the same impression of being stranded on a desert island. Here at Digby the others were strangers, outsiders whose secrets, trophies and victories they did not share.

During the first days of Digby a sort of rampart was erected between them. There was no drawbridge and in the snowed-in citadel the fighters recalled their memories and licked their wounds, looking forward to the following spring.

As soon as the bad weather ended 609 would return south into No. 11 Group's zone of combat as Air Marshal Sholto-Douglas, chief of Fighter Command, had promised.

So they grew used to their misfortune in the icy winds that blew in from the North Sea.

Offenberg was installed in a rather uncomfortable hut which he shared with Jean de Selys. It was of the utmost simplicity.

A few half-open valises, two uniforms hanging in the cupboard, a toilet set on the table, a pair of boots under the camp bed – that was all. A tour round the property consisted of a glance into the mess lounge and the reading of the few notices pinned up in the entrance hall.

****

Sunday, 23rd November

Mass at the camp. One Section of 609 had to escort a few coasters sailing south; we met them off the Wash some minutes' flight from the base. I shall eventually believe that the war is still going on up here.

From time to time the Luftwaffe sends a few bombers into the Digby sector, but very rarely, and since the weather is against this type of exercise I shall have little chance of meeting any Nazi aircraft. The world has had a temporary breakdown, or at least has slowed down in speed. But perhaps it is only a moment's respite before the good times begin again.

In the meantime, as Gilroy says, we are unemployed. No bombers, no fighters. It was different at Biggin Hill. If the mountain wouldn't come to Mahomet then Mahomet went to the mountain. . . .

While we were on the way to our machines, our bald friend Rigler soliloquised: "I wonder what the Saint-Omer boys are doing? I'm beginning to miss them."

"Don't tell me you're homesick for them?"

"I think I am," he said, adjusting his Mae West. "We enjoyed ourselves with those madmen, admit it. And the tricks Groupie played on them! Sending a formation here and they took off. And when they had run out of juice sending another. And if they waited for us on the way out they found another on their tails."

He gesticulated with his hands, describing the imaginary formations. Rigler enjoyed strategy.

"Ah," he sighed, "they were good times although we groused all day. Never mind, we're off to escort these old tubs."

An ace now, Sergeant Rigler, who has won the D.F.M., the highest award an N.C.O. can win, climbed on to the wing of his Spitfire. We took off about 10.00 hours and got into a well-boxed formation. The four of us, wing to wing, climbed on course 170° to 3,000 feet. The sky was overcast above us, and

199

there were no gaps in the compact mass of cloud, no emergency exit to the sky. Well, we should have to remain downstairs ... As we did not yet know the sector I unfolded my map on my knee and tried to get my ground position. Very few landmarks. At any moment we should be flying over Boston, Lincs.

"Blue 1, do you know where we are?"

I had no time to reply before Rigler answered:

"Don't ask such embarrassing questions. There's the railway ... I'm turning to port and we shall soon come out over the coast. We're flying over the Wash."

"Blue 1 to Blue 4. Convoy to starboard at ten o'clock."

Yes, the cargo vessels were there spitting black smoke. A dozen of them ... I ordered line abreast. The manoeuvre carried out, we dipped our wings and flew diagonally across the convoy. After notifying control we did our shepherd act circling over the convoy, making out to sea and returning. The water below was a muddy yellow, dotted here and there with sandbanks along the shore.

After flying for about an hour and a half Digby Control called me. My hands were frozen in spite of my fur gloves and my feet were just as cold. In actual fact I could not feel them at all.

I was pleased to be going home.

Lunch in the mess. Half an hour before dusk I took Roger Malengrau and Rigler with me to carry out a patrol on the route Boston-Hull-Sheffield. Night was falling rapidly.

Returning to our point of departure I caught sight of the flare path lights at Digby. As soon as I had touched down I found to my amazement that I was on a strange airfield and that the landmarks were new to me. And yet when I called Digby they had given me permission to land. Where the hell was I? How incredibly stupid. A few moments later a British Squadron Commander explained the mystery and laughed at my discomfiture.

I was at Wellingmore, five miles from my own base, and I had mistaken the two fields.

It was as simple as that. I returned to Digby by car. At dinner half an hour later, a few pilots began discussing at the top of their voices the qualities needed for night fighters, the need to be a good navigator. They were doing their best to pull my leg.

"I've seen Hurricane types who returned in a fast launch," said Banham, who is a great wit when the occasion arises. "Tell me, Pyker, how come that you set off in a Spit and came home in a car?"

As I decided to keep a straight face the affair ended with a few tankards and beer and some yarns ... of fighter pilots.

****

Editor's Note.—The year hurried to its close at great strides. The pilots of 609 had found a small pub near Digby where the food was excellent. When the menu in the mess did not satisfy them, they drove to the "Musicians' Arms" to eat a pheasant or some soufflé omelettes. Between training flights and an odd patrol they played games and Jean Offenberg was initiated into the mysteries of Squash.

Yvan Dumonceau and Roger Malengrau put in for leave and it was granted. Gilroy also decided to return home for a few days and handed over the Squadron to Pyker. A new word was on the lips of the pilots at the moment: Pearl Harbour. The alarming news arrived of the sinking of the *Repulse* and the *Prince of Wales*, the pride of the Navy, off the Malay coast. The Japs invaded the Philippines and the Dutch East Indies. They were advancing on Singapore. Some British pilots were transferred to units in the Middle East. One Belgian, Van Aerenbergh, was posted to the Upavon Flying School as instructor.

To fill the gaps four sergeants landed at Digby and two of them – Young and Paterson – were posted to B Flight under Offenberg's orders.

A few sorties broke the monotony. At times they telephoned to Maurice Choron who was also bored to death at Heston, or invited Mike Robinson, their former squadron commander.

One day Maurice, who visited 609 as often as possible, arrived at Digby in a Miles Magister trainer and announced his arrival by a number of spectacular flick rolls a few feet above the ground. This delighted the boys but earned him a rocket from the Canadian station commandant, Group Captain Campbell. The little Corsican was threatened with a court martial for having infringed R.A.F. regulations by performing low flying aerobatics.

"Don't worry, Maurice," said Offenberg. "Mike Robinson will be here in a minute. He'll explain things to Campbell this evening in the mess." As soon as Robinson heard what had happened he promised to have a chat with the Group Captain.

"We'll meet tonight and have a couple of drinks," he said. "It'll be all right."

That evening at mess they noticed that the Commandant was missing and Robinson, having failed to buttonhole the irascible Canadian, found an excellent way of arranging things. As soon as he learned that the "Old Man" was in his office he put on his gloves, adjusted his scarf and climbed into his own Spitfire. He then proceeded to carry out a series of hair-raising aerobatics a few feet from the ground. He skimmed at a couple of feet over the Group Captain's office and with a last wave set off south and was lost to view.

Maurice Choron did not get sent for a court marital.

Alex Nitelet, who had been shot down over France the previous August, paid a visit to his old comrades at arms as soon as he returned to England. Shot down by an Me, he baled out and managed to get back to this country via Spain and Portugal. He had lost an eye.

On the 21st January 1942, Offenberg wrote a few brief words in his diary: *"I take up the youngsters – Blanco has arrived from Heston and has been posted to my Flight. Lallemand has been promoted Flying Officer."*

From the 22nd, the pages remain blank and time has set the seal of melancholy of fifteen years oblivion upon them.

At Brussels on the 24th January 1942 about eight o'clock in the evening Jean's family had foregathered at 43 Square Riga as they had done every evening for nearly two years.

With the curtains drawn and safe from prying enemy ears and eyes they listened to the B.B.C. bulletins. The news was about as depressing as it could possibly be, but there was a ray of light in their darkness. The unknown voice poured out honeyed words and told them that the dawn would soon be breaking. The Russians were on the banks of the Donetz and would soon be going over to the offensive in the Ukraine. Bardia had been recaptured by the Eighth Army, the Desert Rats. . . .

Dawn was about to break . . . There was every chance now that America with its power and resources was in the war. The legend of Hitler's invincibility – he had not found easy victories on the East Front – had been destroyed by the Russian people.

"We are no longer alone," said the voice, "and the whirlwind will be conquered."

Mme. Offenberg, prematurely aged by these two war years, who trembled each day for her youngest son of whom she had news so rarely, turned to Francis, her other son, and said:

"The news could have been worse. . . ."

Francis, his ear glued to the set, motioned her to be silent. What was going on? A bugle sounded a well-known note, a sad air whose notes were muffled in this parlour with the curtained windows. It was the Last Post, the sad trumpet call for those who have died in action. Then the Brabançonne was played.

"Someone's been killed," said Francis. "A Belgian this time. . . ."

It was not the first time they had heard a broadcast of this type but today the atmosphere was heavier and there was a certain tense anxiety in the air.

Mme. Offenberg stood up. The announcer said:

"This evening we have learned with regret that the best of the Belgian fighter pilots has been killed on active service. It is Flight Lieutenant Jean Offenberg, D.F.C."

"It's Jean," said Francis simply.

Deeply upset, Mme. Offenberg rushed to her bedroom and sank down on the bed weeping, stifling her sobs with a handkerchief between her teeth. . . .

Hot tears fell on her counterpane and all she could murmur was: "Jean is dead. Jean is dead. . . ."

*   *   *

Yes, Jean was dead. On the 22nd January when summer and autumn had long since died. The north wind was icy. The Digby airfield was covered with snow but the weather was clear enough for flying. Offenberg, who had not flown since the 16th, decided to profit by the clear sky to do a formation flight with one of the new pilots, a Belgian, Pilot Officer Roelandt. He had just joined the Squadron.

"We won't stay up too long," he said. "The weather won't hold. Come along."

"I'm with you."

The two Spitfires took off to the north and the hoar frost on their wings soon melted.

For more than an hour they practised over the field. Offenberg gave his orders over the intercom.

"Echelon to port."

"Echelon to starboard."

"Line abreast."

The last manoeuvre was carried out immediately by Roelandt who was in position next to his leader, his left wingtip almost touching Offenberg's right wingtip.

Pyker was pleased with his pupil. He "stuck" well and had his aircraft well under control.

He waved in encouragement and Roelandt smiled.

"One more figure and we'll call it a day. You're doing well."

A silence.

"Line astern, Blue 2."

Roelandt obeyed at once and took up his place behind his leader, slightly lower so as not to be caught in the slipstream.

And then, without Offenberg noticing, another Spitfire enjoying himself on a solo attacked their formation which was within range of him.

It was Sergeant Renzi of 92 Squadron who was killing the time as best he could. He attacked from 90°. Offenberg was watching the sky behind him and at the same time his pupil, who noticed nothing. Why should he have been paying attention when there were no enemy about over his own field?

Sergeant Renzi approached fast. 300 yards ... 200 ... 50 ...
Offenberg saw him.

He passed too near, and sideslipped. Offenberg pulled his stick and gave full gas. The other machine did the same and it was a collision.

Offenberg's Spitfire, its tail unit cut off, continued to climb for an instant and then turned over on its back. The debris of the Spit flew around Roelandt's machine for a fraction of a second.

Would Pyker jump? No.

He went into a vertical dive. He was at only 1,000 feet, too low for a parachute to have opened.

Two seconds later it was all over. The two fighters crashed. The disconsolate Roelandt looked at the wreckage of the two machines on the white snow. The wings detached from the fuselage made a huge cross on the snow-covered English countryside.

*　　*　　*

Offenberg's mother will never read this book, for the shock of her son's death killed her. Nor did she read her son's diaries for by the time they reached the Offenberg family she was already dead.

As for Jean, he was buried at Digby in the county of Lincoln-shire on the afternoon of the 26th January 1942 by the Catholic padre of the station. His brothers in arms acted as pall-bearers and carried his coffin to the cemetery of Scopwith in the sun-light which made the snow sparkle. The pilots had kept watch round his coffin in the small chapel. That was all they could do for Pyker except to stand now motionless in the cemetery so as not to break the silence and the peace.

And thus as the coffin was lowered into the earth he had at his side faithful wingers such as had protected him in so many combats with the enemy.

The evening of the funeral Father Morris wrote a letter to a colleague which is a fine testimony:

"I had the privilege and honour of burying him this after-noon. According to all I have heard of him it is both consoling and encouraging to know that a saint sometimes slips unseen among the others. Offenberg did not receive the Last Sacra-ments, but I am convinced that he did not need them."

A few days later, the 15th February, Jean de Selys-Long-champs, who later became famous for attacking Gestapo H.Q. in the Avenue Louise, Brussels, wrote a letter to Jean's uncle liv-ing in the Argentine. This is an extract from that letter, written the day after Pyker's death by a fellow pilot who had flown with him:

"I do not know whether you know your nephew well. Jean was the greatest, the most magnificent of us. Entering the R.A.F. in August 1940 as a Pilot Officer, he was promoted Flight Lieutenant within a year, leading an operational flight. In May 1941 he was awarded the D.F.C. for good conduct and exceptional courage which had obtained him six certain victories and five probables. On the 21st July 1941 the Minister for National Defence decorated him with the Belgian Croix de Guerre in the name of our King.

"I cannot explain to you all that Jean meant to us. He was a symbol of integrity, a permanent example, an inexhaustible source of hope in the future, in our future, in the future of our country, in our King and all that we hold dear. We felt rather than realised his quality and the moral support that radiated from him in hours of discouragement and weariness and his unshakeable support in combat.

"His presence brought such a wealth of freshness and in-nocence into the tortured violent hours we lived through. His death has been a terrible shock for us. We felt in it the ineluctable hand of Providence. His hour sounded at the very moment we were pleased to see him enjoying a well-earned rest.

"If his death surprised us he was not caught unawares. Perhaps you know how devout he was. Our only consolation, and I think you will feel the same, is that he is now at peace, a peace infinitely more precious than he could have enjoyed here below.

"We have buried him in a small cemetery in the English countryside. There remains the mark he has left on us which is too deep not to be an example in our future work. Having had the honour to serve in his Squadron and in addition to have been his friend, I shall not forget what I have learned from him.

"According to his express wishes, his effects have been sent to an English family of whom he was very fond and with whom he spent most of his leave. They will forward them to his parents as soon as it is possible."

* * *

In the enclosure of honour in Evère cemetery there is a simple wooden cross bearing the name OFFENBERG.

Together with my son I took a few crocuses that had just blossomed in my garden. A child's hand placed the flowers on the cold earth where he rests as though to thank this unknown friend whom he knew only from his fine story.

As he remained there open-eyed and seemed no longer to understand as he saw the mound I said to him: "Come, he's very tired. Let him rest. He was so very tired."

The boy took my hand and together we walked along the deserted peaceful avenues into the sunlight which already heralded the spring.

Woluwé-Saint-Lambert.
10th March 1956

The following is a list of the principal combats recorded by Jean Offenberg himself on the 29th December 1941. When we consider the innate modesty and honesty of this pilot, the list is an exact reflection of his legendary career.

AERIAL COMBATS 1940-1941

Country	Date	Type of Aircraft	Results
	1940		
Belgium	10th May	1 Do 17	Damaged
		1 Do 17	Not observed
		1 Do 17	Confirmed
England	8th Sept.	½ Do 275	Damaged
	27th Oct.	1 Me 109E	Probable
	1st Nov.	1 Me 109E	Confirmed
	6th Nov.	1 Me 109	Confirmed
	9th Nov.	1 Ju 88	Damaged
	11th Dec.	1 He 111	Confirmed
	1941		
	5th May	1 Heinkel 60	Damaged
		1 Heinkel 60	Confirmed
		1 Me 109E	Confirmed
		1 Me 109E	Not observed
	21st June	1 MeF	No result
	22nd June	1 MeF	No result
		1 Me 109E	Damaged
	27th June	1 Me 109	No result
		1 Me 109	No result
	7th July	1 Me 109E	Confirmed
	9th July	1 Me 109	Missed
		1 Me 109	No result
		1 Me 109	Not observed
	19th July	1 Me 109	Probable
	24th July	1 Me 109	No result
		1 Flak Ship	

Country	Date	Type of Aircraft	Results
	1941		
England	31st July	1 E Boat	
		1 Minesweeper	
	6th Aug.	1 Me 109	Probable
		1 Me 109	Not observed
		1 Me 109	Not observed
	19th Aug.	1 Me 109	Not observed
	27th Aug.	1 Me 109	Probable
	29th Aug.	1 Me 109	Not observed
		1 Me 109	Probable
	27th Sept.	1 Me 109	Damaged
	13th Oct.	1 Me 109	Damaged
	27th Oct.	1 Me 109	No result

Killed on active service 22nd January 1942.